Fish Market

A Cookbook for Selecting and Preparing Seafood

by KATHY HUNT

RUNNING PRESS
PHILADELPHIA · LONDON

Published by Running Press, A Member of the Perseus Books Group
All rights reserved under the Pan-American and International Copyright Conventions

Printed in China

Books published by Running Press are available at special discounts for bulk purchases in the United States by corporations, institutions, and other organizations. For more information, please contact the Special Markets Department at the Perseus Books Group, 2300 Chestnut Street, Suite 200, Philadelphia, PA 19103, or call (800) 810-4145, ext. 5000, or e-mail special.markets@perseusbooks.com.

ISBN 978-0-7624-4474-8

Library of Congress Control Number: 2012955885

E-book ISBN 978-0-7624-4826-5

9   8   7   6   5   4   3   2   1
Digit on the right indicates the number of this printing

Cover and interior design by Amanda Richmond
Edited by Geoffrey Stone
Typography: Edmond Sans, Lomba, and Janda Elegant Handwriting

Running Press Book Publishers
2300 Chestnut Street
Philadelphia, PA 19103-4371

Visit us on the web!
www.runningpresscooks.com

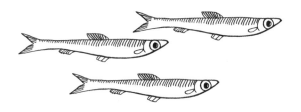

for Sean
and the late
Clifford R. Williams

Contents

ACKNOWLEDGMENTS ...5

INTRODUCTION ...6

CHAPTER 1: **A BEVY OF BIVALVES** ...19

CHAPTER 2: **A COLLECTION OF CRUSTACEANS** ...40

CHAPTER 3: **SMALL, SAVORY, OILY FISH** ...64

CHAPTER 4: **RICH, MEATY, OILY FISH** ...86

CHAPTER 5: **FIRM, FLAVORFUL FISH** ...121

CHAPTER 6: **MILD, WHITE-FLESHED FISH** ...147

CHAPTER 7: **DELICATE, FLAKY DELIGHTS** ...176

CHAPTER 8: **FABULOUS, SOMETIMES FORGOTTEN SEAFOOD** ...199

CHAPTER 9: **SEAFOOD SIDES** ...222

ECO-RATING CHART ...239

BIBLIOGRAPHY ...240

INDEX ... 242

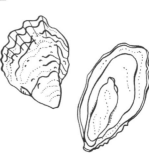

Acknowledgments

Many thanks to Vince Smith, Kathy McGowan, Brande Plotnick, Rob Plotnick, and Van Morgan for their culinary prowess, enthusiasm, and feedback. They are all masters of the kitchen.

Additionally, I must thank Sharon Burke, Jason and Rachelle Hafer, Tom and Laura Ransom, Kirsten Van Vlandren, Tim and Gaye Freeman, Fred Greenspoon, Lisa Hancock, and Gwyneth Turner for bravely sampling my test dishes.

I am indebted to my agent, Sharon Bowers of the Miller Agency, and Running Press editor Kristin Green Wiewora for choosing to work with me and to designer Amanda Richmond for her beautiful work. Without them there would be no *Fish Market*.

I owe a special thanks to food historian and cookbook author Francine Segan. She helped a journalist who loved cooking and travel become a journalist who writes about her loves.

Had it not been for food aficionado and fishing buddy Frank Wilmer, I may never have known the joys of eating wild mushrooms plucked directly from the forest floor or of filleting my own fish. He's helped shape the knowledge and palate of this former suburban kid.

For decades Vasiliki Kolovos has shared her wisdom and recipes. A former restaurant owner, her cooking in general and kourabiedes cookies in particular are among my fondest food memories.

Similarly, Elizabeth Theisen has encouraged and inspired me in the kitchen. She, along with Christina Brazier, Patricia Jones, and Luong Vo, helped to fuel my passion for cooking.

I've been fortunate to have a tight-knit group of childhood friends rooting for me throughout my life and writing career. Among them I must single out Marilee Morrow, Nickie Kolovos, and Amy Lambo Hawthorne. Each uniquely aided me in seeing this book come to fruition.

Likewise, Sean Dippold has played an invaluable role. Friend, husband, proofreader, kitchen assistant, global adventurer, daring dining companion—he does it all with good humor, patience, love, and grace. My gratitude to him is boundless.

While my late parents, Patricia and William Hunt, taught me how to discern between good and bad cooking, it was my late uncle Clifford R. Williams who imparted the pleasures of eating. The earliest supporter of both my writing and my experiments in the kitchen, Cliff embraced all foods but especially those shared with family and friends. I live and cook by his example.

Introduction

Depending upon our backgrounds and where we live, most of us eat only a smattering of fish and shellfish. Until I moved away from my hometown outside of Pittsburgh, Pennsylvania and started seriously traveling and cooking, that certainly was the case for me. With no fishermen in my family, we ate what was available at our local markets and stuck to the seafood that my mother and her mother before her had cooked—cod, flounder, haddock, tuna, and the occasional salmon loaf or cake.

Restaurants provided me with my first taste of more exotic seafood. At the age of nine I discovered clam fritters, followed shortly thereafter by linguine with clam sauce. These became my go-to meals whenever my family dined out. They also made me wonder what other unusual, tasty seafood was swimming about.

Meeting people, making new friends, and being invited to special events similarly broadened my horizons. At an Italian-American friend's Feast of the Seven Fishes I tried my first sweet squid. At another friend's parents' cocktail party the preteen me snuck in a salty bite of salmon roe. Novel and exciting, they were a far cry from the fish found in my family's kitchen.

Travel additionally expanded my palate. How could I visit New Orleans and not have crayfish or spend a week in the Florida Keys and not try conch? I couldn't and didn't. My attitude regarding seafood—and food in general—was to eat as the locals did. In Brussels I had mussels. In Cambodia I ate snakehead fish. In every region and country I tried what was to me a new fish.

Cooking brought all of these experiences together. Through classes, cookbooks, handwritten recipes, and attempts to replicate others' dishes I established a firm culinary foundation in seafood. I likewise became a passionate proponent of eating fish and shellfish.

Why Seafood?

I think that a better question might be, "Why *not* seafood?" Low in fat and high in nutrients, seafood is a regular source of protein for me, and health authorities seem to agree with that habit. The latest U.S. dietary guidelines advise Americans to consume twice as much fish as they currently do to reduce the risk of heart disease. It's advice not to be taken lightly. Research has shown that eating two (three-ounce) servings of fish per week lessens the likelihood of dying from heart disease by 36 percent. Studies have also indicated that increased seafood consumption may lower the occurrence of strokes, depression, Alzheimer's disease, and even cancer.

What makes fish and shellfish so magical is their richness in omega-3 fatty acids. Especially common in fatty, deep-water fish, these acids are known to lower bad cholesterol or low-density lipoprotein levels, which contribute to cardiovascular disease. Omega-3s may also increase good cholesterol or high-density lipoproteins, which help transport cholesterol through the bloodstream. That's nothing to sneeze at.

Beyond nutrition and healthfulness, seafood offers an alternative to consuming factory-farmed animals. Too often industrialized cows, pigs, and chickens live their short lives in appalling conditions. They lack room to roam, graze, and, in some instances, even breathe. Such is not the case with fish and shellfish. Whether puttering about in the ocean, rivers, or man-made ponds or lakes, they retain their intended lifestyles and exist relatively cruelty-free. If, like me, you're concerned about animal welfare but you don't want to give up eating all animal proteins, you can keep seafood in your diet without much guilt. (Of course, sustainability and freshness are important factors to consider: read more about both on pages 10–11.)

Likewise, it doesn't hurt that sustainably farmed seafood is much richer in flavor than the less-humane alternatives. A fish that has lived in its natural environment, swum freely, and consumed the foods that it's meant to eat possesses a taste and texture unparalleled to any bland, mass-produced meat or poultry. Healthy, flavorful, and incredibly easy to prepare, fish and shellfish are a blessing on nights when I'm juggling six different activities and don't have time to while away hours at the stove. I just season a fish fillet or steak with sea salt and ground black pepper and then plop it on the grill, under the broiler, or on the stovetop. Within minutes of it hitting the heat I have a tasty meal. If I want to dress up the fish, I drizzle a little lemon juice, melted butter, or hot sauce over the top. In a snap dinner is ready.

My Seafood Journey

My initial interest in seafood stemmed from medical concerns and the resultant culinary disasters that they introduced. When I was fourteen, my father had a massive heart attack at a high school football game. After recovering from this near-fatal event, he radically altered his—and our family's—eating habits. Gone were the cholesterol- and fat-laden prime rib, rib-eye steak, and roast beef dinners. Instead, we ate heart-healthy meals of broiled flounder, baked haddock, and the occasional salmon cake.

Unfortunately, my mother, the self-appointed cook of our household, had little enthusiasm for the kitchen. As a result, she made our seafood suppers about as seasoned and succulent as sandpaper. I, however, knew there must be a better way. Inspired and armed with copies of Irma Rombauer's *The Joy of Cooking* and *Jane Grigson's Fish Book*, I began a war against dry, dull seafood.

Early on I learned two invaluable rules. First off, keep the preparations simple. Most seafood requires only a splash of lemon juice or dab of butter and dash of salt and pepper to make it shine. In other words, skip the elaborate, time-consuming recipes. All you need to do is cook, season, and serve.

Second, don't overcook seafood. Fish need merely a few minutes on a hot grill or in a preheated oven or pan. Any longer and the flesh becomes dry and tough. Take it from me—no one enjoys food that bears a strong resemblance to cardboard.

Over the years I've tacked on additional standards, including buying safe, sustainable seafood. This topic gets a lot of airtime, yet it still leaves most of us wondering what qualifies as both environmental and consumption-friendly. We know that farmed fish addresses the problem of overfishing wild populations, but it also adds to the concerns about water pollution and chemically tainted foods. Meanwhile, wild seafood avoids the issue of pollutants but increases the likelihoods of marine bycatch and depleted fish stocks. It's enough to make seafood fans abandon cooking and order pizza instead.

Selecting Seafood

In this book I have tried to take the confusion out of choosing seafood.
For each fish and shellfish, I indicate when it is ecologically safe or unsound to consume. I also point out which seafood is high or low in contaminants and provide possible alternatives for those fish. Follow these basic guidelines and you can make sound seafood choices.

Once you've teased out the reliable options, you'll need to determine which fish is freshest and best for purchase. To do this, I follow a few simple rules:

- Look for firm, blemish-free skin and glistening but not soggy flesh.
- If you find a whole fish, its eyes should be bright and its appearance lifelike.
- Fillets should have minimal gaping and no browned areas.
- Whatever you do, steer clear of strong-smelling fish. This is a sure sign that the fish has been hanging around too long at the market.

The criteria for shellfish are quite similar:

- The shells should be whole, firm, and free of cracks or breaks.
- Odors should be minimal; ideally, they should smell sweetly and of the sea.
- If you're dealing with bivalves, the shells should be closed. If opened, they should shut when you tap on them.

If you can, purchase a whole fish. You can then either fillet it at home or have your fishmonger clean and fillet it for you. By acquiring whole fish, you ensure that what you've purchased is truly the fish that you desire and not a cheaper substitute.

Obviously, you want to work with a trustworthy market. Clean, well-refrigerated, and well-lit seafood cases are good signs. Whole fish stored in ice and fillets and steaks placed on ice are also positive indicators. Seafood sitting inside grimy cases in pools of icy slush is a sure sign of a careless seller.

Everyone benefits from a skilled and knowledgeable fishmonger. In situations where you're not certain which fish or how much to buy, a helpful, well-informed fishmonger will guide you in the right direction and work to find the best fish for you.

To find my cadre of fishmongers, I started by asking avid home cooks and chefs who supplied their seafood. Names acquired, I then visited the seafood departments of those grocery stores and seafood shops. There I checked out the atmosphere and talked to the people behind the counters.

At each stop I asked the same series of questions:

- How often and on what days does the seafood department receive seafood?
- From where does their seafood originate?
- Do they order fresh, whole fish or only frozen fillets and steaks?
- Will they fillet whole fish for their customers?
- Could they order a specific fish for me? If so, whom do I see about that?

Is what they have behind the counter all that they ever sell, or do they offer a range of seafood not on display today?

If the people behind the counter couldn't answer my questions or direct me to someone who could, I scratched that shop off my list. If they only sold defrosted salmon and tuna steaks, shrimp, scallops, and frozen squid rings and crab claws, they, too, were nixed. By the end of my friendly interrogations I'd found a handful of seasoned seafood sellers whom I continue to buy from and chat with about fish.

THE SCOOP ON ECO-RATINGS

The environmental ratings referenced in this book are based upon assessments from the Environmental Defense Fund's Seafood Selector and the Monterey Bay Aquarium's Seafood Watch. The terminology comes directly from the EDF's Seafood Selector.

In terms of rankings "eco-best" refers to seafood from either wild, healthy, and sustainably fished or soundly farmed populations. To fish sustainably, fishermen must leave marine habitats intact or inflict only minimal harm. Furthermore, bycatch is nominal. To farm safely, one must strictly limit environmental pollution, chemical usage, and the risks of disease and escaped fish. "Eco-best" seafood contains few contaminants such as polychlorinated biphenyls (PCBs) and mercury. It can be safely eaten at least once per week.

"Eco-okay" consists of seafood with an uneven track record. Some have elevated levels of contaminants. Others may have damaged habitats, reduced populations, or questionable fishery management. Consume these fish and shellfish in moderation, no more than twice a month.

The label "eco-worst" says it all. Due to overfishing, extensive bycatch, habitat destruction, widespread pollution, disease, escapes, and the presence of chemicals, this seafood should be avoided. Substitute an eco-friendlier fish or shellfish for any possessing an "eco-worst" rating.

Keep in mind that seafood ratings are not static. As fishing practices and environmental factors improve or worsen, rankings will shift. For up-to-the-minute statuses consult the Environmental Defense Fund, Monterey Bay Aquarium, or any knowledgeable and reputable fishmonger.

Cleaning Fish

Usually you can rely upon your fishmonger to gut, scale, skin, and fillet seafood for you. Adept with a knife, he can do these tasks in a matter of minutes. But when you or loved ones go fishing and return home with coolers filled with whole fish to clean, you're on your own. That's where some basic knife skills come in to play.

Keep in mind that no matter how good your knife skills are, they won't matter much if you use a dull knife on your seafood. Whenever your chef's knife blade begins to feel dull to the touch, run both sides of the blade over a series of oiled sharpening stones or through an electric knife sharpener. This practice will ensure clean, easy cutting and a long-lived, well-maintained knife. Sharpening stones and electric sharpeners are available at cookware shops and some hardware and home goods stores.

Likewise, you should always hone your chef's knife before each use. Honing realigns the blade's edge, which shifts after repeated cutting. To hone your knife, take the steel, a three- to fourteen-inch rod of textured metal, and, grasping it by the handle, run the knife blade over the steel at a twenty-degree angle. Do this five times on each side of the blade. For detailed instructions on sharpening and honing knives, see the Culinary Institute of America's *The Professional Chef's Knife Kit*.

REMOVING THE SCALES

To begin, you'll need to decide whether or not to remove the scales. A few fish, such as turbot, don't have scales so you won't need to worry about them. If the fish does have scales, they usually can be taken off either by scraping the surface of the fish with a knife or by brushing them off with your fingers.

Holding the fish by the tail over a bag or your kitchen sink, run the back of your knife or fingers from the tail downward toward the head. Do this over the entire body until the scales have been dislodged. Note that running water over the fish as you're scraping or brushing will help to loosen the scales.

GUTTING THE FISH

I promise—gutting sounds far more gruesome than it is. Using a small, sharp knife, cut into the underside of the fish; you'll start at its jaw and move downward to the anal opening known as the vent. Once the fish is opened, scoop out the organs with your fingers or a spoon and throw them out. Scrape out any remaining membranes or viscera and then rinse the fish under running water.

REMOVING THE GILLS

If you're cooking a whole fish, the next step is to take out the gills. Simply cut these out with a knife and discard them.

REMOVING THE HEAD, TAIL, AND FINS

Once scales, organs, and gills have been disposed of, you can either take off the head and tail or move on to the fins. When cooking for squeamish friends, I do lop off the head and tail. Both are easy to remove.

To take off the head, insert the blade of a sharp, heavy knife behind the gill covers and cut downward. Flip the fish over and do the same on the other side. If the head doesn't come off with this second cut, you may have to pull or snap it off the backbone.

For the tail, slice it off where the tail meets the body. You can either toss out the head and tail or save them to make stock, see page 158.

The final step in cleaning is to remove the fins. For this I use sharp kitchen scissors. Just snip off the fins and pull out the bones. You can either discard or keep the fins for stock.

To Skin or Not to Skin

As I've experimented with cooking fish over the years, I've learned the benefits of keeping the skin on. It keeps the flesh moist. It also flavors it. In cases of delicate fish, such as sole or trout, it holds the meat together as it cooks.

Yet, in some instances, I do need to remove the skin before cooking. Some fish—mahi mahi, catfish, and cod, among others—merely have tough, bad tasting, or inedible skin that should be discarded before cooking. Fortunately, skinning is easy to do.

To start this process, place your fish on a clean, flat surface. Holding it by the tail, use a chef's knife to make a small, vertical cut just before the tail begins. Pull the knife forward slightly so that you expose a bit of the meat and create a flap of skin. Angle your knife downward and forward, sliding the blade under this flap. Keeping your knife as close to the inside of the skin as possible, ease the blade downward and toward the head. Once you've reached the head of the fish, pull or cut off the skin. Trim off any extra skin that may have been left behind. That's it. You've just skinned a fish.

Cutting Steaks and Fillets

Don't expect to master cutting steaks and fillets on your first or even fourth try. With some practice, though, you can become fairly accomplished at both.

STEAKS

Of the two cuts, I find steaks to be more forgiving. As long as I have a sharp, heavy chef's knife, I usually can create decently sized and shaped steaks.

To cut steaks, you'll need a bigger fish: one that weighs at least four pounds. Almost any larger fish can be made into steaks. This includes the aforementioned tuna, salmon, and swordfish, as well as bluefish, carp, cobia, mackerel, sablefish, halibut, snapper, and so on. De-scale, gut, and remove the fins on this fish. The skin stays on to help hold the steak together during cooking.

Once you've cleaned your fish, measure out how big you want your steaks to be. A good guideline for this is a commercially produced beef steak. In terms of thickness it will run between one and two inches. Cut vertically from backbone to belly to make each steak: you should get about three ample-sized steaks. Rinse the steaks off and refrigerate or freeze until you're ready to cook them.

FILLETS

Fillets are a bit trickier. If you come across a boatload of inexpensive mackerel, try practicing on them. Mackerel are the quintessential roundfish, representative of pretty much any fish that isn't a flat, side-swimming flatfish. Thanks to their price, availability, and uncomplicated bone structure, these guys are ideal for learning how to fillet properly.

If you have a roundfish with scales and you don't plan on skinning the fish, you'll need to remove the scales. See the Cleaning Fish section, pages 11–12, for details on how to do this.

Once the fish is cleaned and de-scaled or skinned, lay it on its side with its back facing you. Insert your chef's or filleting knife behind the gills. With the blade planted half an inch into the flesh, slice downward along the backbone from head to tail. Turn the fish around so that the belly faces you and repeat this cut from head to tail. Make a final vertical cut near the tail to release the fillet. Flip over the fish and repeat these steps to remove the other fillet.

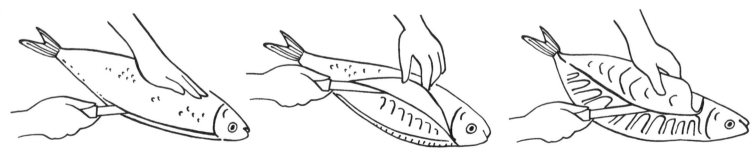

For flatfish, such as flounder and sole, clean the fish, take off the scales, and lay the fish with its eyes looking upward on a clean, flat work surface. Cleaning and filleting tasks can be carried out with a chef's knife. For those wishing to acquire additional knives, a filleting knife could be used in place of the chef's knife. Using a sharp knife or kitchen shears, snip off the fins.

Place your knife at the base of the head and make a deep, diagonal incision here. It should be deep enough for you to hit bone. Locate the backbone and insert your knife over the top of it. Start slicing horizontally from head to tail. You'll want to cut over, not through, the backbone, so keep your knife above it. Go through the small bones in the thicker part of the fillet and then move toward the belly, slicing through the side bones. As you reach the end of the fillet, pierce the skin with your knife and release it. Flip over the fish and carve the next fillet in the same manner.

At this point you can trim the edges of the fillets and pluck out the bones with seafood pliers or tweezers. You could also leave the bones in and remove them from the cooked fillets before serving.

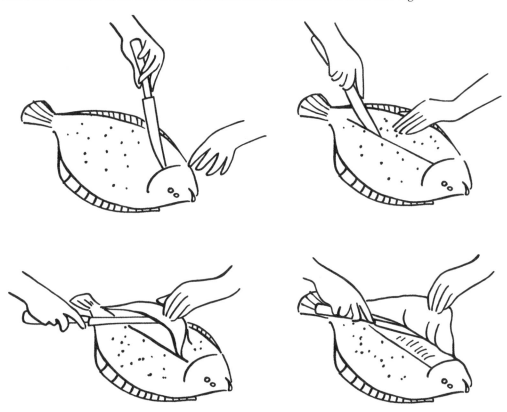

Cooking Equipment

You don't need a kitchen full of fancy pots and pans to cook seafood properly. There are, however, a few pieces of equipment that I've found particularly useful. Some things, such as aluminum foil, parchment paper, a cutting board, ovenproof baking dish, and large, rimmed baking sheet, you probably already have on hand. If you don't have them, you'll want to stock up on these items. You may also want to invest in the following pieces of equipment:

ESSENTIALS

Boning knife: Slender and more flexible than a chef's knife, a sharp, five-inch boning knife enables me to remove bones from fish with ease.

Chef's knife: A multitasker's dream, a freshly sharpened, eight-inch chef's knife can clean and fillet fish, chop vegetables, herbs, and fruit, and do most other knife work.

Paring knife: This can be used to clean and open bivalves and crustaceans.

Six- to eight-quart stockpot with lid: A lidded, heavy-bottomed stockpot is great for making soups, chowders, and stews. Its size and accompanying lid also make it a good vessel for steaming fish and shellfish.

Twelve-inch nonstick skillet or frying pan: I find nonstick pans ideal for browning or pan-searing fragile seafood, such as scallops, flounder, and sole.

Fish turner or spatula: Slender and slotted, a fish spatula allows me to flip fish fillets and steaks without difficulty. It also encourages unwanted oils to drain off the fish.

Metal or bamboo skewers: I use these for threading and cooking fish kebabs.

Needle-nose seafood pliers/tweezers: These are ideal for removing pin bones in fish.

Rubber spatula: I use this with non-stick skillets so that I don't mar their surfaces.

Instant-read thermometer: An instant-read thermometer clears up any questions or concerns about seafood doneness.

NON-ESSENTIAL TOOLS

Clam and oyster knives: Relatively inexpensive, these small knives work wonders when opening oysters and clams. Each one is designed for its specific bivalve.

Fish fillet knife: I like to think that my seven-inch fish fillet knife enables me to cut plumper, nicer-looking fillets. Truthfully, if you're skilled at filleting, any sharp, thin knife will do.

Heavy-duty kitchen scissors: Sharp, heavy kitchen scissors are handy for removing fins.

Sauté pan: Constructed for sautéing, my four-quart sauté pan also works nicely for poaching and pan-frying.

Twelve-inch bamboo steamer: This multitasking tool can be used to steam dumplings, as well as seafood.

Fish grill basket with nonstick finish: This is perfect for turning whole fish on a grill. The nonstick surface makes the basket a breeze to clean.

Seafood crackers: These are great for cracking open lobster and crab claws.

Cut-resistant glove: I slip my shellfish-holding hand into this glove before prying open those hard and sometimes uncooperative shells. What I spent on a cut resistant glove I save on bandages and emergency room visits.

Candy/deep-fry thermometer: In the rare instances where I deep-fry seafood, this inexpensive thermometer lets me know when the oil is piping hot and ready for frying.

Cedar or maple grilling planks: I haul out these planks to cook whole fish, fillets, and steaks on my grill. Planks add a nice, woody flavor and provide a safe, gentle cooking surface for delicate fish.

Keeping Your Knives Sharp

Expert knife skills won't matter much if you use an unsharpened knife. Whenever your knife's blade starts to feel dull, run it through an electric knife sharpener or over a series of lightly oiled sharpening stones. This will ensure clean, easy cutting and a long-lived, well-maintained knife.

If sharpening with stones, begin with the coarsest grit. Set the stone on a flat work surface and spread a few drops of honing oil—available at cookware, knife, and some hardware stores—over it. Position your knife at a twenty-degree angle to the stone. Placing your fingertips on the blade to keep it under even pressure, draw the blade, from tip to heel, over the top of the stone. Do this ten times on each side before switching to a finer grit stone. Once you've finished sharpening your knife, wipe the oil from the blade and stones and move on to honing.

You should hone your knife before each use. This realigns the blade's edge, which shifts during repeated cutting. To hone a knife, take the steel, a three- to fourteen-inch, textured metal rod, and grasping it by the handle, pull the knife's blade, from heel to tip, over it at a twenty-degree angle. Repeat this step on the other side of the steel and blade. Alternating between the two sides, make ten strokes total across the steel. When done, you'll have a straight blade that's ready for some serious knife work.

Ingredients

Unless otherwise specified, I use unsalted butter, fine sea salt, skim organic milk, freshly squeezed citrus juice, and organic greens. When I need grated citrus zest, I buy organic lemons, limes, or oranges. If I'm only using the juice, I save a few cents and choose the conventional options.

All cheeses are full fat. All wines are dry. All flour is unbleached. All eggs are large and cage-free. You won't see any recipes calling for curly parsley; all the fresh parsley used is Italian flat-leaf.

Depending upon your location, you may have difficulty tracking down some seafood. Whenever possible, I list substitutes for harder-to-find fish. Often recipes within the same chapter are interchangeable (e.g., the sardines discussed in Small, Savory, Oily Fish (page 64) can stand in for herring recipes in that chapter). Frequently fish from one chapter can be substituted for fish in another. If you live in a landlocked region or one that lacks a diverse seafood market, you should still be able to make almost all of the recipes.

A few recipes call for unusual or exotic ingredients. I think specifically of the tamarind paste in Sesame-Crusted Salmon with Sweet Tamarind Sauce from chapter 4 (page 111) and garam masala and black mustard seeds in Catfish Curry from chapter 6 (page 150). In those instances I cite where the item can be purchased in stores and online.

A Bevy of Bivalves

If you're looking for simple yet sumptuous seafood, I can think of no better group to turn to than the bivalve. Whether flat, globular, scalloped, or smooth, these marine invertebrates are some of the most uncomplicated and tastiest seafood around. From petite, half-inch bay scallops to hefty, twelve-inch Japanese oysters these members of the mollusk family share a major trait—they possess two hinged shells, or valves, held together by a single muscle. Break apart the shells and you've got four of the world's most beloved delicacies: clams, mussels, oysters, and scallops.

With the exception of scallops, which are shucked immediately after harvesting, bivalves are sold live and in their shells. To pick out good, live bivalves, I look for ones with shells that close tightly when tapped. I avoid those that don't respond to tapping or that smell unpleasant, and any that have broken or damaged shells.

Similar to most seafood, bivalves need only minimal preparation. In the case of oysters, for instance, I can execute the three S's: scrub, shuck, and serve them on the half-shell with a squeeze of fresh lemon juice.

Bivalves respond well to a wealth of cooking methods. You can broil, grill, steam, sauté, or roast them. Stuff them with herbs and bake them. Coat them with breadcrumbs or a batter and pan- or deep-fry them. I've made all four into soups and stews as well as casseroles and pies. At times the preparation possibilities seem limitless.

Clams

Clams hold a special place in my heart, because they were the first bivalves that I consumed. Centuries before my happy introduction to clams, these mollusks were prized for both their function and form. Native Americans had a particular affinity for clams. Coastal tribes harvested them for food. Most importantly, they taught early colonists to eat these tidal-based creatures. If it weren't for the Native Americans' culinary resourcefulness, I may never have had that addicting first bite of clams.

There are two varieties of clams: hard-shell and soft-shell. Possessing a hard, grayish shell less than two inches in diameter, the East Coast littleneck is the smallest hard-shell clam. Registering at two and a half inches in diameter, the cherrystone comes next followed by the quahog or chowder clam, which measures between three to six inches across. Hard-shells, such as Pacific littlenecks, Manilas, pismos, and butter clams, all hail from the West Coast.

Contrary to their name, soft-shell clams have brittle, thin shells that don't close completely, due to long, protruding siphons or necks. Steamers and razor clams fall into the soft-shell category, as does the monstrously large geoduck, pronounced "gooey duck." Amazingly, its neck can jut out several feet.

For both soft- and hard-shell clams, size matters. The smaller the clam, the more tender the meat. Large clams, such as quahogs, usually end up chopped or minced and added to chowders or formed into fritters. Small clams tend to be steamed. All should be cooked gently so that they don't become tough and chewy.

To store fresh, live clams, I place them in an empty bowl in my refrigerator. I never put them under plastic wrap or water. That's the quickest way to end up with a fridge full of stinky, dead clams. I try to cook them within a day or two of purchase. The fresher they are, the tastier they will be. They particularly shine when seasoned with such flavorings as butter, olive oil, soy sauce, white wine, basil, garlic, ginger, parsley, and red pepper flakes.

Both farmed and soft-shell clams receive an eco-best rating and can be consumed often.

Clam Fritters with Spicy Rémoulade

My first experience with clams came in the form of fritters. As a nine-year-old I didn't have a palate refined or experienced enough to appreciate the accompanying rémoulade sauce. I just dunked the hot clam fritters into ketchup. Over the years I've grown to love the French mustard-mayonnaise dressing known as rémoulade. However, when I'm pressed for time, I still dig out a bottle of ketchup and start dipping my clam fritters. If you can, take the time to make the following spicy rémoulade. You won't regret it.

It may seem as though I'm cheating a bit in this recipe by using canned clams. In the case of fritters, inexpensive canned clams save time and work well, but feel free to substitute with fresh clams if you've got the time to spare.

SERVES 6

For the rémoulade:

1 cup mayonnaise
2 teaspoons Dijon mustard
2 teaspoons freshly squeezed lemon juice
2 teaspoons capers, drained and rinsed
1 tablespoon chopped fresh tarragon
2 tablespoons chopped fresh flat-leaf parsley
1 garlic clove
$1/4$ teaspoon ground hot paprika
$1/2$ teaspoon sea salt
1 teaspoon hot sauce

For the fritters:

$1^1/2$ cups unbleached all-purpose flour
1 teaspoon baking soda
1 teaspoon sea salt
$1/2$ teaspoon freshly ground black pepper
$1/2$ teaspoon cayenne pepper
1 (12-ounce) bottle lager beer
2 (6.5-ounce) cans chopped clams, drained
5 cups grapeseed oil, plus more as
   needed for frying

TO MAKE THE RÉMOULADE, pulse the mayonnaise, mustard, lemon juice, capers, tarragon, parsley, garlic, paprika, salt, and hot sauce together in the bowl of a food processor or blender. Once blended, spoon the dressing into a small bowl and refrigerate until ready to use.

FOR THE FRITTERS, in a large bowl mix together the flour, baking soda, salt, black pepper, and cayenne. Pour in the beer and stir until no lumps remain. Add the clams and stir again until all are coated. At this point you will have a fairly thick batter.

Pour 5 cups of vegetable oil (or enough to reach a depth of 3 inches) into a deep fryer or deep, 8-quart, heavy-bottomed stockpot. Heat the oil on medium-high. When ready, the oil will shimmer and its temperature will read between 350°F and 365°F on an instant-read thermometer.

Working in batches, spoon one heaping tablespoon of batter per fritter into the hot oil. Whatever you do, don't overcrowd the fritters or else they won't cook evenly. Turn them occasionally in the oil. Cook for 2 to 3 minutes or until the fritters are light brown, then remove them with tongs or a slotted spoon. Place them on paper towels to absorb the extra oil. Place the fritters on a large platter with the bowl of rémoulade and serve immediately.

HOW TO CLEAN YOUR CLAMS

With hard-shell clams I take a stiff bristled brush and, placing the clam under running water, scrub the shell until it's clean. Soft-shells require a bit more work. An hour or so before cooking them, I'll rinse the clams and then place them in a bowl of salted water to soak. Live clams will push salt water, along with any dirt and debris, out of their shells. Use salted water and the clams do the cleaning for you. This should remove much of the sediment inside. After soaking them for roughly thirty minutes, drain the clams, rinse them again, and start shucking.

CLAM SHUCKING

First off, pick up a clam knife or good paring knife. Believe me, it's worth the ten to thirteen dollar investment; butter, steak, and chef's knives just don't do the job.

Knife and clams acquired, place a heavy, folded dishtowel in the palm of one hand and your knife in the other hand. Put the clam in the towel so that its hinge faces you. Wedge your clam or paring knife between the two shells. Wiggling the knife to gain leverage, slide it from end to end. This will separate the shells.

Using the tip of your knife, scrape out the meat in the top shell and drop it into the bottom. Do the same with the bottom shell's meat, being careful to reserve the clam liquid. (It's best if you do this over a small bowl.) Remove the meat and start cooking.

Littleneck Linguine with Brown Butter

Since medieval times French chefs have incorporated brown butter, or *beurre noisette,* into their cooking. They use it to enliven steamed vegetables, dress up calves' brains, and add a kick to fish. It lends a luscious and intensely nutty flavor that I adore.

In this dish, linguine with clam sauce gets a makeover, the red sauce replaced with velvety brown butter. It's a simple change with a divine result. If you can't find littlenecks, substitute any other small, hard-shelled clam.

SERVES 4

1¹/₂ cups dry white wine

3¹/₂ to 4 dozen (about 4 pounds) littleneck
  clams, scrubbed

10 tablespoons unsalted butter, cut into pieces

1 pound linguine

2 tablespoons minced fresh flat-leaf parsley

¹/₂ cup grated Pecorino Romano cheese

Place the white wine in a medium stockpot and bring to a boil over medium-high heat. Add the clams, cover, and cook until the clams open, 5 to 8 minutes.

In a small saucepan, melt the butter over medium heat, swirling the pan over the heat. Continue cooking and swirling the pan. A foam will form and then slowly disappear. At this point the butter should be turning golden in color. Three to 4 minutes after foaming, the bubbling butter should begin to smell nutty and bits of milk solids will begin to turn brown. Give the butter a final swirl, remove from the heat, and set aside.

Cook the linguine according to the package instructions. Drain it, and place the pasta in a large bowl. Add the clams to the pasta. Pour the brown butter over the clams and linguine and, using two forks, toss together so that the pasta is coated. Sprinkle the parsley and Romano cheese over the pasta and toss again. Serve immediately.

Grilled Clams with Lemon-Basil Butter

As with most shellfish, I've found that clams respond remarkably well to grilling. They take almost no time to prepare. Cleanup is likewise minimal. Plus, grilled clams require little adornment. If you don't have time to whip together lemon-basil butter, you could always top these with a squeeze of lemon juice, a dollop of hot, barbecue, or cocktail sauce, or a splash of soy sauce.

SERVES 6

Freshly squeezed juice of 1 lemon

Grated zest of 2 lemons

3 tablespoons minced fresh basil

$^1/_2$ teaspoon freshly ground black pepper

1 stick ($^1/_2$ cup) unsalted butter, melted and cooled

5 dozen (about $7^1/_2$ pounds) medium, hard-shelled clams such as top neck or cherrystone, scrubbed

Preheat the grill on high.

Add the lemon juice and zest, basil, and pepper to the melted butter. Stir together and set aside.

Cover the grill grates with foil and then place the clams on top of the foil. Cover the grill and allow the clams to cook for 8 to 10 minutes, until their shells have popped open and begun to steam. After tossing out any unopened clams, place the grilled clams in a bowl or on a platter and drizzle the lemon-basil butter over them. Serve immediately.

Mussels

Similar to their clam brethren, mussels possess a lengthy culinary history. Unlike clams, which won over early American settlers, mussels originally wowed European diners. Archeological evidence indicates that Europe has been consuming these dark blue- to black-shelled mollusks for over twenty thousand years.

What's the attraction to mussels? Granted, I'm wooed by the facts that they grow in abundance and are available year-round. I also appreciate that their method of collecting food—filtering the ocean water to extract miniscule marine life—helps to keep their habitats clean. What has completely sold me, though, is the taste. Mussels possess creamy, sweet, juicy meat slightly reminiscent of lobster. I get the flavor of lobster for a fraction of the price. Can't beat that!

Although dozens of species exist, I most often encounter blue or common mussels, and so, unless otherwise indicated, that is the species I use in my recipes. Found on the Mediterranean, Atlantic, and Pacific coasts, blue mussels range from two to three inches in length and have dark blue shells. Every now and then I see green-lipped mussels. Imported from New Zealand, green-lipped mussels can grow up to eight inches long. As you might guess from their name, they have bright green shells.

In terms of quality, the tinier the mussel is, the better the dining experience will be. As with all bivalves and shellfish, avoid those with broken or damaged shells. Steer clear of overly heavy or lightweight and rattling ones. The former may be weighed down with sand. The latter may contain a dead mussel.

Mussels are at their best when cooked the day that they're purchased (or, even better, the day that they're harvested). In a few instances I've had no choice but to cover fresh mussels with a damp towel and refrigerate them. They will keep for up to two days this way. If they smell fishy or funky, though, they should be discarded.

Mussels also come packed in oil and in plain and smoked versions. Frozen New Zealand mussels, either whole or on the half-shell, are also available.

When setting out to cook mussels, I keep in mind their flavor affinities. Their sweet, juicy meat favors such ingredients as celery, chives, clams, curry powder, garlic, lemon, mustard, onions, pasta, potatoes, shallots, spinach, tarragon, and tomatoes. In terms of cooking liquids I would recommend a Belgian or Belgian-style beer, cream, olive oil, Pernod, red wine vinegar, vermouth, or dry white wine.

The mussels in American markets are primarily farmed-raised on ropes in the ocean. Because this practice does not damage the environment and because the mussels' filter-feeding system helps to keep the ocean clean, these bivalves are an ecologically safe seafood choice. In fact, environmental experts rank them as an "eco-best" food.

SCRUB-A-DUB-DUB: WASHING LIVE MUSSELS IN A TUB

Look at a mussel and the first thing that you'll notice is a cluster of scruffy threads attached to it. Collectively called a beard, these fibers allow the mussel to cling to and grow on rocks, poles, and other substrate. While useful to the mussel, they're of no value to the cook and should be scraped off with a knife.

Under running water and using a stiff, bristled brush, scrub the de-bearded mussels. Toss out any with cracked, damaged, or opened shells. If the mussels seem heavy or unusually dirty, soak them in a tub under running water for an hour before draining and washing off again.

Belgian Steamed Mussels

Appropriately enough, I first tasted Belgian steamed mussels, or *moules marinière,* in the Flemish city of Ghent. On a brisk, late December afternoon, as local Belgians rushed about the cobbled streets, I snuck into a little pub to warm up and grab a bite to eat. While the pub's name has vanished from my memory, its delectable moules frites still linger on my palate. Served with a plate of Belgian-style frites and a mustard-mayonnaise sauce, those tender, succulent mussels remain a highpoint of my visits to Belgium.

In this recipe I've omitted the side of frites. Needless to say, if you have time to make thick-cut fries, do so. Otherwise, crusty bread is a good substitute and a great way to sop up all the delicious broth.

SERVES 4

3 tablespoons unsalted butter
2 shallots, minced
1 garlic clove, minced
$^1/_2$ teaspoon dried thyme
$^1/_2$ teaspoon dried tarragon
$^1/_2$ teaspoon dried marjoram
$^1/_2$ teaspoon freshly ground black pepper
$1^1/_2$ cups Belgian beer (such as Duvel or Leffe Blond) or a Belgian-style beer (such as Victory Brewing Company's Golden Monkey or Brewery Ommegang's Hennepin Farmhouse Saison)

4 pounds mussels, debearded and cleaned
3 tablespoons fresh flat-leaf parsley, minced

In a medium stockpot melt the butter over medium heat. Add the shallots and garlic and sauté for 3 minutes before adding the thyme, tarragon, and marjoram. Stirring occasionally, cook until the ingredients have softened but have not started to brown, about 1 minute. Add the pepper and beer and bring the ingredients to a boil over medium-high heat. Add the mussels and then cover the pot with a lid. Reduce the heat to medium and allow the mussels to steam for 5 to 8 minutes.

Once most of the mussels have opened, take the pot off the burner. Shake the pot several times to coat all the mussels with the sauce. Throw out any that haven't opened. Add the parsley and toss to combine. Spoon the mussels and broth into four bowls and serve.

Mussels Provençal

Featuring the flavors of the South of

France, this dish can be served as either a starter or an entrée. For a spicier version, replace the capers with 1 teaspoon of crushed red pepper flakes.

SERVES 4 AS AN ENTRÉE OR 6 AS AN APPETIZER

3 tablespoons olive oil
1 medium yellow onion, diced
$1/4$ teaspoon sea salt
4 garlic cloves, minced
1 medium red bell pepper, diced
$1^1/_2$ teaspoons dried thyme
1 teaspoon dried basil
1 teaspoon capers, drained and rinsed
1 (28-ounce) can diced tomatoes with their juices
1 cup dry white wine
Freshly squeezed juice of 1 lemon
$1/_2$ teaspoon freshly ground black pepper
4 pounds mussels, debearded and cleaned
$1/_2$ cup chopped fresh flat-leaf parsley

In a medium stockpot heat the olive oil over medium heat. Add the onion and salt and sauté until soft and somewhat translucent, 5 to 7 minutes. Add the garlic, bell pepper, thyme, and basil and sauté for another 5 minutes. Tumble in the capers, tomatoes, white wine, lemon juice, and black pepper and bring to a boil.

Simmer for 5 minutes to marry the flavors. Taste and adjust the seasonings, and then add the mussels.

Cover the pot and allow the mussels to cook until the majority of them have opened, 5 to 8 minutes. Don't overcook the mussels as this will make them tough. Add the parsley and toss to combine. Spoon the mussels into a large bowl, pour the sauce over top, and serve.

Broiled Stuffed Mussels

This recipe works well with clams and oysters, too. However, you might need to adjust the cooking times by a few seconds, depending upon the size of bivalve used.

SERVES 4

1 cup dry white wine
4 pounds mussels, debearded and cleaned
$^{1}/_{2}$ cup grated Gruyere cheese
$^{3}/_{4}$ cup plain white breadcrumbs, toasted
2 tablespoons chopped fresh flat-leaf parsley
$^{1}/_{2}$ teaspoon dried marjoram
$^{1}/_{2}$ teaspoon sea salt
$^{1}/_{4}$ teaspoon freshly ground white pepper
$^{1}/_{8}$ teaspoon ground nutmeg
2 to 3 tablespoons olive oil, as needed

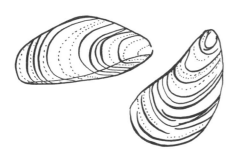

Place the white wine in a medium stockpot and bring to a boil over high heat. Add the mussels, cover, and steam for 5 to 8 minutes, until the mussels open wide. Discard any unopened ones. Using a fine mesh sieve, strain the liquid into a bowl and reserve it for later.

Place the mussels on baking sheets and allow them to rest at room temperature for 10 minutes or until they're cool enough to handle.

In a small bowl mix together the cheese, breadcrumbs, parsley, marjoram, salt, pepper, and nutmeg. Add 4 to 6 tablespoons of the reserved cooking liquid. If the filling still seems dry, add a smidgen more. You want the stuffing to be soft and moist but not soggy.

Preheat the oven's broiler on low.

Remove the top shell of each mussel and discard it. Top each uncovered mussel with 1 to 1$^{1}/_{2}$ teaspoons of stuffing. Drizzle a little olive oil over each.

If using more than one baking sheet, place the sheets, one at a time, on the rack closest to the broiler. Broil until the stuffing has turned golden brown, 1 to 2 minutes. Be sure to watch the mussels so that they don't overcook or blacken. Serve immediately.

Oysters

The most coveted of all bivalves, oysters have been culinary darlings for centuries. Their heyday came in the nineteenth century when oyster quantities were high and costs were low. At that time diners in North America and Great Britain consumed oysters as if there were no tomorrow. A slew of oyster-based dishes, including Oysters Rockefeller (oysters on the half shell topped with spinach, butter, breadcrumbs, and seasonings and baked until golden brown) and angels on horseback (bacon-wrapped oysters on toast), came into being. Whether consumed on the half-shell or in a prepared dish, people just couldn't get enough of these delectable shellfish.

Unsurprisingly, overconsumption during the late nineteenth century led to shortages and higher prices. Fortunately, thanks to the increased presence and popularity of farmed oysters in the twentieth century, the oyster market rebounded. At present farmed oysters are relatively inexpensive and plentiful, making them an "eco-best" seafood choice. That, paired with the fact that oysters are also high in omega-3 fatty acids and iron and low in calories and fat, is great news for those of us who adore this gray, rough-shelled bivalve.

There are four major species of commercially harvested oysters—Eastern (or Atlantic), Pacific (or Japanese), European flat, and Olympia. Within these species there exist countless types, including such familiar favorites as Eastern Bluepoints, Wellfleets, and Chincoteagues. Their names are based upon their geographic origin (Chincoteagues from Virginia, Wellfleets from Massachusetts).

Sizes can vary anywhere from the one-and-a-half-inch Olympia to the twelve-inch Japanese. As with the other bivalves, the smaller the oyster is, the more tender it will be.

When buying oysters, consider the season as well as the size. Most oyster eaters know about the no "R" rule— don't bother consuming oysters in a month without an "r" in its name. During the months of May through August oysters spawn, becoming watery and not terribly tasty. Do as I do and enjoy these soft, creamy delicacies from the fall through the spring, and opt for farmed rather than wild oysters, as these are the eco-friendliest.

Similar to clams and mussels, live oysters should have solid, closed shells. If slightly ajar, the shells should snap shut when tapped. If an oyster rattles when you shake it, toss it in the discard pile; chances are it's dead.

Oysters can be stored in the refrigerator (in a bowl, covered with a damp towel) for up to a week. If at all possible, I use them right away. I live by the adage "faster usage, better flavor."

If you don't want to fiddle around with oyster knives and shells, you can buy pre-shucked oysters. Before taking them home, check to ensure that the oysters' liquid appears clear, not murky. You can also find canned, frozen, and smoked oysters in grocery, gourmet, and seafood stores.

If you decide to go the raw route with oysters, keep in mind that the majority of seafood-related illnesses are caused by consuming raw shellfish. When you cook shellfish, you kill naturally occurring bacteria. Eat them uncooked and you ingest the bacteria and any accompanying pathogens. How a person's stomach deals with these additions varies. In other words, proceed carefully.

Like all bivalves, oysters do well when baked, broiled, grilled, or steamed. They also can be fried, poached, roasted, or sautéed. Their briny flavor goes nicely with black pepper, butter, cayenne pepper, chives, cream, garlic, lemon, olive oil, parsley, shallots, soy sauce, thyme, and white wine. Fennel, potatoes, spinach, and tomatoes likewise complement oysters' salty taste.

THE FINE ART OF OYSTER SHUCKING

First of all, I suggest that you acquire a sturdy oyster knife. An oyster knife has a short, stiff blade and an angled tip. This angled tip helps in prying open the shells.

I'd also advise stabilizing your oyster so that it doesn't wobble as you work. Some cooks form a mound of sea salt or ice and plop the oyster on top of that. I've used salt as well as a nest of clean kitchen towels to hold my oysters in place. If your knife skills are lacking, consider wearing a mesh, cut-resistant glove on the hand that will hold the oyster. You can also place a heavy dishtowel in the palm of that hand to protect it from slipping or jabbing knives.

Once a stable surface is established, place the oyster's rounded edge down on your work area. Insert the knife between the shells and turn it as you would a key in a lock. This should snap the shell open. Slide the knife from end to end to separate the shells.

Using the tip of your knife, scrape out the meat in the top shell and drop it into the bottom, then loosen the meat from the bottom shell. Be careful to reserve the liquid. If you're serving the oyster on the half shell, leave the meat in the bottom shell. Otherwise, remove the meat for cooking.

Oyster Shooters

This adults-only appetizer couldn't be quicker to make. For those abstaining from alcohol, replace the vodka with three tablespoons of a mild salsa.

SERVES 2

2 shucked oysters

Dash of freshly ground black pepper

1 teaspoon freshly squeezed lemon juice, divided

6 tablespoons vodka, divided

1 tablespoon tomato juice, divided

1 tablespoon hot sauce, divided

Season the oysters with pepper. Place each oyster in a 3-ounce shooter or cordial glass. Add a half-teaspoon of lemon juice to each glass and then pour 3 tablespoons vodka over each oyster. To finish, add equal amounts of tomato juice and hot sauce to the shooters. Bottoms up!

OYSTERS ON THE HALF SHELL

As a child, I thought that oysters on the half shell were the height of culinary sophistication. In reality, though, they require no cooking at all and very little preparation. What could be simpler? You simply serve a raw oyster in its bottom shell on a bed of crushed ice. To consume, place a dash of lemon juice, hot sauce, or vinegar or a smidgen of horseradish or cocktail sauce on the oyster. Open your mouth, tip your head back, and slurp up the oyster and all its amazing juices.

Angels on Horseback

Angels on horseback dates back to Victorian England when oysters were plentiful and primarily the food of the poor. When scallops were used in this recipe, folks referred to the repast as archangels on horseback. In Victorian times, both angels and archangels on horseback were known as savories—small, savory dishes that followed dessert. They were believed to cleanse the palate and prepare stomachs for the final drink of the night. Eventually, angels on horseback, along with other savories, were relegated to the category of appetizers. Clever names and history notwithstanding, any dish that involves bacon, plump oysters, and buttered toast, has to be good.

SERVES 6 TO 8

1 to 2 teaspoons sweet paprika
24 medium oysters, shucked
12 strips good-quality bacon, sliced in half
6 slices country white bread
Salted butter, as needed

Preheat the broiler on high. Line a baking sheet with aluminum foil

Sprinkle a smidgen of paprika over each oyster, wrap it in a piece of bacon, and secure it with a small metal skewer. Place the bacon-wrapped oysters on the baking sheet and place them directly under the broiler. Broil until the bacon has become crisp, 4 to 6 minutes, turning once during the cooking time.

While the oysters are broiling, toast the bread, and then butter it and cut each slice into quarters. Place each oyster on a toast quarter and serve immediately.

EASY OYSTER CLEANING

Cleaning oysters is the easy task. It's the shucking that's a bit of an art form. To clean your oysters, scrub them with water and a stiff, bristled brush. Make sure that all the dirt has been removed from the shells before moving onto the trickier step of shucking.

Oyster Po' Boys

The following recipe was inspired by Chef John D. Folse's The Encyclopedia of Cajun and Creole Cuisine. For the optional hot sauce I use the Louisiana original, Tabasco.

SERVES 6

Grapeseed oil, as needed
6 half-baguettes or hoagie/sub rolls
1 large egg, beaten
2 cups skim milk
2 teaspoons Dijon mustard
1 teaspoon sea salt
1 teaspoon freshly ground black pepper
2 cups unbleached all-purpose flour
1 cup cornmeal
2 tablespoons garlic powder
$1/2$ teaspoon cayenne pepper
4 dozen oysters, shucked
6 tablespoons good-quality mayonnaise
4 ripe tomatoes, thinly sliced
2 cups shredded romaine or Bibb lettuce leaves
Dash of hot sauce (optional)

Preheat the oven to 375°F.

Add oil to a depth of 4 inches in either a deep fryer or an 8-quart, heavy-bottomed stockpot, and heat over medium-high heat. When ready, the oil will be between 350°F and 365°F on a thermometer. (Note: If using a deep fryer, follow the manufacturer's instructions for oil amounts and heating temperatures.)

Slice the rolls lengthwise and place them on a baking tray, crust side down. Set aside.

In a mixing bowl combine the egg, milk, mustard, salt, and black pepper. In a separate mixing bowl combine the flour, cornmeal, garlic powder, and cayenne. Set both bowls aside.

Place the rolls in the oven, turn off the heat, and allow them to become crispy and warm, 8 to 10 minutes.

Dip the oysters in the egg batter and then in the cornmeal-flour mixture. Fry the oysters in batches of three for 3 minutes, or until they are golden on all sides and float to the surface. Remove and place them on paper towels to absorb the excess oil, and then cover to keep them warm. Repeat this process until all the oysters are fried.

Remove the rolls from the oven. Spread a tablespoon of mayonnaise on each one. Place an equal number of tomato slices on the bottom half of each and sprinkle with shredded lettuce. Place a few oysters on top of the lettuce. Splash on a dash of hot sauce, if desired, cover with the top half of the roll, and secure with a toothpick. Slice the sandwich in half and serve immediately.

A SHORT HISTORY OF THE PO' BOY

The official sandwich of New Orleans, the po' boy's origin varies from source to source. Two tales, though, prevail. In the early nineteenth century, Madame Bégué, the owner of a French Market coffee stand, gave away sandwiches made from French baguettes to penniless New Orleanean children. Her food was "for a poor boy." The second story involves the New Orleans streetcar strike of 1929. In it two former streetcar workers, Bennie and Clovis Martin, handed out free food to any striking laborer or poor boy who stumbled upon their French Market restaurant.

While these first po' boys featured potatoes and brown gravy, today's popular offerings include fried oysters, shrimp, or hot roast beef with gravy. What they all share in common is their succulence. As my husband's cousin Mike Malloy, a longtime New Orleans resident and culinary professional, says, "The more napkins required, the better the po' boy."

OYSTERS ROCKEFELLER

A New Orleans original, Oysters Rockefeller was created in 1889 by Chef Jules Alciatore at his family's famed French Quarter restaurant Antoine's. Alciatore reputedly named his dish in honor of the industrialist John D. Rockefeller, who, like the oyster's buttery sauce, was wildly rich.

Although Alciatore kept the exact ingredients a secret, countless interpretations of his recipe do exist. All feature oysters on the half shell topped with a mixture of chopped greens, butter, breadcrumbs, and anise-flavored liqueur.

To whip up a dozen of your own Oysters Rockefeller, you'll need $3/4$ cup cooked and drained spinach; 3 tablespoons plain breadcrumbs; 3 scallions, coarsely chopped; $1/2$ celery stalk, coarsely chopped; 4 tablespoons unsalted butter; 2 teaspoons anise-flavored liqueur such as Pernod; salt and freshly ground black pepper to taste; a dash of hot sauce; and 12 small to medium oysters on the half shell. Preheat the oven to 450°F. Put everything but the oysters in a food processor and pulse until minced. Cover the bottom of a baking sheet with a thick layer of coarse sea salt. Spoon the stuffing over the oysters and lay them on the prepared baking sheet. Bake until the oysters are plump and juicy and the topping is golden brown, 12 to 15 minutes.

Scallops

Plump, versatile, and protected by two gorgeous, fan-shaped shells, the scallop has a lot going for it. It's blessed with a firm texture and a complex yet delicately sweet taste. Almost translucent when raw, it turns a lovely pearl color when cooked. In terms of cooking it responds well to a plethora of techniques, including sautéing, pan-searing, grilling, broiling, and poaching. It can also be made into a gratin, stir-fry, ceviche, or tartare.

Scallops generally fall into two broad groups—bay and sea. Hailing from the East Coast, tiny bay scallops grow to roughly a half-inch in diameter and are sweeter and juicier than sea scallops. Bay scallops are also less abundant; as a result, they cost considerably more. Bay scallops are harvested from October through January and April through May, except for Nantucket bay scallops, which are in season from November to early January.

Sea scallops, which come from the North Atlantic, range from one and a half inches to nine inches in diameter. While chewier than the bay scallops, they are still as moist, and because they are harvested year-round they are widely available and considerably less expensive.

Bay and sea scallops differ from all other bivalves in one respect—you'll almost never have to shuck them, unless you gather them yourself. Because their shells never close completely, scallops spoil easily. To avoid this, fishermen shuck the scallops right after harvesting them. Everything is discarded but the meaty muscle; this propels a scallop through the water and is what we cook and eat.

When selecting scallops, take color, luster, and odor into consideration. The flesh should be somewhere between a pale pink and light beige. Unless it has been soaked in a water solution, which increases its weight and cost, a scallop will not appear bright white. The scallop's meat should have a glistening sheen and smell sweet rather than pungent or fishy. Ask your fishmonger for dry-packed or untreated scallops to ensure that you get the best quality.

Back at home, immediately refrigerate your scallops. You should use them within two days.

Avocados, bell peppers, carrots, chiles, corn, edamame, mushrooms, spinach, and tomatoes are perfect complements to scallops. Bright and simple seasonings such as basil, chervil, parsley, thyme, ginger, garlic, scallions, shallots, lemon, lime, cayenne, salt, white and black pepper, butter, cream, vinegar, and dry white wine give the mild bivalves a flavor boost.

Similar to the other bivalves, scallops, especially when farmed, are a sound, eco-friendly seafood choice.

Vietnamese Scallop Boat Salad

Inspired by my husband's Saigon-born-and-bred stepfather, this salad combines the gentle flavor of sea scallops with the spicy, piquant punch of Asian condiments.

SERVES 4 TO 6 AS A SMALL PLATE/APPETIZER

1/2 cup plain rice vinegar

2 tablespoons rice wine

2 tablespoons reduced-sodium soy sauce

2 tablespoons olive oil

1 tablespoon sugar

1/2-inch piece ginger, peeled and grated (about 1 tablespoon)

1 stalk lemongrass, trimmed and sliced

2 teaspoons fish sauce

2 tablespoons grapeseed oil

1 pound large sea scallops

Sea salt, to taste

Freshly ground black pepper, to taste

4 firmly packed cups (about 4 ounces) mixed greens, washed and dried

1 small red bell pepper, cored, and cut into long 1-inch-wide strips

1 small orange or yellow bell pepper, cored, and cut into long 1-inch-wide strips

1 red chilie pepper, seeded and diced

In a small bowl whisk together the vinegar, rice wine, soy sauce, olive oil, sugar, grated ginger, lemongrass, and fish sauce. Set the dressing aside.

Heat the oil in a large, nonstick frying pan over high heat, until it starts to smoke. Season the scallops with salt and pepper and place them in the frying pan. Reduce the heat to medium-high.

Cook the scallops until brown on the bottom, 3 to 4 minutes, and then flip them over and fry for another 3 to 4 minutes, until the other side is browned and the scallops have lost their opaqueness. Remove them from the hot pan.

Toss the mixed greens with the dressing and place equal portions of salad on 4 to 6 plates. Place one strip of red and one strip of orange bell pepper horizontally in the middle of each salad. Lay another strip of red and orange pepper vertically across the other two strips. These will be the "boats" for your scallops as they sail across the sea of greens.

Put an equal number of scallops in each boat. Sprinkle the chile pepper over the scallops and serve.

Scallop and Mushroom Pie

Like many Americans, I seem to have spent an inordinate number of vacation days eating and drinking in the pubs of Ireland. On these trips I gorge myself on fish and chips, salmon cakes, oysters, and, of course, a pint or two of Guinness. However, what I enjoy most are the crusty potato-topped fish pies. Back at home, when I'm yearning for a bit of Irish pub grub, I whip up my own version of this classic dish, using scallops, mushrooms, and a little bit of sherry.

SERVES 6

1 pound Idaho potatoes, peeled and cut into chunks

5 tablespoons unsalted butter, divided

1³/₄ cups skim milk, divided

Sea salt

10 ounces cremini mushrooms, stems discarded and caps sliced

2 garlic cloves, minced

1¹/₂ pounds sea scallops

1 tablespoon unbleached all-purpose flour

2 tablespoons sherry

Preheat the oven to 350°F. Butter a 2-quart baking dish.

Boil the potatoes in a large pot of water until fork tender. Drain the water from the pot and, using a potato masher or ricer, mash the hot potatoes with 1 tablespoon of the butter and 1 cup of the milk until no lumps remain. Season with salt to taste and set aside.

Melt 3 tablespoons of the butter in a medium sauté pan. Add the mushrooms and sauté on medium-high heat for 5 minutes. Add the garlic, stir together, and then add the scallops. Cook for 10 to 12 minutes, until the scallops are opaque. Remove the scallops from the pan and place them on a warm plate.

Keeping the pan over medium-high heat, add the remaining ³/₄ cup milk and swirl it around to deglaze. Add the flour and stir until the sauce is well combined and thick with no lumps. Return the scallops to the pan. Add the sherry and stir.

Pour the contents of the sauté pan into the greased baking dish. Spread the mashed potatoes evenly over the filling. Dot the top of the potatoes with the remaining tablespoon of butter and place the dish in the oven. Bake for 20 minutes or until the top of the potatoes is golden brown. Serve immediately.

Pan-Seared Scallops with Sherry Vinegar Reduction

Sweet and savory, these pan-seared scallops pair nicely with a subtle, cheese-laced polenta.

SERVES 4 TO 6

3 tablespoon olive oil, divided
2 tablespoons minced shallot
1 cup sherry vinegar
1 tablespoon light brown sugar, firmly packed
1 pound large sea scallops
Freshly ground white pepper, to taste
Sea salt, to taste
Parmesan Polenta, page 237

Heat 1 tablespoon of the olive oil in a small frying pan over medium heat. Add the shallot and sauté until softened, 3 to 5 minutes. Remove from heat.

Pour the sherry vinegar into a separate frying pan and bring to a boil over high heat. Reduce the heat and stir in the brown sugar and shallots. Simmer until the liquid has thickened and reduced to $1/2$ or $1/3$ cup. When finished, the sauce will be dark and syrupy. Set aside.

In a large nonstick frying pan, heat the remaining 2 tablespoons of olive oil on high. Season the scallops with salt and pepper, add them to the pan, and reduce the heat to medium-high. Sear the scallops until brown on the bottom, 3 to 4 minutes. Flip them over and fry the other side until browned, another 3 to 4 minutes.

Place the scallops on dinner plates with the polenta. Gently reheat the sherry vinegar reduction over medium heat and then drizzle it over the scallops. Serve immediately.

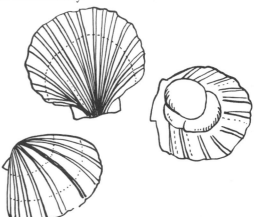

A Collection of Crustaceans

By definition, crustaceans are marine invertebrates with rigid exo-skeletons and jointed appendages. In simpler terms, these guys possess shells, usually five pairs of legs, and occasionally claws: they include shrimp, crab, crayfish, and lobster. The lesser-known langoustine, lobsterette, and prawn are also among the thirty-eight thousand crustacean species in existence.

Although they vary in size and appearance, crustaceans grow in the same way. They shed their shells in order to form new, larger ones. During this regrowth period they are known as soft-shells. Some soft-shells, such as blue crabs, are considered a delicacy.

While crustaceans may all grow the same way, they don't show up at markets in the same form. Lobsters and crabs are sold live, raw (cleaned or uncleaned), and pre-cooked (fresh or frozen). Similarly, you may come across live, fresh, or frozen crayfish. Shrimp are shipped frozen and then either left as is or defrosted and displayed. Yet, frozen shrimp could also come shelled or unshelled, raw or cooked.

What this means to me is that I have a wide range of things to consider when buying crustaceans. With live ones I look for liveliness. If they're not moving around, I don't buy them. Likewise, I check to ensure that their holding tanks look clean. If the water is murky, I move on to the frozen ones.

Defrosted crustaceans should smell of saltwater and nothing else. If I get a whiff of ammonia or other unpleasant odors, I pass on purchasing them. I also skip those with damaged, yellowing, or spotted shells.

Live crustaceans should be consumed the day you buy them. Fortunately, it doesn't take much planning or effort to prepare a crustacean. Simply heat enough water to boil or steam the shellfish. After cooking it, pair it with lemon juice, clarified butter, or cocktail sauce. *Voila!* A fast and easy feast!

Should you crave a fancier dish, know that crustaceans can be prepared using a variety of techniques. They may also be baked, broiled, grilled, sautéed, deep- or pan-fried, stewed, and poached. Easy, versatile, and tasty, they're a delight to cook and eat.

Crabs

Crab is easily one of America's most popular shellfish. From my perspective, it's no wonder why. With its firm yet moist texture and sweet yet slightly salty flavor, crab pleases a wide range of tastes. Because it can be prepared in a host of ways, it's a great food for beginning cooks as well as skilled chefs. Think of it as the "something for everyone" shellfish.

All crabs possess more or less the same shape, though they differ in terms of size and region of origin. They have two strong claws for capturing and crushing prey and eight legs for walking or swimming.

Out of forty-five hundred species of crab, I regularly consume eight types.

From the Pacific Coast I get the succulent, pink-fleshed *Dungeness crab*. Weighing between one and four pounds, it has a meatiness that reminds me of lobster.

Hailing from the North Pacific are *king* and *snow crabs*. Kings thrive in the waters near Alaska and Japan. Weighing as much as twenty pounds, they can measure up to ten feet from tip to tip. Snow crabs can grow up to three feet across. King and snow crabs are sold primarily as frozen legs.

Found in the Atlantic, *Jonah* and *rock* or *peekytoe crabs* were once considered worthless bycatch, or marine life that's unintentionally caught with other species. In fact, upon finding these guys in their lobster pots, lobstermen would toss them out. However, tastes and attitudes change. In the 1990s Jonah and peekytoe became prized for their sweet, moist, and firm meat.

The *stone crab*, caught mainly off the southeast coast of the U.S., possesses a sweet, succulent, solid flesh that makes it a favorite with diners. Since only the claw meat is eaten, fishermen just twist off the claws and throw the live crabs back into the water so they can grow new ones.

Featuring a blue-green shell and blue claws, *blue crab* comes from the Gulf and Atlantic coasts, particularly the Chesapeake Bay. It is consumed both whole and in its soft-shell state, weighing between one to two pounds, and its sweet, soft, and flaky meat, is a favorite among consumers. Unfortunately, this popularity, along with habitat changes, has caused its numbers to dwindle. A more eco-friendly choice would be either stone or Dungeness crab.

You can buy live, hard-shell crabs year-round in coastal regions. Live soft-shells can be found from April to mid-September, peaking in June and July. You can get hard-shells live or cooked whole and frozen. You will also find them cooked, picked, and pasteurized or as frozen claws. Whole, frozen soft-shells are available throughout the year.

When you purchase live crabs, make sure that they're active and perky. Throw them in the fridge as soon as you get home and cook and eat them that day. When cooked and refrigerated, crabs will keep for a few days, but their flavor will fade quickly.

How best to cook crabs? The easiest methods are boiling or steaming and serving them with clarified butter or lemon wedges. However, they also can be baked, broiled, grilled, sautéed, or stir-fried. Soft-shells can also be deep-fried, pan-roasted, or used in tempura. All crabs go well with avocados, bell peppers, grapefruit, onions, shrimp, and tomatoes. Seasonings such as basil, chives, flat-leaf parsley, tarragon, cayenne, black and white pepper, Old Bay Seasoning, garlic, ginger, mayonnaise, Dijon mustard, hot sauce, and vinegar also boost their flavor.

Overall, crab is an ecologically okay shellfish choice. Some populations, such as blue and Russian king crabs, have lost their habitats and are decreasing in number. However, others, such as trap-caught stone and Dungeness crabs, are harvested in sustainable manners and are found in abundance. Choose your crab wisely and enjoy in moderation.

HOW TO CLEAN AND EAT A WHOLE COOKED CRAB

To get the most meat for your efforts, you will need a small wooden mallet and a sharp paring knife. To start, twist off the claws and set them aside. Using a paring knife or your fingers, pull off the triangle-shaped apron, gills, and intestines on the bottom of the crab. Throw these away. Holding the top shell at the front, pull it off and discard. With your hands tear the crab in half and then twist off the legs. Once the crab has been broken down, you're ready to start eating.

Take the tip of a paring knife and pick the meat off of the body. Do the same with the legs and claws. To reach the claw meat, you may need to strike the claws with a mallet. This will crack open the shell and expose a solid strip of meat. If the legs are small, you can just squeeze or suck the meat from them.

Dungeness Crab Salad

With a crab as succulent and tender as Dungeness, the simplest preparations are often the best. If you cannot find Dungeness crabmeat at your local market, substitute Jonah crab. You could also replace the crabmeat altogether and feature lobster here instead.

SERVES 4 TO 6

1 cucumber, peeled, seeded, and diced

1 ripe mango, peeled, seeded, and diced

1/4 cup chopped sweet yellow onion

6 cups (about 5 1/2 ounces) tightly packed mixed greens

1 tablespoon chopped chives

1 tablespoon grated orange zest

1/4 cup freshly squeezed orange juice

1/3 cup olive oil

1 teaspoon sea salt

1/4 teaspoon freshly ground black pepper

1 pound cooked fresh Dungeness crabmeat

1 avocado, sliced

In a large bowl toss together the cucumber, mango, onion, and mixed greens. In a small bowl whisk together the chives, orange zest and juice, oil, salt, and pepper. Pour all but one tablespoon of the dressing over the salad and toss again to combine. Add the remaining dressing to the crabmeat and toss until completely mixed. Spoon the greens onto four plates and top each salad with the sliced avocado and crabmeat. Serve.

Crab Cakelets

If you live in the Mid-Atlantic or have ever visited Maryland's Chesapeake Bay area, you've undoubtedly seen a crab cake or two. Long associated with this region, the fried crabmeat patty remains a quintessentially American dish. It first appeared in print back in 1939 in Crosby Gaige's New York World's Fair Cookbook and has won over countless diners ever since.

A variation on traditional crab cakes, these cakelets make wonderful appetizers, as well as a main course. Figure one to two per person as an appetizer and two to three as an entrée. I find that they go beautifully with a side of Warm Summer Corn Salad (page 228) or with a splash of lemon juice.

MAKES 20 (2-INCH) CAKELETS

2 teaspoons plus 2 tablespoons olive oil, divided
3 tablespoons minced shallot
1 pound fresh lump crabmeat
1 large egg, lightly beaten
$1/4$ cup good-quality mayonnaise
2 teaspoons Dijon mustard
$1/4$ teaspoon cayenne pepper
$1/8$ teaspoon paprika
$1/4$ teaspoon sea salt
$1/4$ teaspoon freshly ground black pepper
1 tablespoon minced fresh flat-leaf parsley
2 to 4 tablespoons plain breadcrumbs
$1/3$ cup unbleached all-purpose flour
2 tablespoons unsalted butter
Lemon wedges, for serving (optional)

Heat 2 teaspoons of the olive oil in a small frying or sauté pan over medium heat. Add the shallot and sauté until soft, about 2 minutes. Remove the pan from heat and cool for 5 minutes.

In a medium bowl mix together the shallots, crabmeat, egg, mayonnaise, mustard, cayenne, paprika, salt, black pepper, and parsley. Add just enough breadcrumbs so that the mixture binds together (no more than 4 tablespoons).

Place the flour on a shallow plate. Heat the butter and the remaining 2 tablespoons of oil over medium heat in a large, nonstick frying pan.

While the butter and oil are heating, form the crab cakelets. Take one heaping tablespoon of crab mixture and, using your hands, shape it into a 2-inch-round patty. Dredge both sides of the cakelet in the flour and set aside. Repeat with the remaining crab mixture.

Pan-fry the cakelets in the hot butter-oil mixture for 10 minutes, gently flipping them over after 5 minutes so that both sides turn golden-brown. Serve warm.

Spicy Crab Stew

I like to think of spicy crab stew as a lazy cook's gumbo. In this case I'm the lazy cook. My spicy crab stew possesses the colors and aromas associated with the Southern Louisiana specialty but without the customary okra, sausage, and rice of Creole and Cajun gumbos. Even without pork, this is a dish that both meat and seafood lovers will adore.

SERVES 6

2 tablespoons olive oil
3 garlic cloves, minced
1 large red bell pepper, diced
1 large yellow onion, diced
1 (28-ounce) can diced tomatoes with their juices
1 dried bay leaf
$1/2$ teaspoon cayenne pepper
$1/2$ teaspoon freshly ground black pepper
$1/2$ teaspoon ground cumin
$1/4$ teaspoon garlic powder
$1/8$ teaspoon ground nutmeg
4 cups vegetable stock
1 (8-ounce) bottle clam juice
1 pound fresh lump crabmeat
1 teaspoon sherry wine vinegar
Sea salt, to taste
Handful of fresh, flat-leaf parsley, chopped

Heat the olive oil in a medium stockpot over medium-high heat. Add the garlic, bell pepper, and onion and sauté until softened, about 5 minutes. Add the tomatoes, bay leaf, cayenne, black pepper, cumin, garlic powder, nutmeg, vegetable stock, and clam juice and stir to combine. Bring the ingredients to a boil, reduce the heat to low, and simmer uncovered for 15 to 20 minutes, stirring occasionally.

Skim off the top of the soup and pull out the bay leaf. Pour half of the soup—about 4 cups—into a bowl or blender. Purée the soup until smooth with an immersion blender or traditional blender, then return the puréed soup to the original stockpot. Stir in the crabmeat and vinegar. Simmer for 10 minutes, stirring periodically. Season to taste with salt, and adjust the other seasonings if necessary. Ladle the stew into bowls, sprinkle chopped parsley over top of each, and serve.

Crayfish

Crayfish resemble tiny lobsters and are found in freshwater lakes, rivers, swamps, wetlands, and canals across the globe. Similar to their fellow crustaceans, the meat of these two- to eight-ounce critters is white, sweet, and succulent. It's much more tender, though, than lobster. If the characteristics sound appealing but the name doesn't ring a bell, try, instead, "crawfish," "crawdad," or "mudbug." In the American South this three- to six-inch crustacean goes by any one of these monikers. It was in Louisiana—the so-called "crawfish capital of the world"—that I first fell for the moist, sweet, flavorful nature of this petite crustacean.

The bulk of American crayfish indeed comes from Louisiana, where they have been farmed since the eighteenth century. Fishermen trapped crayfish in the wild and relocated them to ponds or fields. There they farmed the crustaceans in rotation with crops of rice, providing them with natural vegetation for food. This sensible aquaculture system continues today, making American farmed crayfish a reliably safe, eco-friendly seafood choice.

Crayfish are sold whole and alive or frozen. As is always the case with live fish, look for movement. When touched or picked up, they should move around and spread their claws.

These crustaceans are particularly perishable, so cook them within a day of purchase. If you buy them frozen, defrost them in the refrigerator overnight.

To clean crayfish, before or after cooking, twist the tail off of the head and peel off the shell. If you choose to devein the tail, which is not necessary but is sometimes more aesthetically pleasing, use the tip of a small, sharp knife to lift the vein up and out.

Raw crayfish meat is grayish-white. When cooked, the meat turns white, and the shell become scarlet red—just like a miniature lobster.

Crayfish respond well to boiling, broiling, steaming, and deep-frying. In Louisiana natives hold crawfish boils and festivals featuring boiled crayfish, crayfish gumbo, stew, pie, jambalaya, and étouffée. In Sweden, where this shellfish is equally popular, families throw summer crayfish parties at which they serve mounds of boiled and chilled crayfish. Whether in Louisiana or Sweden, diners crack open the small tails to enjoy the sweet, moist meat and suck the juices from the heads.

While purists claim that crayfish need no adornments, I've found that this shellfish perks up with the addition of a seasoning or two. The sweet, rich taste marries well with garlic, flat-leaf parsley, tarragon, thyme, olive oil, and dry white wine. It also pairs nicely with asparagus, avocados, zucchini, carrots, leeks, mangoes, morel mushrooms, hazelnuts, rice, and bacon.

SWEDISH CRAYFISH BOIL

To turn a Louisiana crawfish boil (page 49) into a Swedish crayfish boil, withhold the garlic, onions, potatoes, and corn. Replace the cayenne, paprika, salt, and pepper with a mixture of $^1/_2$ cup salt, 3 tablespoons sugar, and a bunch of fresh dill. Boil the crayfish with the salt, sugar, and dill. Drain, chill, and serve the crayfish alongside crisp bread, a strong Scandinavian cheese, and beverages such as beer, schnapps, or aquavit.

Crayfish Étouffée

Étouffée is a zesty Cajun stew of vegetables and crayfish served over rice. Based on the French technique of braising or stewing, it's a great way to showcase Louisiana's beloved shellfish.

SERVES 4

4 tablespoons unsalted butter

$1/4$ cup olive oil

$1/2$ cup plus 2 tablespoons unbleached all-purpose flour

1 small yellow onion, diced

3 celery stalks, diced

1 large green bell pepper, diced

1 (14.5-ounce) can diced tomatoes with their juices

5 garlic cloves, minced

$1^1/2$ pounds crayfish tails, cleaned (page 46)

1 tablespoon chopped fresh tarragon

1 teaspoon freshly ground black pepper

1 teaspoon chili powder

1 teaspoon dried thyme

$1/8$ teaspoon cayenne pepper

2 cups vegetable stock

2 tablespoons dry sherry

$1/3$ cup chopped fresh, flat-leaf parsley

1 teaspoon sea salt

3 to 4 cups steamed white rice, for serving

Hot sauce, for serving

In a medium stockpot heat the butter and olive oil over medium-high. Whisk in the flour and stir until a thick paste forms. Reduce the heat to low and continue cooking, stirring vigorously, until the roux thickens, darkens, and gives off a pleasant, nutty aroma, about 5 minutes.

Add the onion, celery, bell pepper, tomatoes, and garlic and cook until softened, 2 to 3 minutes. Add the crayfish tails, tarragon, black pepper, chili powder, thyme, and cayenne, and stir to combine. Add the stock and $1/2$ cup water and stir to form a thick sauce. As the étouffée cooks, you may need to add more water to maintain a thick, saucy consistency.

Bring the ingredients to a boil and then reduce the heat to medium. Allow the ingredients to simmer, uncovered, for 20 minutes, stirring intermittently and adding water as necessary. During this time the flavors will meld together and the stew will thicken; adding water will prevent it from becoming solid or paste-like. After 20 minutes the stew should be fragrant, thick, and chunky.

Add the sherry and parsley, stir, and simmer uncovered for another 5 minutes. Season to taste with salt. To serve, spoon the étouffée over white rice and top with a dash or two of hot sauce.

Louisiana Crawfish Boil

In Louisiana crawfish boils occur throughout the winter and spring. That's when crayfish are in season and at their heaviest.

If using live crayfish, I soak them repeatedly in a tub of cold water, rinsing them off under running water after each wash. When the crayfish no longer turn the water in the tub a muddy, dirty color, I know that they're clean. Before placing them in boiling water, I always check for and discard any dead crayfish.

SERVES 6

1 bottle lager beer
2 large yellow onions, quartered
10 garlic cloves, smashed
2 tablespoons cayenne pepper
1 tablespoon sweet paprika
1 tablespoon freshly ground black pepper
$^1/_3$ cup plus 1 tablespoon sea salt
$^1/_2$ pound smoked sausage, sliced
6 ears of corn, shucked and halved
$1^1/_2$ pounds red bliss potatoes, scrubbed
4 pounds whole crayfish, cleaned

Place the beer, onions, garlic, cayenne, paprika, black pepper, salt, and about $2^1/_2$ gallons of water in a very large stockpot over medium-high heat. Cover the pot and bring the ingredients to a boil. Once the water is boiling, add the sausage, corn, and potatoes, cover, and cook for 10 minutes. Add the crayfish, cover, and cook for an additional 5 minutes: the potatoes should be soft and the flesh of the crayfish should be firm.

Turn off the heat and allow the crayfish to sit in the seasoned water for 15 to 30 minutes, until they're infused with flavor. Drain and serve the corn, potatoes, and crayfish on a large platter.

Crayfish and Mushroom Risotto

Oyster mushrooms add an extra dash of earthiness to the crayfish. You can also make this risotto with 1 pound (36- to 40-count) cleaned, North American farmed shrimp.

SERVES 4

1/3 cup olive oil

1 large shallot, minced

3 ounces oyster mushrooms, chopped

Grated zest and juice of 1 lemon, divided

2 cups Arborio rice

4 cups warm chicken stock, divided

1 pound crayfish tails, cleaned (page 46)

1 teaspoon sea salt

1/2 teaspoon freshly ground black pepper

Parmigiano-Reggiano cheese, grated, for serving

In a large saucepan heat the olive oil over medium-high heat. When the oil starts to shimmer, add the shallot and mushrooms and sauté for 3 to 5 minutes, or until the shallot is translucent and the mushrooms are soft. Add the lemon zest and rice, stir, and cook until the rice has become slightly opaque, 1 to 2 minutes.

Add the lemon juice and 1/2 cup of the chicken stock to the rice. Stirring constantly, cook the ingredients over medium-high heat until the stock has been absorbed by the rice. Add another 1/2 cup of stock, stirring continually. Continue adding stock and stirring regularly until all the stock has been absorbed and the rice is just firm to the bite, about 15 minutes.

Tumble in the crayfish tails and stir to combine. Simmer for 3 to 5 minutes, until the tails have turned snow-white in color. Season with the salt and pepper, and add some Parmigiano-Reggiano cheese to taste. Spoon the risotto into shallow bowls and sprinkle more cheese over top of each. Serve immediately.

Lobster

I tend to think of lobster as a luxury item, something to indulge in on holidays, vacations, and special occasions. Yet, until the nineteenth century, this shellfish was so common in America that it was used as bait. In fact, during colonial times I could have walked along the beaches of Plymouth at low tide and plucked lobsters weighing as much as forty pounds right from the shoreline.

Initially snubbed by aristocrats, these hard-shelled giants were consumed mostly by the poor and the Native Americans until the nineteenth century, when the wealthy developed a taste for lobster. By the 1840s the East Coast lobster had reached Chicago and the Midwest, where diners considered it a symbol of fine dining and of personal affluence. Within seventy years, as the cravings heightened and the supplies dwindled, lobster moved from the status of mundane staple to rare treat.

As a result of overfishing, both the supply and the size of lobsters has decreased. Forget about those forty-pound behemoths. Today's trap-caught lobsters are categorized by size as "chickens" (1 pound), eighths ($1^1/8$ pounds), and quarters ($1^1/4$ to $1^1/2$ pounds). Occasionally you'll encounter larger ones, but the aforementioned sizes are the most common. Almost half of any lobster's weight comes from its claws.

Fresh lobsters are available throughout the year. The most economical time to buy one is in the spring and summer, at the height of harvesting. As with all crustaceans, a live lobster should be active. When you straighten its tail and then let go, the tail should curl back under its body. Its shell should also be firm, thick, and healthy look-

LOBSTER BOIL

Boiled lobster is one of the easiest shellfish dishes to prepare. All that you need is a large stockpot, water, sea salt, and lobster. Be sure to allot one $1^1/2$-pound lobster for each guest.

To kick off your lobster boil, bring a large stockpot filled with water to a boil over medium-high heat. Add 2 tablespoons of sea salt. Drop the lobster one at a time into the water and cover the pot. Generally, you cook a lobster 8 minutes for the first pound and then 4 minutes for the next pound. For instance, a $1^1/2$-pound lobster will boil for about 10 minutes and a 2-pounder would cook for 12 minutes. When the lobster has finished cooking, its shell will be bright red. To ensure that it's truly done, insert an instant-read thermometer in the tail meat. If the thermometer reads 140°F, the lobster can be removed from the pot. Allow it to rest for 5 minutes before serving with butter and lemon juice.

ing. A lobster's color varies according to its habitat. Some appear greenish-blue. Others are reddish-brown. The crustacean only turns scarlet red after being cooked.

Lobster must be cooked the same day that it's purchased. Because it will die in fresh water, transport it in seawater or wrap it in a wet cloth and lay it on ice. Then store it on ice in a cooler until it's time to kill and cook it.

Since bacteria breeds quickly in dead lobsters, this crustacean must either be killed immediately before being cooked or be boiled alive. Those squeamish about killing or boiling live lobsters can buy cooked, whole lobsters. You can also purchase frozen lobster tails.

Boiling remains the simplest—and, in my opinion, the best—way to prepare lobster. I get a lot of taste for very little effort. The shell of the lobster flavors the bubbling water, which, in turn, flavors the lobster meat.

Along with boiling, lobster responds well to baking, broiling, grilling, pan roasting, poaching, sautéing, and steaming. Although its sweet meat doesn't require more than a drop of lemon juice or clarified butter, it is enhanced by a variety of foods and seasonings. Basil, bay leaf, chives, cilantro, parsley, tarragon, cayenne, red curry, garlic, lime, coconut milk, cream, orange juice, vanilla, vinegar, and dry white wine all magnify lobster's taste. Avocados, carrots, celery, corn, onions, peas, pineapple, potatoes, rice, and tomatoes also pep up this crustacean.

While the American, trap-caught lobster has experienced setbacks, it still ranks as an eco-okay food choice.

——— REMOVING MEAT FROM A WHOLE COOKED LOBSTER———

Removing lobster meat sounds a bit harder than it is. Holding the tail section in one hand and the head in the other, twist the two ends, pulling the tail away from the head. While pressing down on the tail's shell, roll it over your work surface until you hear the shell crack. From here, just peel off the shell, leaving behind a big chunk of meat.

For the claws, use the heel—the thick part of the blade, right before it enters the handle—of your chef's knife to crack them open. Place the heel, with the blade facing downward, on the claw and press down, cracking the shell. With your fingers pry the shell off, revealing a solid piece of claw meat. Finally, cut into the knuckles with your chef's knife and pull out the meat.

WORKING WITH A LIVE LOBSTER

No matter what technique you choose to prepare a lobster, always kill it right before cooking. To ensure a relatively humane death, put the lobster in a cooler filled with iced salt water. Cover the cooler and let it sit in the frigid water for thirty minutes. According to food scientist and author Harold McGee, this will anaesthetize the lobster, thus easing your conscience and its pain slightly.

Leaving the bands on its claws, lay the lobster stomach side down on a clean cutting board. Grasping the lobster's body with your free hand, insert the sharpened tip of a chef's knife into the base of its head. If you're unsure where the base is, look for a cross mark on the top of the shell and insert your knife here. Then push the knife all the way down, splitting the head in half and killing it instantly. Once you've done this, then boil or steam the lobster.

When grilling, broiling, or baking lobster, split the crustacean in half before cooking. After splitting the head in two, position your knife by your initial cut, facing the blade toward the tail, and cut through the shell and tail meat. Once the lobster is halved, remove the sac in its head as well as the runny, green tomalley (liver) located near the head sac. The head sac should be discarded. The tomalley, though, can be reserved for use in sauces.

Lobster-Corn Chowder

At the end of summer my husband
and I usually set off for the Mid Coast of Maine, where we visit friends and gobble up countless lobster specialties. One dish that I make sure to order again and again is lobster-corn chowder. When I'm back at home and craving a taste of New England, I whip up this version.

SERVES 6 TO 8

3 tablespoons unsalted butter
1 stalk celery, diced
1 medium yellow onion, diced
2 carrots, finely chopped
1 Yukon gold potato, peeled and
    cut into $^1/_2$-inch cubes
$2^1/_2$ cups fresh or frozen corn kernels
1 teaspoon sweet paprika
$5^1/_2$ cups chicken stock
$^1/_2$ cup light cream
1 pound cooked lobster meat, cut into chunks
Sea salt, to taste
Freshly ground black pepper, to taste

Melt the butter in a medium stockpot over medium heat. Add the celery, onion, carrots, and potato and sauté until softened but not browned, 5 to 7 minutes.

Add the corn and paprika and stir to combine. Add the chicken stock, bring the ingredients to a boil, reduce the heat to low, and simmer until the potatoes are tender, about 10 minutes. Skim off any scum that rises to the top of the soup.

Add the cream and the lobster meat and season to taste with salt and pepper. Stir gently to combine and bring the chowder back to a simmer. Taste and adjust the seasonings before serving in warmed soup bowls.

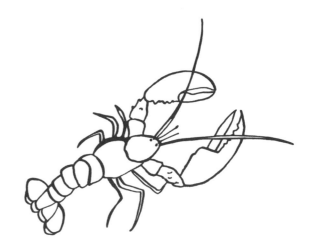

Grilled Lobster with Lime-Herb Butter

Grilled lobster can be prepared over hot coals outdoors or in a grill pan on your kitchen stove. Indoors, you lose a bit of the flavor and romance of cooking over an open fire, but you can still create a delectable meal.

Instead of working with two live lobsters, you can use four (5- to 6-ounce) lobster tails in this recipe.

SERVES 4

$1/2$ cup (1 stick) unsalted butter,
    at room temperature
1 garlic clove, minced
Grated zest and juice of 2 limes
3 tablespoons minced fresh cilantro
$1/4$ teaspoon ground white pepper
1 teaspoon sea salt
2 live (3-pound) lobsters
2 to 3 tablespoons olive oil

Preheat your grill on high.

In a small microwavable bowl, use a fork to mix together the butter, garlic, lime zest and juice, cilantro, pepper, and salt. Warm the ingredients in the microwave for 10 to 15 seconds, until the butter has melted. Set aside.

Kill, split, and clean the lobsters. (See Working with a Live Lobster, page 53, for details.) Brush olive oil over the lobster halves and place them on the hot grill, cut side down. Grill for 2 to 3 minutes and then turn the halves over. Drizzle some of the lime-herb butter over the top of each lobster. Cook for an additional 2 minutes.

Place the grilled lobster on plates and serve immediately with any remaining lime-herb butter.

Open-Faced Lobster-Avocado Roll

For this recipe you need two and a half cups lobster meat, which you'll get by steaming two (1½-pound) lobsters and removing the meat. To save a little time and money, you can also use frozen lobster meat. Just defrost in the refrigerator overnight. If authenticity is what you crave, replace the baguette with four toasted hot dog buns. Serve these open-faced rolls with a side of Mango-Tomato Salsa (page 223).

SERVES 6

2½ cups cooked lobster meat,
    cut into small chunks

1 teaspoon freshly squeezed lemon juice

½ cup plus 1 tablespoon good-quality mayonnaise

2 scallions, whites and 1 inch of greens,
    finely chopped

⅓ cup chopped celery (about 1½ stalks)

Freshly ground black pepper, to taste

1 to 2 tablespoons unsalted butter, softened

1 large French bâtarde or other long, slender bread,
    sliced and cut into 6 equal sections

2 avocados, pitted, sliced, and sprinkled with
    lime juice

In a medium bowl, toss the lobster with the lemon juice. Add the mayonnaise, scallions, and celery and stir to combine. The salad should be moist, but the flavor should not be overwhelmed by mayonnaise. Season with pepper to taste. Refrigerate until ready to use.

Preheat the oven broiler on low. Butter the sliced sides of the bâtarde pieces and place them on a baking sheet sliced side up. Place the sheet directly under the broiler and broil until the butter has melted and the corners of the bread have turned golden in color. Remove the bread from the oven and spoon equal amounts of lobster salad on each piece. Top with avocado slices and serve.

ICONIC NEW ENGLAND CUISINE

The origins of the lobster roll remain a mystery. Some suspect that it evolved as a more portable way to eat lobster salad. Others assume it was a reaction to the twentieth-century creation of the hot dog bun and the public's desire to try different foods on this new type of bread. No matter how it originated, the lobster roll remains a symbol of New England cuisine.

Long associated with the state of Maine, lobster rolls pop up everywhere from upscale restaurants to roadside shacks. I first sampled one of these juicy sandwiches at the humble Red's Eats in Wiscasset, Maine. The Red's Eats lobster roll season runs from mid-April to mid-October, and has for more than seventy years. During those six months the roadside stand sells seven and a half tons of fresh lobster meat. That's a lot of lobster rolls!

Shrimp

Today they're the most popular shellfish in America, but it wasn't until the early twentieth century that shrimp were nationally available. Unless you lived in the South where they were sold live, you missed out on these flavorful crustaceans. In the early 1900s advances in fishing trawler refrigeration allowed the commercialization of shrimp fishing. This, in turn, prompted the nationwide craze for the crustacean.

More than 300 shrimp species exist worldwide, but the most common in the U.S. are: Gulf White, Gulf Pink, Gulf Brown, Ecuadoran or Mexican White, Chinese White, Black Tiger, and Rock. As the names suggest, Gulf shrimp hail from the Gulf Coast, Chinese and Black Tiger come from Asia, and Ecuadoran or Mexican White originate in those countries. Of these Black Tiger is the largest, growing up to one foot in length. It's also one of the more expensive. As a general rule, the larger the shrimp, the higher the price.

Since what's considered medium-size by one producer may be dubbed large by another, I select my shrimp by count and not by size. Count is just the number of shrimp that it takes to make a pound. The smaller the number in the count, the larger the shrimp will be. That way, the inconsistencies won't affect my cooking. For example, I may need only ten colossal shrimp to make a pound but a count of thirty-six to forty-five small shrimp to get the same weight.

When I purchase fresh shrimp where I live, what I get are frozen shrimp that have been defrosted and put on display in a glass seafood case. As there's no benefit to defrosted shrimp, I go with bags of frozen. That way I don't have to use it right away. Nor do I need to fret over how long it's been hanging around in the case.

If you opt for defrosted shrimp, smell it before buying. If you got a whiff of ammonia or other off odors, move on. Likewise, stay away from those with pitted, yellow, spotted, or mushy shells. Avoid buying imported shrimp, especially white and tiger shrimp, as foreign fisheries frequently have lax or no environmental regulations. Instead, look for farmed shrimp from North America, which possess an eco-best rating. These fisheries adhere to strict regulations and provide the eco-soundest shrimp choice for consumers.

When selecting frozen shrimp, stick with unpeeled and uncooked. Unpeeled shrimp tend to have more flavor and texture than peeled. Plus, you can use the leftover shells to make a rich stock.

Shrimp last up to three months in the freezer. To defrost, I put the frozen shrimp in my refrigerator to thaw overnight. I've also placed them in cold water to defrost. As time-saving as microwaving may sound, it actually robs them of moisture and nutrients. Cook shrimp within two days of defrosting. Once cooked, they will last for three days in the refrigerator.

It's no great wonder why shrimp are such a popular shellfish. They're extremely versatile and easy to prepare. I can bake, boil, broil, deep-fry, grill, poach, roast, sauté, steam, or stir-fry these little guys. I can serve them with a splash of lemon juice or cocktail sauce, lay them over a bed of lettuce or pasta, layer them in a sandwich, or feature them in a stir-fry. They require only a minimal amount of cooking—just until they turn pink and curl slightly—and have a wonderfully nutty taste.

Among the ingredients that favor shrimp best are cayenne pepper, curry powder, Old Bay seasoning, black and white pepper, salt, saffron, chives, cilantro, flat-leaf parsley, thyme, garlic, chile peppers, lemon, mustard, olive oil, vinegar, dry white wine, rice wine, and Sauternes. Shrimp also go well with avocados, red bell peppers, carrots, celery, mushrooms, onions, scallions, shallots, tomatoes, beans, bacon, clams, and crab.

TO DEVEIN OR NOT TO DEVEIN

When you devein a shrimp, you remove its intestinal vein, that slender, dark line running along its back. Though it is commonly done for aesthetic reasons, it's not technically imperative that you devein, unless you are butterflying a shrimp or cooking extra-large or jumbo shrimp, which might have gritty deposits in that area.

To devein shrimp, grab an inexpensive deveining knife or a sharp paring knife. Insert the blade tip beneath the vein on the shrimp's back and pull upward. The vein usually comes out in one swift swipe. Discard the vein and move on to the next shrimp.

Sautéed Ginger-Scallion Shrimp

This is my go-to recipe for parties and special occasions. Easy and filling, it wins over hungry diners, as well as mingling guests.

SERVES 2 AS LARGE PLATES OR 4 AS APPETIZERS

3 tablespoons olive oil

3 scallions, whites and 1 inch of greens, cut into matchsticks

2 inches fresh ginger, peeled and cut into matchsticks

2 garlic cloves, cut into matchsticks

1 pound (16- to 20-count) shrimp, peeled

2 to 3 tablespoons dry sherry

Freshly ground white pepper, to taste

Heat the oil in a large sauté or frying pan over medium heat. Add the scallions, ginger, and garlic and sauté for 2 minutes. Add the shrimp and toss to combine. Cook for 4 to 7 minutes, turning the shrimp over once or twice, until the shrimp have curled and turned coral-pink in color. Add the sherry and white pepper and toss to combine again. Serve immediately.

EVERYONE'S FAVORITE APPETIZER

How many times have you gone to a party and found all the guests hovering over the shrimp cocktail tray? I personally have lost count. What I do know is that in most instances the host will have spent far too much money on a premade, store-bought platter that could easily have been pulled together at home.

To create shrimp cocktail for 10 to 12 guests, you'll need 3 pounds of 16- to 20-count shrimp, a small stockpot filled with salted water, 1 large bowl of iced water, and more ice as needed.

Bring the salted water to a boil. As it's heating, devein the shrimp (page 59), leaving the shells on.

Once the water has boiled, add the shrimp. Cook until the shrimp turn coral in color and begin to curl, 1 to $1^{1}/_{2}$ minutes. Using a strainer or slotted spoon, remove the shrimp and place them in the bowl of iced water. Allow the shrimp to cool, adding more ice as needed, for 5 minutes.

Drain and peel the shrimp. Place them on a platter and serve with cocktail sauce, hot sauce, or lemon juice.

Sizzling Garlic Shrimp

Whenever I have a chance to go out for tapas, I insist on ordering at least one plate of gambas al ajillo (garlic shrimp). Widely popular in Spain, this dish features shrimp coated in olive oil and cooked with garlic and chiles in individual earthenware cas-seroles. Since I don't have the space to store all those terra cotta dishes, I make garlic shrimp at home in a shallow frying pan.

Serve these alongside slices of toasted French baguette or bâtarde to sop up the roasted garlic and oil.

SERVES 4

¹/₂ cup olive oil
4 cloves garlic, thinly sliced
2 to 3 dried chiles de arbol, split open,
    seeds removed
1 pound (16- to 20-count) shrimp, peeled
Sea salt, to taste
Ground black pepper, to taste
Handful of fresh flat-leaf parsley, chopped
1 French baguette, lightly toasted and sliced

Heat the oil in a medium frying or sauté pan over medium heat. Add the garlic and chiles and cook for 1 minute, stirring constantly. Add the shrimp, sprinkle with salt and black pepper, and sauté for 3 to 4 minutes, until curled and coral in color.

To serve, split the shrimp and flavored oil between four small, warmed bowls or pour the shrimp and oil in one warmed serving bowl. Scatter the flat-leaf parsley over top.

Spice-Peppercorn Shrimp

When laid over a bed of mixed greens and dressed with balsamic vinegar, these shrimp make for a lovely lunch or light dinner. I've also served them on their own with a squeeze of lime juice as a zesty hors d'oeuvre.

SERVES 6

1 teaspoon coarse sea salt

1 tablespoon chili powder

1 tablespoon curry powder

1 teaspoon sweet paprika

1 teaspoon cardamom

1$^1/_2$ teaspoons whole white peppercorns

1$^1/_2$ teaspoons whole rose or pink peppercorns

$^1/_4$ cup olive oil

2 egg whites, lightly whisked

2 pounds (21- to 30-count) shrimp, peeled

2 limes, quartered, for serving

Using a mortar and pestle or a spice grinder, grind together the salt, chili powder, curry powder, paprika, cardamom, and peppercorns. Spread the spice mix onto a salad plate.

Heat the olive oil in a large sauté or frying pan over medium-high heat. As the oil is heating, prepare the shrimp. Dip each shrimp into the whisked egg whites and then into the spice-peppercorn mix, pressing to coat the entire shrimp.

Working in batches, place the coated shrimp in the pan and cook for 3 minutes. Flip the shrimp over and cook for another 2 to 4 minutes, until they are curled and cooked through. Remove from the heat and serve with the limes.

Shrimp Paella

Named for the two-handled pan in which it's traditionally cooked, as well as the region from which it originated, paella remains one of the signature dishes of Spain. Originally it consisted of short grain rice cooked with snails, rabbit, chicken, saffron, garlic, and olive oil. It has since gone on to include tomatoes, butter beans, shellfish, and a variety of other ingredients.

SERVES 4

3 cups chicken stock

1 cup clam juice

$1/4$ teaspoon saffron threads

$1/4$ cup olive oil

1 large yellow onion, diced

4 garlic cloves, minced

1 tablespoon sweet paprika

$1/8$ teaspoon cayenne pepper

2 cups short-grain rice

2 cups (31- to 35-count) shrimp, peeled and cut into chunks

1 medium red bell pepper, seeded and diced

1 small ripe tomato, seeded and diced

1 teaspoon sea salt

Handful of fresh flat-leaf parsley, roughly chopped

Preheat the oven to 450°F.

In a medium saucepan heat the chicken stock and clam juice over medium heat until hot. Add the saffron and set aside.

Heat the olive oil in a 14-inch oven-safe frying or paella pan over medium heat. Add the onion and garlic and cook until softened, about 5 minutes. Stir in the paprika and cayenne and cook for an additional minute.

Add the rice to the pan and stir until all the grains have been coated with oil. Add the shrimp, bell pepper, tomato, salt, and the heated stock and stir the ingredients together. Gently place the pan in the oven and bake, uncovered, for 15 to 20 minutes, or until all the liquid has been absorbed and a thin crust has formed on top. Remove the paella from the oven and garnish with the chopped parsley. Serve immediately.

Small, Savory, Oily Fish

I have a slew of finicky friends who snub small, savory, oily fish. That's a shame, for this group contains some of the most flavorful, healthful, and ecologically sound seafood around. These fish brim with omega-3 fatty acids, which aid in cardiovascular health. They're rich in protein and Vitamin D. On top of that, they're accessible, easy to prepare, and delicious. Anchovies, herring, and sardines fall into this category as do butterfish and shad.

Found in cold as well as warm waters, these silvery-skinned, fatty-fleshed fish swim in massive schools near the water's surface. Their size and plentitude make them a popular food source for other fish. In fact, they're sometimes referred to as prey or bait fish. If you have ever dined on salmon or tuna, you have, indirectly, eaten a small, oily fish.

Unlike most seafood, the fish in this category are often sold canned. After being beheaded and filleted, anchovies, herring, and sardines are salt-cured or preserved in oil. They're then packed in tins and sent to markets. Herring may also be smoked or pickled in vinegar and spices. Stored in unopened cans, these fish keep for one year. However, it's best to check the expiration date on the packaging to ensure freshness.

If you live along a coastline or have access to a well-stocked seafood department, you may find these types of fish sold whole and fresh on ice. In this state the soft-boned fish taste spectacular. If you buy fresh, look for plump flesh, shiny eyes, and unbruised skin.

Because of their high oil content, small, savory, oily fish are quite perishable and should be used within a day of purchase. Remember to refrigerate the fish on ice until you're ready to clean and cook them.

Canned or salted oily fish need very little preparation. You can bake or broil them, add them to salads, sauces or dips, or put them in casseroles or atop pizzas. When fresh, they can be grilled, fried, marinated, sautéed, braised, broiled, or baked. Just remember that in most cases, you cannot substitute salted or canned for fresh.

Anchovies

I'll always remember my first startling bite of anchovy. On a lunch date with my dad when I was still in elementary school, I sneaked a bite of his Caesar salad and chomped right down on a salty, slightly nutty anchovy. I was both stunned and intrigued. How had that teensy but powerful fish found its way into an otherwise bland salad? Most importantly, why had I never seen it before and where could I get more?

Had I grown up in Europe, I never would have questioned the presence of the anchovy. Derived from the Spanish word *anchova*, this fish has been a favorite of Europeans for centuries. Since the 1500s cooks there have utilized its luscious, oily taste to perk up countless dishes. Yet, in the U.S. we use this dart-like fish sparingly, saving it for pizzas or Caesar salads. What we don't eat ends up getting processed into fishmeal and oil, which seems wasteful for such a full-bodied, omega-3-packed food.

Although anchovies are found in all the warm oceans, the most prized come from the Mediterranean Sea. There, the supply is plentiful and the risks of contaminants and unintentionally caught marine life, known as bycatch, are low. In Turkey, home to the anchovy's greatest enthusiasts, people bake it into breads and pen poems about their beloved *hamsi*.

The diminutive anchovy runs about three to four inches from head to tail. It has gleaming, silvery skin and soft, off-white to gray flesh. A fragile fish, it bruises easily and spoils quickly. As a result, fresh anchovies must be stored on ice in the refrigerator and cooked within a day of purchase.

In the U.S. anchovies are usually filleted, salt-cured, and canned in oil. Frozen, whole anchovies, which we would dub "fresh," are, however, becoming more common in grocery stores.

Fresh anchovies impart a rich, buttery flavor that goes well with capers, garlic, olives, parsley, tomatoes, lemon, cheese, eggs, pasta, and white wine vinegar. Oily and soft, they are perfect for baking, broiling, grilling, marinating, pan-frying, and smoking.

Unlike their fresh counterparts, canned anchovies taste quite salty. As a result, they cannot replace fresh ones in recipes. Use canned to garnish pizzas, spice up salads and sandwiches, and enhance sauces. To reduce their saltiness, soak them in cold water for twenty to thirty minutes. Then drain and gently pat them dry before cooking.

Low in contaminants and high in population, anchovies are a wonderful, eco-friendly fish to eat.

ANCHOVY CLEANING

Thanks to their small size and delicate bodies, whole anchovies are easy to clean. Just run your fingernail—or a small knife if you're a bit squeamish—along the anchovy's belly, slitting it open. Pull out and discard the innards and rinse clean. From here you can remove the fillets by running your finger along the backbone and gently pulling off each fillet. The bones and head can then be thrown away.

CAESAR AND HIS SALAD

Although most diners associate Caesar salad with anchovies, the original salad recipe didn't contain them. Conceived by Tijuanan restaurant owner Caesar Cardini in 1924, the first salad featured whole Romaine lettuce leaves, which diners were to eat with their fingers. The lettuce was dressed in a mixture of 2 mashed and sautéed garlic cloves, 2 cups croutons, $1/4$ cup grated Parmesan cheese, $1/2$ cup olive oil, several dashes Worcestershire sauce, juice of 1 lemon, 2 raw eggs, and ground black pepper. Tossed tableside, the unusual salad garnered countless fans and imitators.

Wanting a subtler taste to his salad, Caesar initially opposed the inclusion of anchovy fillets. Nonetheless, the salad went on to contain and become defined by them. Mashed into a paste and then whisked into the olive oil, the fillets added complexity and flavor to this dish.

Please note that due to the risk of salmonella, raw eggs should not be consumed by children, the elderly, the ill, or pregnant women.

Marinated Anchovies

Known as *boquerones*, marinated anchovies are one of Spain's most popular tapas dishes. For this recipe you will need to purchase fresh anchovies. To clean the fish, follow the instructions in the sidebar Anchovy Cleaning on the opposite page or ask your fishmonger to fillet them for you. Note that the anchovies must marinate for two days, so you'll have to plan accordingly. The vinegar and lemon juice denaturates the proteins in the raw anchovies, making the suitable for eating. Eat these on their own or with thin slices of baguette.

SERVES 6

1 pound filleted fresh anchovies
1 cup white wine vinegar
3 tablespoons freshly squeezed lemon juice
1 tablespoon grated lemon zest
2 garlic cloves, minced
$1/2$ teaspoon capers, rinsed and drained
2 tablespoons extra-virgin olive oil
Freshly ground black pepper, to taste
Handful of fresh flat-leaf parsley, roughly chopped
1 French baguette, thinly sliced and lightly toasted under the broiler (optional)

Place the anchovies, vinegar, lemon juice and zest, garlic, and capers in a shallow dish and toss to combine. Cover the dish and refrigerate for two days. By this point the flesh will have turned white.

After two days, strain the liquid from the anchovies, leaving behind the minced garlic, capers, and lemon zest. Place the anchovies, garlic, and zest in a serving bowl. Drizzle the olive oil and black pepper over top and toss to combine. Sprinkle the parsley over the anchovies and serve with the sliced baguette, if desired.

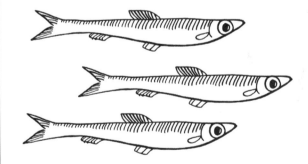

Cannellini-Anchovy-Tomato Pita

This makes a lovely appetizer as is.
However, if you're craving a more substantial dish, you can use the toppings on a bed of mixed greens and add a drizzle of good balsamic vinegar. When served alongside the sliced pita, it becomes a hearty meal.

SERVES 6 TO 8 AS AN APPETIZER

1 (2-ounce) can anchovy fillets, drained and chopped

1 (15-ounce) can diced tomatoes, drained

1 (15-ounce) can cannellini beans, drained and rinsed

1 tablespoon minced red onion

1/2 teaspoon dried thyme

2 tablespoons olive oil

1 tablespoon freshly squeezed lemon juice

1/4 teaspoon freshly ground white pepper

4 white pitas, toasted and cut into quarters

In a medium bowl combine the anchovies, tomatoes, beans, onion, thyme, oil, lemon juice, and pepper. Cover and refrigerate for 30 to 60 minutes to allow the flavors to meld.

When you're ready to eat, spoon the ingredients onto the pita quarters and serve.

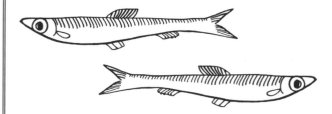

Fettuccine with Anchovy Sauce

This quick and easy meal requires little time or effort. Yet, the resulting Mediterranean-inspired entrée is quite impressive. To add a little heat to your sauce, toss in a half teaspoon red pepper flakes when sautéing the anchovies, nuts, and garlic.

SERVES 4

3 tablespoons olive oil
1 (2-ounce) can anchovy fillets, drained and minced
2 garlic cloves, thinly sliced
2 tablespoons coarsely chopped walnuts
1 pound fettuccine or other long, wide pasta
Freshly ground black pepper, to taste
Grated Parmesan cheese, to taste

Bring a medium stockpot of salted water to a boil over medium-high heat.

Heat the olive oil in a large sauté pan over medium heat. Add the anchovies, garlic, and walnuts and sauté until the garlic turns golden, about 2 to 3 minutes. Turn off the heat and set the pan aside.

Cook the pasta in the boiling water according to the package instructions. After reserving a half cup of salted cooking water, drain the pasta. Add the reserved water to the anchovy-garlic mixture and heat on medium, stirring occasionally, until the ingredients are well incorporated and the sauce doesn't look runny, 2 to 4 minutes. Taste the sauce and season to taste with black pepper.

Tumble the pasta and sauce into a serving bowl, sprinkle a generous amount of grated Parmesan cheese over top, and toss to combine. Serve immediately.

Jansson's Temptation

A specialty of Sweden, Jansson's Temptation's exact origins remain unknown. Some attribute this anchovy-onion-potato casserole to a nineteenth-century Swedish religious reformer who loved anchovies, onions, and spuds. Others point to an early twentieth-century Stockholm hostess who dubbed her party dish "Jansson's Temptation" in honor of a 1928 film of the same name. No matter how Jansson's Temptation got its start, it continues to be a beloved staple of Swedish smorgasbords. Whenever I'm in Stockholm, I make sure to have at least one meal of Jansson's Temptation. Warm, savory, and filling, it's the perfect pick-me-up on dark winter days and cold spring nights.

For a slightly different take on this classic, replace the anchovies with five ounces of smoked salmon or four ounces of canned sardine or herring fillets.

SERVES 4 TO 6

$1/4$ teaspoon freshly ground white pepper
$1/4$ cup plain white breadcrumbs
2 tablespoons grated Pecorino Romano cheese
2 tablespoons unsalted butter
2 small white onions, halved and thinly sliced

$1^1/_2$ pounds Idaho or russet potatoes, peeled, halved, and sliced into $1/4$-inch thick crescents
2 (2-ounce) cans anchovy fillets, drained
$3/4$ cup heavy cream
$1/4$ cup whole milk
1 tablespoon salted butter, melted

Preheat the oven to 400°F. Grease a 2-quart baking dish. In a small bowl mix together the pepper, breadcrumbs, and cheese and set aside.

Melt the unsalted butter in a medium frying or sauté pan over medium heat. Add the onions and sauté until golden in color, about 7 minutes.

Place half of the potatoes in the bottom of the prepared baking dish. Layer the onions, followed by the anchovy fillets and remaining potatoes, over them. You may need to press down on the layers so that everything fits snugly in the dish.

Whisk together the cream and milk and pour it into the baking dish. Sprinkle the breadcrumb mixture over the potatoes and then drizzle the melted butter over the top. Bake for 45 to 50 minutes, until the potatoes are soft and golden-brown. Serve warm.

Butterfish

Found in small schools along the Atlantic and Gulf Coasts, the moist and fatty butterfish only recently entered the culinary scene. In the nineteenth century farmers used it as fertilizer for coastal crops. As late as the 1930s fishermen tossed it out as bycatch. At that time no one was interested in cooking this squat, snub-nosed peewee. Luckily, tastes changed. Thanks to its soft, buttery flesh and mild, succulent flavor, today's cooks rate it as one of the U.S.'s best table fish.

Round, flat, and with shiny, silver skin, butterfish looks a bit like an oversized coin—hence its other name, dollarfish. It can grow to a maximum length of twelve inches but normally reaches between six and nine inches long. Weight-wise, it tips the scale at one and a quarter pounds. Usually, though, it weighs around four and a half ounces. Because it's so petite, I allot two fish per person when preparing it.

In spite of its rather unique appearance, butterfish tend to be mistaken for other fish, most commonly pomfrets, which are larger relatives of butterfish, but also pompanos and escolars. A good rule to follow is if the fish resembles small, shiny currency, it's the real butterfish.

Although it's caught almost year-round, butterfish tends to peak in late spring and late fall. During that time I see whole butterfish in seafood as well as Asian and Caribbean markets. Look for bright, unbruised, silvery skin. If the butterfish smells bad or overpowering, move on to a different fish.

In terms of cleaning, I usually ask my fishmonger to remove the head and fins for me. I don't bother with the delicate scales; these can be rinsed off under running water. Butterfish will keep on ice in the refrigerator for up to two days.

Cooking butterfish is a breeze. The fish requires no fussy preparations and only takes a few minutes to cook. Once the flesh turns opaque and is easily pierced by a fork, it's done.

Butterfish responds well to such techniques as grilling, broiling, and baking. It also tastes wonderful when pan-fried or sautéed. Its fatty, omega-3-rich flesh favors such diverse ingredients as brown sugar, chiles, garlic, ginger, red onion, shallots, lemongrass, lemon, lime, coconut, soy sauce, tamarind, turmeric, and shrimp,

No environmental studies have been carried out for butterfish, so there are no eco-recommendations.

Sautéed Butterfish

In this recipe I sometimes replace the shallots with two minced garlic cloves or a half cup of sliced yellow onion. When I do this, I also switch out the cut limes for lemons. All versions of sautéed butterfish are equally delicious.

SERVES 4

3 tablespoons olive oil

$^1/_2$ cup unbleached all-purpose flour

$^2/_3$ cup cornmeal

1 teaspoon freshly ground black pepper, plus more for seasoning

$^3/_4$ teaspoon sea salt, plus more for seasoning

2 eggs

2 tablespoons skim milk

8 to 10 butterfish (about 3 pounds), heads removed, gutted and rinsed

2 shallots, minced

2 limes, cut into wedges for serving

Heat the oil in a large frying or sauté pan over medium heat. While the oil is heating, mix the flour, cornmeal, 1 teaspoon pepper, and $^3/_4$ teaspoon salt together on a plate. In a shallow bowl, whisk together the eggs and milk.

Season the butterfish with salt and pepper to taste. Dip a butterfish into the eggs and then dredge it through the flour-cornmeal coating. Repeat until all are coated.

Toss the shallots into the hot oil and sauté for 1 minute. Raise the heat to medium-high, add the butterfish, and cook for 3 to 4 minutes. Turn the fish over and cook on the other side for 2 to 3 minutes. When finished, the skin will be brown and the flesh opaque and tender. Serve immediately with lime wedges on the side.

Grilled Cambodian Butterfish

Although butterfish neither comes from Cambodia nor makes an appearance in traditional Cambodian cooking, the sweet fattiness of the fish provides a good balance to the subtly spicy flavors of Cambodian cuisine. Serve this with a side of steamed rice and a dash of soy sauce.

SERVES 4

8 to 10 butterfish (about 3 pounds), heads removed, gutted, and rinsed

$1/3$ cup plus 1 tablespoon canned unsweetened coconut milk

3 tablespoons freshly squeezed lime juice

1 teaspoon fish sauce

2 fresh kaffir lime leaves, cut into strips, or 1 tablespoon grated lime zest

2 garlic cloves, crushed

1 shallot, halved and sliced

1 small red chile, sliced

$1/2$ inch piece ginger, peeled and finely chopped (1 tablespoon)

1 teaspoon sugar

$1/4$ teaspoon freshly ground black pepper

3 to 4 cups steamed rice, for serving

Reduced-sodium soy sauce, for serving

Place the butterfish on a large shallow plate or pan.

In a small bowl whisk together the coconut milk, lime juice, and fish sauce. Add the lime leaves or zest, garlic, shallot, chile, ginger, sugar, and black pepper and stir to combine. Pour the marinade over the butterfish, cover, and refrigerate for 30 to 60 minutes, turning the fish over once after 15 to 30 minutes.

Preheat the grill on high.

Remove the butterfish from the refrigerator and drain off the marinade. Place the fish in a grill basket or on a sheet of aluminum foil that has been greased on one side with olive oil. Grill for 3 to 4 minutes on each side. The flesh will be opaque and tender when finished. Serve warm over steamed rice, and pass the soy sauce at the table.

Herring

I 'm forever amazed that a petite little fish like herring could have such a huge impact on human history. Battles have been waged and named for it. International economic alliances have been founded over it. Political powers have risen and fallen with its own rise and fall in population. Easily netted and consumed, herring sustained much of northern Europe for centuries and captivated American fishermen up to the twentieth century.

Along with its former abundant supply, wide range of distribution, and ease of catch, herring kept and traveled well. This portability enabled sailors to consume it at sea and explorers and vagabonds to devour it on the road. Herring's ability to be eaten raw, preserved, fermented, or cooked made it a major food source for the masses for centuries. Its culinary prominence spawned several specialties, including kippers, bloaters, and rollmops. In essence, this was a fish for anyone and everyone.

Unfortunately, herring's popularity led to it being overfished. Only in recent years has its population recovered enough to make it an eco-okay seafood choice. Even so, most historians consider the low-contaminant, high-in-omega-3-fatty-acid fish to be one of the world's most important foods.

This bright-eyed, silver-scaled, saltwater fish swims in enormous schools in the cold waters of the North Atlantic and Pacific Oceans. You can find it as far down as the Chesapeake Bay on one side of the Atlantic and the north of France on the other. On the West Coast it extends up to the Arctic Sea. It's at its best in spring and summer, right before it begins to spawn.

Larger than the anchovy but smaller than butterfish, herring ranges in size from five to seven inches. It boasts a high fat content—around twenty percent right before spawning—and fine, soft, off-white meat. Its fat makes it quite rich and delectable; it also makes it highly perishable. Herring should be stored on ice in the refrigerator for no longer than two days.

Unless you live along a coastline, you may not have access to fresh herring. If you do stumble upon whole, fresh herring, keep an eye out for those with bright scales and firm bellies. The plumper they are, the more flavorful they will be.

Enjoyed around the globe, herring is sold fresh or preserved. In terms of preservation it can be salt-cured, pickled, or smoked. You can also buy its gold-colored roe, which is renowned for its delicate taste.

Fresh herring can be pan-fried, grilled, baked, broiled, or hot-smoked.

Herring works well with such seasonings as allspice, bay leaf, parsley, tarragon, coriander seeds, dill, mustard, soy sauce, vinegar, and white wine. It likewise goes with bacon, butter, cream, garlic, onions, and potatoes. Any recipe using sardines or mackerel can also be applied to herring.

DEBONING HERRING

You won't have to work very hard to clean a whole, fresh herring. First, you'll need to remove its scales. See Cleaning Fish on page 11 for details on how to do this.

After removing the scales, grab a sharp knife or kitchen scissors and slit open the herring's belly from the head almost to the tail. Pull out the innards and backbone and discard them. If you cannot snap off the head, cut it off with your knife or scissors. Rinse off the fish again. From here you can preserve it in salt or vinegar, hot-smoke or grill it, bake, fry, or broil it.

Pickled Beet and Herring Salad

Scandinavian in origin, this tart, cold salad is known in that region as sillsalad. The beets turn all the ingredients a reddish-purple hue, making for a vibrant-looking-and-tasting repast. To cook the beets, scrub them clean and immerse them in simmering water and cook for half an hour or until fork-tender. Sillsalad is frequently served with sour cream, but in this case I've opted for a lower-calorie drizzle of sweetened lemon juice.

SERVES 4 TO 6

1 (7-ounce) container pickled herring, drained and diced

3 cups (about 1³/₄ pounds) cooked beets, chilled and diced

¹/₄ cup diced yellow onion

1 green apple, peeled, cored, and diced

2 tablespoons minced fresh tarragon

3 tablespoons cider vinegar

3 tablespoons extra-virgin olive oil

Sea salt

¹/₄ teaspoon freshly ground white pepper

2 tablespoons freshly squeezed lemon juice

1 teaspoon sugar

In a medium serving bowl mix together the herring, beets, onion, and apple. In a separate bowl, whisk together the tarragon, vinegar, olive oil, salt to taste, and pepper and pour it over the salad. Cover and refrigerate until chilled.

Before serving, whisk together the lemon juice and sugar. Drizzle over the salad and serve.

Scottish Fried Herring

In Scotland herring is traditionally
fried in bacon fat. If you don't eat pork, you can also
fry the fish in an equal amount of salted butter.

SERVES 6

1 cup rolled oats

$1/2$ teaspoon sea salt, plus more for seasoning

$1/2$ teaspoon freshly ground black pepper,
 plus more for seasoning

$1/2$ teaspoon onion powder

$1/4$ cup unbleached all-purpose flour

2 large eggs

6 large fresh herring, cleaned and deboned
 (page 75)

5 tablespoons salted butter, divided

Pulse the oats, salt, pepper, and onion powder in a food processor or blender until coarsely ground and well blended.

Spread the oat mixture and flour onto two separate plates.

Whisk the eggs with 2 tablespoons of water.

Season the herring with salt and pepper to taste. Dip the fish into the flour and then into the egg, making sure that it is evenly coated. Press the fish into the oats. Repeat with the remaining herring and set aside.

Melt half of the butter in a large, nonstick frying pan over medium heat. Add the herring and cook on one side until golden-brown, about 2 to 3 minutes. Add the remaining butter to the pan, flip the herring, and cook on that side until golden brown, 1 to 2 minutes. Remove from the pan and serve hot.

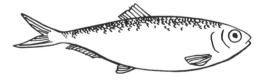

Smoked Herring Tea Sandwiches

Although at heart this is a deli offer-ing, smoked herring tea sandwiches make wonderful canapés. Serve them as an appetizer, snack, or part of an afternoon tea spread. You can also keep the bread slices whole and enjoy the sandwiches for lunch or dinner. In true deli style I like to eat these with half-sour or dill pickles and a few spoonfuls of tart coleslaw.

SERVES 4 TO 6

1 teaspoon drained and rinsed capers

1 teaspoon freshly squeezed lemon juice

2 tablespoons chopped fresh dill

$^1/_2$ teaspoon kosher salt

$^1/_4$ teaspoon freshly ground black pepper

$^1/_2$ cup sour cream

8 slices fresh rye bread

4 to 8 leaves Bibb lettuce, cut to fit the bread

4 large smoked herring, cut to fit the bread

$^1/_2$ small red onion, thinly sliced

2 hard-cooked eggs, sliced

Dill pickles (optional)

Place the capers, lemon juice, dill, salt, pepper, and sour cream in the bowl of a food processor or blender and pulse until well combined.

On four of the bread slices, layer one to two lettuce leaves, one herring, and equal amounts of onion and egg slices. Spread the sour cream dressing on one side of the other four bread slices and lay these slices of bread on top of the sandwich filling. Slice each sandwich into quarters. Serve with the remaining dressing and pickles on the side.

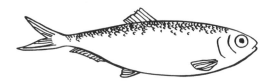

Sardines

Swimming in waters around the globe, this oily fish has long been valued as an inexpensive and flavorful food. By the nineteenth century it had become the center of trade in England's West Country, where fishermen accepted sardines as part of their pay. In the twentieth century this ten- to fourteen-inch fish fed American soldiers during two world wars and provided jobs for vast numbers of workers. In its heyday of the 1920s to 1940s it served as the backbone of America's largest, most profitable fisheries. Monterey, home of California's famed Cannery Row, owes its success to the sardine.

Eventually, the sardine's popularity led to its downfall. Overfishing and the ocean's natural life cycle depleted its supply. Without sardines in the supermarkets shoppers soon turned to and stuck with canned tuna for their cheap, portable, and easy-to-prepare meals.

The iridescent, silver fish have since rebounded and now thrive in American waters. Because of its abundance and carefully controlled fishing practices, the Pacific, wild-caught sardine has become a smart choice for environmentally conscious diners and is an eco-best fish. Thanks to its small size and primarily vegetarian diet, it doesn't accumulate the high levels of mercury that larger, carnivorous fish do. Additionally, it contains large amounts of heart-healthy omega-3 fatty acids and is a good source of protein.

Beyond its environmental and health benefits, the sardine woos me with moist, rich meat reminiscent of hearty tuna. It also gains points for its ability to pair well with other foods. Vegetables and fruits as diverse as eggplants, bell peppers, garlic, tomatoes, oranges, and raisins, and such herbs as basil, fennel, parsley, and rosemary all exalt the earthy tang of sardines.

Fresh sardines can be grilled, broiled, or fried. They spice up a variety of dishes, including the Mediterranean dish escabèche and the British specialty stargazy pie. The latter, eye-catching dish includes whole, herb-stuffed sardines whose heads poke out around the edge of a thick piecrust. Presumably, the name "stargazy" comes from the sardines gazing upward at the stars.

Less dramatic but no less delectable are canned sardines. I use them in place of anchovies in Caesar salads, to brighten vegetable hoagies and pitas, and, of course, to adorn pizzas. When I mash canned sardines, I can turn ordinary butter or cream cheese into a zesty spread.

With fresh sardines I look for shiny, silvery skins, bright eyes, and firm, pinkish, moderately oily flesh. Good quality canned ones give off a mild, pleasant aroma. They are packed in oil that is heavy and clear. When cooked, good fresh sardines have a luxurious, meaty flavor.

Similar to anchovies and herring, fresh sardines spoil quite quickly. A simple sniff test will indicate whether they have started to deteriorate.

To clean a sardine, follow the same steps used to clean herring on page 75. Should this task prove too painstaking or unappealing, ask your fishmonger to debone the sardines for you. If all else fails, skinless, boneless sardines are available in cans. Although fresh sardine fans may scoff at the thought of buying canned, there are just as many devotees of tinned sardines. These connoisseurs have favorite vintages and countries of origin. Spain, Portugal, and France compete for the title of top canned sardine producer.

Sardine Spread

I'm a huge fan of quick and easy

appetizers, and sardine spread is unquestionably one of my favorites. I serve it on buttery crackers and baguettes and atop celery, bell peppers, and cucumbers on crudités platters. I even offer it as an alternative to butter at the dinner table. It's a wonderful, all-purpose spread.

SERVES 6 TO 8, ABOUT 1½ CUPS

1 (8-ounce) package cream cheese, softened
1 (3.75-ounce) can boneless, skinless sardines, drained
1 garlic clove, crushed
1 teaspoon freshly squeezed lemon juice
3 tablespoons reduced-fat mayonnaise
Freshly ground white pepper, to taste
Sea salt, to taste

Place all of the ingredients in the bowl of a food processor or in a medium mixing bowl and process or mash together until the mixture is smooth and well combined. Taste and adjust the seasonings as necessary, then cover and refrigerate until firm, at least 30 minutes. Serve chilled.

Onion-Sardine Pissaladière

This is my variation of the flaky tart from Nice, France, known as the *pissaladière*. The authentic French version features onions, anchovies, black olives, and occasionally tomatoes. To recreate that pizza-like treat, replace the sardines in the following recipe with canned anchovies and top the pastry with a generous handful of chopped, oil-cured black olives.

SERVES 4 TO 6

1 sheet frozen puff pastry, thawed

3 tablespoons olive oil

$1^1/_2$ medium white onions, halved and sliced into thin crescents

$^3/_4$ teaspoon sea salt

1 (3.75-ounce) can skinless, boneless sardines

1 teaspoon chopped fresh rosemary

$^1/_2$ teaspoon dried thyme

Preheat the oven to 400°F. Roll out the thawed puff pastry and place it on an ungreased baking sheet.

Heat the oil in a medium frying or sauté pan over medium-high heat. Add the onions and salt and sauté until softened and slightly colored, about 6 minutes. Remove the onions from the pan and spread them evenly over the puff pastry.

Using your fingers, break the sardines into chunks and place them on top of the onions, spacing them evenly apart. Sprinkle the rosemary and thyme over the onions and sardines.

Bake the pissaladière for 15 to 20 minutes, until the pastry has puffed up and the edges have browned slightly. Cut into squares and serve warm.

Herb-Stuffed Sardines

In Sicily, a similar dish of open-faced herb-stuffed sardines is known as *sarde a beccafico*. If desired, you can substitute fresh anchovies for the sardines. Serve this with a splash of lemon juice and Lemony Fennel (page 225).

SERVES 4 TO 6

1 tablespoon olive oil

12 large fresh sardines (2 pounds total), cleaned but with the heads left on

$1/2$ teaspoon sea salt, plus more for seasoning the fish

$1/4$ teaspoon freshly ground black pepper, plus more for seasoning the fish

$3/4$ cup breadcrumbs, toasted

3 tablespoons grated Pecorino Romano cheese

2 garlic cloves, minced

3 tablespoons minced shallot

$1/4$ cup chopped, fresh flat-leaf parsley

2 tablespoons chopped fresh basil

$1^1/2$ teaspoons chopped fresh rosemary

1 tablespoon freshly squeezed lemon juice

4 tablespoons extra-virgin olive oil, divided

Preheat the oven to 400°F.

Grease the bottom of a large baking dish with olive oil. Season the sardines with salt and pepper and then place them on their sides in the baking dish.

In a medium bowl, mix together the breadcrumbs, cheese, garlic, shallot, parsley, basil, rosemary, and lemon juice. Mix in the $1/2$ teaspoon of salt, the $1/4$ teaspoon of black pepper, and 2 tablespoons extra-virgin olive oil. Taste and adjust the seasonings as needed.

Using your fingers or a spoon, spread equal amounts of stuffing inside each sardine. Drizzle the remaining oil over top of the sardines. Bake, uncovered, until the fish is golden and tender when probed with a fork, about 15 minutes. Serve warm.

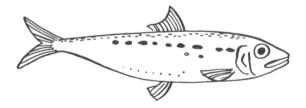

 *Shad*

Springtime on the East Coast means different things to different people.

For me it's all about longer days, warmer nights, and the return of shad festivals. Also known as rock herring and poor man's salmon, shad is one of the most storied fish of the Atlantic. So abundant was shad in colonial times that Native Americans taught settlers how to dry it, cook it, and also use it as fertilizer. George Washington's troops consumed it as part of their rations. At Monticello Thomas Jefferson stocked his pond with the rich, oily fish so that he could eat it year-round. Among gourmands its moist, bright orange roe became a sought-after delicacy. Yet, today, as a result of overfishing, pollution, and loss of habitat, I'm hard-pressed to find shad in markets, restaurants, or even at those spring festivals held in its honor.

The largest member of the herring family, shad lives in the Atlantic Ocean from Florida to Labrador in North America and from the Mediterranean to Southern Ireland in Europe. Introduced to the Pacific Coast in the late 1880s, it now thrives in the Columbia River region. Chances are that, if I do come across shad in my local markets, it will have originated in the Pacific Northwest.

Weighing between three and five pounds and possessing silver-green skin, shad resembles a portly herring. Unlike herring, though, it has an elaborate skeletal system, with a second set of bones running perpendicular to the main. This makes it extremely difficult to fillet. Yet, if you find a skilled fishmonger to fillet it for you, you'll experience a fish like no other. Moderately firm and oily, its beige meat gives off a distinctly sweet, nutty, full-bodied taste. It's high in omega 3-fatty acids, and it's low in toxins and mercury.

Shad is at its best in the spring, as the fish eat heavily before spawning, making themselves plump and juicy. When purchasing shad, look for moist, sweet-smelling meat and roe. If you're fortunate enough to find whole or filleted shad, you can bake, broil, pan-fry, or sauté it. Its roe can be broiled, poached, or sautéed. When the roe's center develops a pinkish hue, it's done cooking.

Although neither meat nor roe need much to boost their flavors, the two do go well with such ingredients as paprika, chervil, sorrel, tarragon, thyme, chives, flat-leaf parsley, celery, potato, shallot, onion, apple, lemon, bacon, butter, apple cider, and white wine.

Because of extreme overfishing, shad is not a sound seafood option. Its population remains in decline and shows no signs of rebounding in the foreseeable future.

Simple Shad

Because shad is such a bold-flavored fish, it requires few additional ingredients. Just add a dash of salt and pepper, set out some lemon wedges, and you've got a delicious meal. You can use this simple preparation with butterfish, salmon, and other oily, flavorful fish.

SERVES 4

1 tablespoon olive oil
2 tablespoons unsalted butter
4 (6- to 8-ounce) shad fillets, bones removed

$^1\!/_2$ teaspoon sea salt
$^1\!/_2$ teaspoon freshly ground black pepper
2 lemons, cut into quarters

Heat the oil and butter in a large frying pan over medium heat.

Season the shad fillets with the salt and pepper and then place the fillets, skin side down, in the pan. Cook until the skin browns, 2 to 3 minutes. Flip the fillets and cook for an additional 2 to 3 minutes, until the fish is firm and flakes when probed with a fork. Serve with the lemon quarters.

SAUTÉED SHAD ROE

Sautéed roe is a vintage delicacy that is rarely encountered in the present. Made of the eggs of fish such as carp, herring, mackerel, or shad, it's a surprisingly simple yet satisfying dish.

Along with 12 ounces of shad roe, you'll need $^1\!/_2$ stick unsalted butter, 2 tablespoons freshly squeezed lemon juice, and a dash each of salt and black pepper.

Melt the butter in a nonstick frying pan over medium heat. Swirl it around the pan and then add the roe.

Cook the roe on one side until lightly browned, about 3 minutes. Turn it over and allow the other side to brown, about 3 minutes. When finished, the centers should look pink.

Remove the roe from the pan. Add the lemon juice to the remaining butter in the pan and whisk together over medium heat for 1 minute. Pour the liquid over the roe and season with salt and black pepper. When finished, you'll have enough to serve 4.

You can also broil, poach, or salt the shad eggs. Salted roe is more commonly known as caviar.

Blackened Shad

I first encountered blackened shad in the early nineties when a friend invited me to her New Jersey town's annual spring shad festival. Cooked on a griddle and served unadorned on a hamburger bun, blackened shad remains one of my favorite springtime foods. You can serve this with or without the bun and with a side of Tomato-Onion-Cucumber Salad or Mango-Tomato Salsa (both on page 223). If you can't find shad, substitute catfish or tuna steaks and adjust your cooking times accordingly.

SERVES 4

1 tablespoon sweet paprika
1 tablespoon garlic powder
1 teaspoon cayenne pepper
1 teaspoon freshly ground black pepper
$1/2$ teaspoon dried marjoram
$1/2$ teaspoon dried oregano
$1/2$ teaspoon sea salt
$1/4$ teaspoon chili powder

2 tablespoons olive oil, divided
4 (6-ounce) shad fillets, bones removed
4 hamburger buns

On a small plate mix together the paprika, garlic powder, cayenne, black pepper, marjoram, oregano, salt, and chili powder.

Heat 1 tablespoon of the olive oil in a large, non-stick frying pan over medium heat.

Brush the remaining oil onto one side of the shad fillets. Dredge the oiled side of the fillets through the spice mixture and place the fish, seasoned sides up, in the pan. Cook until the fillets begin to brown on the bottom and feel tender when probed with a fork, about 5 minutes. Gently flip the fillets and cook on the seasoned side for 1 minute, until firm and completely cooked through. Serve on a bun.

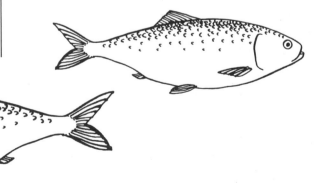

Rich, Meaty, Oily Fish

Whenever I invite steak fans over for dinner, I don't rush out and stock up on T-bones or porterhouses. Instead I turn to rich, meaty, oily fish. Thanks to their fattiness and savory, mildly beef-like flavor, these are the fish that meat-lovers adore. In fact, two members, swordfish and tuna, have become especially popular as alternatives for traditional steaks. They, along with all other meaty fish (salmon, bluefish, carp, mackerel, and sablefish), respond well to such beef-friendly cooking techniques as grilling, broiling, braising, and marinating.

Like the small, savory, oily fish, these guys are rich in protein and omega-3 fatty acids, which aid in cardio-vascular health.

Due to their high oil content rich, meaty, oily fish are extremely perishable. If you acquire them fresh, place them on ice and refrigerate immediately. You must use the fish within a day or two. After two days the risk of spoilage becomes too great to cook and consume them.

Along with the aforementioned cooking methods, this group can be pan-fried, poached, sautéed, and seared. Smoking works wonders on bluefish, carp, sablefish, salmon, and mackerel. Try smoked salmon or sablefish and cream cheese on a bagel and you'll see what I mean. Salmon and tuna are also delicious when served raw in sushi and tartare.

 # Bluefish

Known as the bulldog of the ocean, bluefish is one tough fish. This fatty, silver-skinned guy prowls the temperate and semitropical seas, mercilessly attacking fish—and sometimes fishermen—and killing far more than it can eat. Its fighting spirit has made it a favorite of sportsmen, while its bold, moist, omega-3 fatty acid–rich meat has earned it the devotion of diners.

Bluefish inhabit the warm waters of the Atlantic Ocean and Mediterranean Sea. They are especially popular in Turkey, where fishmongers display the fish with their gills turned inside out to illustrate freshness. Drop by any Turkish seaside restaurant and you'll undoubtedly find this juicy, coarse-textured fish on the menu.

This fish can grow to over thirty pounds and four feet in length. When acquiring bluefish, I stick to those weighing between three and five pounds and under two feet long. The larger fish not only have a stronger, somewhat overwhelming flavor but also have increased levels of mercury and PCBs.

Because of its high oil content, bluefish quickly turns rancid after being pulled from the water. As a result, it doesn't transport well and is rarely found far from where it lives. To avoid spoilage, buy or catch bluefish locally. Refrigerate it in crushed ice and cook it the same day.

When selecting bluefish, whether you're in the market for whole fish, steaks, or fillets, look for glistening meat ranging in color from beige to blue-gray. The fish itself should smell fresh and clean. It should be stored on ice at the market and refrigerated at home.

Similar to other oily fish, bluefish shines when baked, braised, broiled, grilled, pan-seared, sautéed, or hot-smoked. (See the sidebar Smokin' on page 102 for instructions on how to hot-smoke fish.) Its rich, fatty flesh calls for acidic ingredients, such as lemon, lime, orange, tomato, cider and red wine vinegars, and wine. Chile peppers, garlic, marjoram, oregano, rosemary, thyme, cumin, paprika, olive oil, and sugar also complement it. Although it is softer and more fragile than mackerel, bluefish makes a fine substitute for mackerel in recipes.

Due to overzealous commercial and sport fishing, the population of bluefish dropped dramatically in the twentieth century. However, this fast-growing species is now recovering, making U.S. wild-caught bluefish an eco-okay seafood choice. Just keep in mind that the larger the fish, the higher the likelihood of it containing mercury and PCBs.

Turkish Bluefish Grill

It's not often that your first taste of a food is sublimely perfect. Yet, that's how it was for me with bluefish. Over a dozen years ago I had freshly caught, whole bluefish on a rooftop facing the majestic Blue Mosque in Istanbul, Turkey. Like the exotic setting, the full-flavored fish surpassed all my expectations. Cooked gently over a bed of charcoal and then lightly dressed with a tart lemon-parsley sauce, it was succulent, savory, and utterly delicious.

To emulate that memorable late-night meal, I pair this bluefish with sliced, seasoned, and grilled tomatoes, green peppers, and onions. It will also go nicely with Lemony Fennel (page 225) or Tomato-Onion-Cucumber Salad (page 223).

SERVES 4

$^1/_2$ cup plus 2 tablespoons extra-virgin olive oil
Grated zest of 2 lemons
$^1/_4$ cup freshly squeezed lemon juice
$^1/_2$ teaspoon freshly ground black pepper, plus more for seasoning the fish
$^1/_2$ cup minced fresh flat-leaf parsley

1 (5-pound) whole bluefish, cleaned (page 11)
Sea salt, to taste
1 lemon, sliced into rounds
Handful of fresh flat-leaf parsley, stems and leaves intact

Preheat a charcoal grill on high heat.

Whisk together $^1/_2$ cup of the olive oil, lemon zest and juice, black pepper, and minced parsley. Set aside.

With a sharp knife score the sides of the bluefish, making 2- to $3^1/_4$-inch-deep and 1- to 2-inch-long slashes on both sides. Rub the remaining olive oil into the fish's skin.

Season the inside of the bluefish with salt and pepper and then stuff the lemon slices and parsley stems inside of it.

Place the fish in a grilling basket and lay the basket on the grill. Grill 10 to 15 minutes on each side. When the fish is finished cooking, the flesh will be opaque in color and will flake easily when probed by a fork. Remove the fish from the basket and place it on a large serving platter. Serve a small pitcher of the lemon-parsley sauce alongside the fish.

Baked Bluefish

I've adapted this from avid fisher-man, retired vintner, and entrepreneur Frank Wilmer, who helped me land my first bluefish in the Delaware Bay off the coast of New Jersey. His Irish grandmother used a variation of this recipe to cook the bluefish that Frank would catch along the coast of Avalon, New Jersey. She served her baked bluefish with boiled potatoes or stewed tomatoes. I've found that it also goes well with Crispy Rosemary Potatoes (page 236) or Garlic Mashed Potatoes (page 238).

SERVES 4

1/4 cup olive oil, divided
4 (6-ounce) bluefish fillets, skinned
Sea salt, to taste
Freshly ground black pepper, to taste
4 small sprigs rosemary
2 ripe tomatoes, sliced
1 small yellow onion, thinly sliced

Preheat the oven to 350°F.

Tear off two large sheets of aluminum foil. You should have enough foil to enclose two fillets in each foil packet.

Brush half of the olive oil on one side of the aluminum foil sheets. Lay the bluefish fillets on the greased foil and season them with salt and pepper. Distribute the rosemary, tomato, and onion evenly between the fish packets. Drizzle the remaining olive oil over the vegetables and fish.

Fold the long sides of the foil inward until they touch and then crimp the sides together. Do the same with the short ends of the foil.

Place the fish packets on a baking sheet. Bake for 15 minutes or until the fish flakes when probed with a fork and an instant-read thermometer inserted into the fillets reads about 135°F. Remove the fish and allow them to rest in the enclosed packets for 5 minutes before serving.

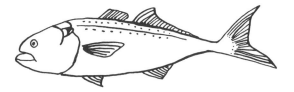

Carp

I'm probably not alone in thinking of carp as both an aquaculture dream and nightmare. This hardy, quick-growing fish flourishes in freshwaters around the globe. Got a freshwater pond in above-freezing temperatures? You can grow carp. Firm fleshed and strong flavored, it thrives on a vegetarian diet. Unfortunately, because it's so voracious and hardy, it tends to push out other fish species. In the late nineteenth century, after it had decimated the habitats of trout and other venerated fish, Americans eradicated this lively herbivore from their waters.

While it has yet to regain a foothold in the U.S. culinary scene, carp remains a darling of Asian, Central European, and Jewish cooking. In China it's both a prized food and an ornamental pet. In the Czech Republic it's a traditional holiday dish. It's also the primary ingredient in the Jewish specialty gefilte fish.

In the wild, carp can grow to forty inches in length and fifty pounds in weight. Farmed carp typically weigh between three and seven pounds.

Generally, carp have small eyes, large scales, and olive-gray skin. Although edible, the skin is tough, hard to remove, and not very appetizing. If you can, save yourself some time and trouble ask your fishmonger to clean these fish for you.

Similar to other oily fish, carp spoils quickly. To prevent this from happening, the fish is kept alive in tanks at markets. When shopping for carp, keep an eye out for small, lively, bright-eyed fish swimming in roomy tanks.

If left on their own, carp prefer to putter about in murky, vegetation-filled water. Unfortunately, this environment gives its otherwise sweet, white meat a muddy tang. To remove the earthy taste, Europeans buy live carp and keep them in water-filled bathtubs for several days; during this time the fish supposedly "swim out" their earthiness. By selecting a carp from a clean tank at the fish market, however, you avoid the unwanted flavor as well as the unusual bathtub guest. If you're still concerned about muddiness, soak the fish for five minutes in a combination of half cup white vinegar and two pints of cold water.

Carp can be prepared whole and as steaks or fillets. They're great candidates for baking, braising, broiling, poaching, and hot-smoking. (See the sidebar Smokin' on page 102 for details on smoking fish.) Carp go especially well with caraway, dill, lemongrass, tarragon, parsley, red chiles, paprika, shallots, garlic, ginger, onion, lemon, butter, sour cream, and white wine.

At present there are no eco-recommendations for carp.

Czech Christmas Carp

Until a Christmastime trip to Prague, I had been unaware of the Czech Republic's long-standing love of carp or of its custom to eat it on Christmas Eve. After pan-frying the fish, cooks there serve it alongside potato salad and followed by hot tea and decorative jam-and-sugar cookies. Uncomplicated yet delicious, it's a meal that's fed families for centuries. If you cannot find carp, substitute catfish or Pacific cod.

Serve with wedges of lemon and a side of Golden Brown Cauliflower (page 233) or Roasted Chestnut-Garlic Brussels Sprouts (page 235).

SERVES 4

$^1/_2$ cup unbleached all-purpose flour,
　plus more as needed
2 large eggs
2 tablespoons skim milk
$^3/_4$ cup plain Panko breadcrumbs
$^1/_4$ cup grated Parmesan cheese
$^1/_8$ teaspoon ground nutmeg
4 (6-ounce) carp fillets, skinned

Sea salt, to taste
Freshly ground black pepper, to taste
$^1/_4$ cup olive oil
Wedges of lemon, for serving (optional)

Place the flour on a shallow plate. In a shallow bowl, whisk together the eggs and milk. On another shallow plate, toss together the breadcrumbs, cheese, and nutmeg.

Season the fish with salt and pepper. Dredge the fillets in the flour, then dip them in the egg and press them in the breadcrumbs to coat on both sides. Set the breaded fillets aside on a clean plate.

Heat the oil in a large nonstick frying pan over medium heat.

Fry the carp until golden-brown and cooked through, 4 to 6 minutes on each side. When finished, the carp will be golden, tender and easily pierced by the tip of a knife. Serve immediately with lemon wedges, if desired.

CZECH REPUBLIC CARP FESTIVAL

Each year on December twentieth the street corners and town squares of the Czech Republic fill with tubs of live *Cyprinus carpio*, a common species of carp grown in and exported from the country's southern lakes and ponds. Throngs of holiday shoppers stand in line for hours to purchase this popular, hardy fish. As custom dictates, they'll serve it as their main course on Christmas Eve.

If the fishmongers do not gut the carp on the spot, the live fish are carried home in plastic bags and released into freshwater–filled bathtubs. There they swim around, supposedly cleaning themselves out, for four days. On December 24th the carp are removed from the bathtub, cleaned, and cooked.

However, not every carp makes it to the dinner table. On Christmas Eve droves of kind-hearted folks transport their live carp to various rivers and release them into the chilly waters. Although the Czechs possess nothing but the best of intentions, the carp rarely benefit from this newfound freedom. The water is simply too cold for the fish and they perish.

Asian-Style Carp

Farmed in China for several millennia and now also farmed in Southeast Asia, carp remains an important and popular food in this part of the world. Pair Asian-style carp with steamed jasmine rice. If you cannot find carp, Pacific cod is a fine substitute.

SERVES 4

2 tablespoons peanut oil

1/4 cup unbleached all-purpose flour, plus more as needed

4 (4- to 6-ounce) carp steaks about 1-inch thick each

Sea salt, to taste

Freshly ground white pepper, to taste

3 1/2 tablespoons reduced-sodium soy sauce

1/4 cup apple cider

1 tablespoon honey

3/4 teaspoon fish sauce

2 cups steamed jasmine or plain white rice, for serving (optional)

Heat the oil in a large frying pan over medium-high heat.

Mound the flour onto a clean work surface. Season the carp with salt and pepper and then dip the fillets in the flour. Place them in the frying pan and cook for 1 minute on each side. Keeping the burner on, transfer the fish to a plate and cover to keep warm.

Pour the soy sauce, cider, honey, and fish sauce into the frying pan. Turn up the heat and bring the liquid to a boil.

Return the carp to the pan, turn the heat down to low, and cover. Cook, flipping the steaks once, until the meat appears tender and flaky, 7 to 9 minutes. Place the carp on a platter.

Taste the sauce and add extra soy sauce, cider, and/or honey if needed. You want the sauce to have a balance of sweet, salty, and sour flavors. Spoon the sauce over the fish and serve immediately with steamed rice, if desired.

Cobia

A curious fish, cobia has several equally curious names: Its brown skin with silvery stripes along its back and sides gives it the nickname "sergeant fish," and its appetite for crab and other crustaceans inspires its other moniker, "crab eater." This seafood diet is what gives cobia its divinely sweet, meaty taste.

Popular along the Gulf of Mexico, the slender, fast-swimming cobia resides in warm waters throughout the world. At one time a sport fish, it is now farmed in the U.S., Taiwan, China, Vietnam, and Belize. Of these producers, America's harvesting techniques are the eco-friendliest. In the U.S. aquafarmers raise cobia in closed re-circulating systems where fish escapes, pollutants, and disease are kept to a minimum. These safe practices have won American farmed cobia an "eco-best" rating.

In the wild cobia can reach up to 130 pounds. On average, though, it weighs between twenty and forty pounds. Similar to carp, cobia possesses a tough skin and firm, pearly white meat.

Cobia is usually sold in steaks or fillets. If you're lucky enough to find it at your fish market, look for firm, sweet-smelling flesh and minimal gaping in the fillets. If the skin has been left on, ask your fishmonger to remove it. Before cooking, always cut out the bloodline that runs along the backbone.

Steaks and fillets will keep for two days in the refrigerator. As with all oily fish, the sooner you cook it, the better it will be.

In my experience the best ways to prepare cobia are to broil, grill, poach, or sauté it. This beefy fish favors such sweet and spicy ingredients as almonds, bananas, coconut, orange, kiwi, lemon, lime, mango, star fruit, cayenne pepper, cilantro, thyme, garlic, and mustard.

Malaysian Fish Soup

Malaysian cooks often feature

whole fish in soups. Since I find that method a bit cumbersome for diners, I cut the cobia into easier-to-manage, bite-size chunks.

If you're not a fan of hotter foods, use half or omit the jalapeño. You will find coconut cream in the international section of supermarkets and in Asian and Latin American markets.

SERVES 4 TO 6

1 tablespoon peanut oil

2 small shallots, minced

4 garlic cloves, thinly sliced

3/4 cup (about 3 ounces) white button mushrooms, sliced

1 large sweet potato, peeled and cut into half-inch cubes

5 cups chicken or fish stock (page 158)

2 stalks lemongrass, chopped

1 1/2 pounds cobia steaks or fillets, skinned and cut into 1-inch chunks

2 tablespoons coconut cream

Sea salt, to taste

1 jalapeño pepper, seeded and sliced

2 scallions, whites and 1-inch of greens sliced

Heat the oil in a small frying or sauté pan over medium-high heat. Add the shallots, garlic, mushrooms, and potato and sauté for 5 minutes. The shallots and garlic will begin to brown, and the mushrooms will have softened slightly.

In a large saucepan or small stockpot bring the stock to a boil. Add the sweet potato mixture and the lemongrass. Simmer over medium heat for 15 to 20 minutes or until the potatoes are easily pierced by a fork.

Skim the top of the soup before adding the cobia and coconut cream. Stir to combine and then reduce the heat to medium-low. Simmer for another 5 to 10 minutes, until the cobia is cooked through. Taste and season as needed with salt. Stir in the jalapeño and scallions just before serving.

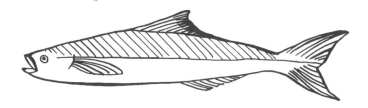

Spicy Citrus Cobia

Serve hot with Lemony Fennel (page 225) or Mango-Tomato Salsa (page 223).

SERVES 4

4 (4- to 6-ounce) cobia fillets or steaks
Grated zest of 2 oranges
Freshly squeezed juice of 1 orange
Grated zest and juice of 1 lime
$1/4$ cup olive oil, plus more as needed
1 teaspoon kosher salt
$1/2$ teaspoon hot paprika
$1/2$ teaspoon freshly ground black pepper

Place the cobia on a large, shallow platter. Whisk together the orange and lime zest and juice, $1/4$ cup of the oil, salt, paprika, and black pepper. Pour the marinade over the cobia, cover with plastic wrap, and refrigerate for 20 to 30 minutes.

While the fish is marinating, preheat the grill on high. Lightly grease the interior of a fish grill basket or a sheet of aluminum foil with olive oil.

Remove the cobia fillets from the refrigerator and place them either in the fish basket or on the foil. Grill for 3 to 4 minutes on each side, until the flesh is opaque and easily flaked. Serve hot.

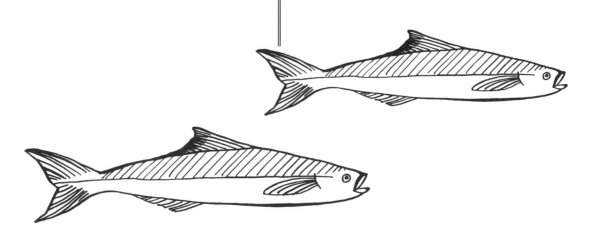

Mackerel

In England the word "mackerel" was once used to refer to excessively vain men. In France it meant "pimp." With its gorgeous, blue-green, tiger-striped back, shimmering silver sides, and stark white belly I can understand why mackerel has caused European tongues to wag for centuries. This is one striking fish.

A relative of the tuna, mackerel can be found in large schools in temperate and tropical seas. Its range reaches from the Mediterranean to Iceland and from Labrador to Brazil. This migratory fish possesses a torpedo-like body that's ideal for speed and distance and a firm, full-bodied flesh that's perfect for cooking.

Mackerel normally vary in length from one to two feet and in weight from one to three pounds. However, the subtropical species known as king mackerel may grow to six feet and weigh over ninety pounds.

According to the U.S. Department of Agriculture, no fish is higher in omega-3 fatty acids than mackerel. That's great news for those concerned about their cardiovascular health. Because mackerel grows quickly and has a relatively low bycatch, it also presents a good option for environmentally conscientious diners.

Fresh one-pound or smaller mackerel tend to be sold whole. Because they lack scales and have easily removable bones, you can quickly fillet them yourself (page 14). Large mackerel usually appear as fillets and steaks but you can also find them smoked, pickled, or salted. In the case of salted mackerel, soak the fish overnight before cooking it, changing the water before bed and in the morning. This reduces its saltiness.

When selecting mackerel, look for the small, Atlantic variety. Unlike the king and Spanish species, Atlantic mackerel is an "eco-best" fish that is low in contaminants such as mercury. It can therefore be eaten safely several times per month.

In terms of physical characteristics, choose fish with a sweet yet beefy smell, brilliant color, firm flesh, and somewhat animated appearance. When displayed on ice, mackerel should appear lifelike and not look dull or dead. Fresh mackerel should be stored in ice until ready to cook. It will only keep for a day, so plan accordingly.

Mackerel's rich, assertive flavor makes it a good match for acidic foods such as lemon, lime, tomato, and vinegar. It also marries nicely with chives, parsley, thyme, garlic, ginger, shallots, scallions, onions, and white wine. In terms of preparation it can be braised, broiled, grilled, marinated, pickled, poached, salted, sautéed, seared, or smoked.

Mackerel Escabèche

Originating in Spain, possibly as a means of preserving fish, escabèche is a dish of poached or fried fish steeped for hours in a spicy, vinegary marinade. Medieval escabèches emphasized sweet-sour pairings, matching raisins, dates, and sugar with ginger, onion, and garlic. In this recipe I take a more modern approach, infusing the fish with fiery Spanish seasonings.

Serve mackerel escabèche with toasted sourdough bread.

SERVES 4

1/4 cup olive oil

4 (4- to 6-ounce) mackerel fillets, skins on

1/2 teaspoon freshly ground black pepper

1 small red onion, halved and thinly sliced

2 garlic cloves, thinly sliced

1 teaspoon coriander seeds, toasted and crushed with mortar and pestle

1 teaspoon sweet paprika

1/2 teaspoon cayenne pepper

1/2 teaspoon sea salt

1/4 teaspoon turmeric

1/8 teaspoon saffron

Grated zest and juice of 1 lemon

2/3 cup apple cider vinegar

Heat the olive oil in a large frying pan over medium-high heat. As the oil heats, season the mackerel with the pepper.

Place the mackerel fillets skin side down in the pan and fry until the skin is crisp and golden brown, about 4 minutes. Turn the fish over and cook for 1 more minute. Remove the fillets from the pan and place them skin side up in a 2- to 3-quart baking dish.

Reduce the heat to medium and add the onion and garlic to the pan. Sauté until softened, 2 to 3 minutes.

Turn off the heat and add the coriander, paprika, cayenne, salt, turmeric, saffron, lemon zest and juice, and cider vinegar to the pan. Stir the ingredients together until well combined.

Pour the warm marinade over the mackerel. Make sure that all the fillets are covered by the liquid. Allow the dish to cool to room temperature; this could take anywhere from 20 to 60 minutes. Once the dish has cooled, refrigerate the mackerel for a minimum of 5 hours and a maximum of 3 days. Serve the fish slightly chilled.

Smoked Mackerel Jackets

Twice-baked potatoes, which my mother always referred to as "jackets," were wildly popular when I was growing up. Here, the potato jackets get stuffed with smoked mackerel, turning them into a hearty, one-dish meal.

SERVES 4

4 large russet potatoes
$1/3$ cup skim milk, warmed
1 tablespoon unsalted butter, softened
$1/2$ teaspoon kosher salt
$1/2$ teaspoon freshly ground black pepper
$1/4$ cup grated Gruyère cheese
1 bunch scallions, sliced
1 pound smoked mackerel fillets, flaked

Preheat the oven to 350°F.

Using a fork, poke holes in the potatoes before microwaving them on high for 8 to 10 minutes or until hot and softened. Cut the potatoes in half and scoop out most of the flesh, leaving behind a small rim of potato in each skin.

Place the potato flesh in a medium bowl and, using a spoon or fork, mash lightly. Add the milk, butter, salt, and pepper and mash again until the mixture is smooth and creamy. Add the cheese, scallions, and flaked mackerel and stir to combine.

Spoon equal amounts of the potato-mackerel mixture back into the skins. Place the filled skins on a baking sheet and bake until warm and golden-brown on top, 10 to 12 minutes. Serve immediately.

Zesty Lime Mackerel

The gentle heat and tartness of this dish can be balanced out by a savory side such as Parmesan Polenta (page 237). If you prefer a hotter dish, double the amount of crushed red pepper in the recipe.

SERVES 4

2 tablespoons olive oil, divided

1¼ pound mackerel fillets, skins on

2 garlic cloves, sliced

3 tablespoons chopped fresh cilantro

Grated zest and juice of 1 lime

1 teaspoon kosher salt

½ teaspoon freshly ground black pepper

¼ teaspoon crushed red pepper

Grease a shallow baking dish with 1 tablespoon of the olive oil. Place the mackerel fillets skin side down in the dish.

In a small bowl, stir together the garlic, cilantro, lime zest and juice, salt, black pepper, crushed red pepper, and the remaining tablespoon of olive oil. Spread the mixture over the top of the fish. Allow the fish to marinate at room temperature for 15 minutes.

Preheat the oven to 400°F.

Bake, uncovered, for 11 to 13 minutes or until the flesh becomes opaque and tender. Serve immediately.

Sablefish

It's not often that I come across a fish suffering from a bit of an identity crisis. Because of its blackish skin and slight resemblance to cod, people often refer to sablefish as black cod. Its buttery texture leads others to call it butterfish. Contrary to these names, sablefish has no ties to cod and is definitely not a butterfish (see page 71 for true butterfish). Nonetheless, I've seen it labeled as smoked black cod at Jewish delis and as butterfish on restaurant menus, even though sablefish's silken, pearly flesh and intense, full-bodied flavor make it very unique.

Hailing from the deep waters of the Pacific Ocean and Bering Sea, sablefish gets its luxurious taste and texture from its diet of crab and squid. It is an extremely palatable fish containing few contaminants, which is why it's considered by many to be Alaska's most valuable fish. Because of its low bycatch and safe working conditions for fishermen, wild-caught Alaskan sablefish is also one of the eco-friendliest.

This slender, oily fish grows to about two feet in length. It typically weighs between three and ten pounds. As a rule, the bigger the sablefish, the better the quality.

When it isn't smoked and marketed as smoked black cod, sablefish is sold as steaks and fillets. Similar to other fatty fish, it spoils easily and should be packed in ice after purchasing. Unlike such oily fish as mackerel, though, it freezes well and can easily be found year-round.

Fresh sablefish is in season from early spring through fall. Keep an eye out for those with soft-textured, glossy meat.

Sablefish is delicious cooked in a variety of ways, including braising, grilling, pan-frying, poaching, roasting, sautéing, steaming, and hot-smoking. Its sweet flavor is balanced out by cabbage, jicama, oyster mushrooms, scallions, garlic, ginger, honey, miso, mustard, sake, sesame oil, and soy sauce. A flexible fish, it can stand in for grouper, mackerel, monkfish, and salmon in recipes.

Hot-smoking seafood can be a gratifying and an appetizing experience, providing a dash of excitement on your dinner plate. Unlike cold-smoking, which can take days, hot-smoking requires only an hour or so to complete. Plus, you don't need any special equipment to hot-smoke. As long as you have a stovetop and a kitchen exhaust fan, you're set.

To begin, soak $1^1/_2$ cups of wood chips in water according to the package directions. As the chips are soaking, coat 1 to $1^1/_2$ pounds of fish fillets or steaks in a brine of $^1/_4$ cup salt and $^1/_4$ cup sugar to 4 cups of water. Allow the fish to brine for 30 to 60 minutes in the refrigerator. When the fish has finished brining, pat it dry with clean paper towels.

If you're smoking your fish on the stove, layer the soaked wood chips on the bottom of a wide, heavy-bottomed stockpot. Place a round, wire cooling rack or metal steamer basket over the chips; you'll want the fish to sit approximately 1-inch above the wood chips. Cover the pot and turn the burner to medium-high heat. Flip on your exhaust fan and wait. Once the chips begin to smoke, lay the marinated fish on the rack, reduce the heat to medium-low, and cover again. After 15 to 20 minutes the fish will be opaque, cooked through, and finished smoking. Keep in mind that the thicker your fish is, the more time it will take to smoke. Similarly, the longer the fish smokes, the bolder its flavor will be.

If you're using a grill, you'll still need to soak the wood chips and brine the fish. Toward the end of the brining period, preheat the grill, either gas or charcoal. For gas, light one side of the grill and turn to high heat. For charcoal, pile the briquettes on one side of the grill and light them. The grill is ready when they're hot and covered in a light dusting of ash. Cover the briquetttes with 1 to $1^1/_2$ cups of soaked wood chips. Once the wood chips begin to smoke, place the fish over indirect heat—not directly over the flames—and cover the grill. Allow the fish to smoke for 15 to 30 minutes, until it is opaque and has reached the desired level of smokiness.

Hot-smoking infuses the seafood with a smoky flavor; it does not extend its shelf life. You should consume the smoked food within a few days.

In addition to sablefish, bluefish, carp, mackerel, salmon, swordfish, and shellfish can be hot-smoked.

Sable and Goat Cheese Omelet

In addition to layering it atop bagels, bread, crepes, or potato pancakes, I like to showcase homemade or store-bought smoked sablefish in an omelet. For a bit of variety, you can replace the goat cheese with shredded Gruyère and add a 1/3 cup of sautéed oyster mushrooms. If you cannot find smoked sablefish, you can also use smoked trout in the omelet. The recipe makes two individual-sized omelets, which is far better than trying to cook one large omelet. Serve either version with fresh fruit and toasted pumpernickel bread.

SERVES 2

1 tablespoon olive oil, divided
1 tablespoon unsalted butter, divided
5 large eggs
Pinch of sea salt
Pinch of freshly ground black pepper
2 ounces good-quality goat cheese, crumbled
2 ounces smoked sablefish, roughly chopped
4 chive stems, finely chopped

Heat half the oil and half the butter in a small non-stick frying or omelet pan over medium heat. Whisk together the eggs, salt, and pepper. Swirl the melted butter and heated oil around the pan so that it's evenly coated. Pour half of the egg mixture into the pan. Reserve the rest of the eggs for the other omelet.

Reduce the heat to medium-low and cook the omelet until it's firm but still moist on top, 7 to 10 minutes. Sprinkle half of the cheese onto the omelet and then layer half of the sablefish over one half of the omelet. Fold the omelet over and press down lightly with a spatula so that it stays closed. Cover and cook for another minute. Place the omelet on a plate, sprinkle the chives over the top, and cover to keep warm.

Heat the remaining olive oil and butter in the frying pan over medium heat. Swirl the liquids around the pan and then pour in the rest of the whisked eggs. Reduce the heat to medium-low. Repeat the remaining steps for the second omelet. Serve hot.

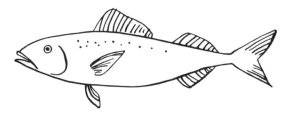

Pan-Seared Sablefish with Soy-Sesame Glaze

Sablefish is considered a delicacy in Japan. In fact, Japan consumes over ninety percent of America's catch of this eco-friendly fish. This dish is a nod to its Japanese popularity and to its affinity to acidic flavors.

SERVES 4

4 (4- to 6-ounce) sablefish fillets, skins on
Freshly ground black pepper, to taste
3 tablespoons soy sauce
1 1/2 tablespoons sesame oil
2 teaspoons rice vinegar
2 tablespoons firmly packed light brown sugar
2 tablespoons peanut oil
2 tablespoons sesame seeds, toasted lightly,
    for garnish

Season the sablefish with pepper.

In a small bowl, whisk together the soy sauce, sesame oil, rice vinegar, and brown sugar. Pour the mixture into a small saucepan and bring to a low boil over medium-high heat. Allow the mixture to boil, stirring periodically, until thickened, 3 to 5 minutes. Remove from the heat and set aside.

Heat the peanut oil in a large frying pan over high heat. Lay the fillets flesh side down and sear for 1 minute. Reduce the heat to medium. Gently flip the fillets and cook until the skin browns and the meat turns opaque, 4 to 6 minutes. Drizzle half of the soy-sesame glaze over the fillets and cook for another minute. Remove the sablefish from the pan, place each fillet skin side down on a plate, and spoon the remaining sauce over each. Sprinkle the toasted sesame seeds over the fillets and serve immediately.

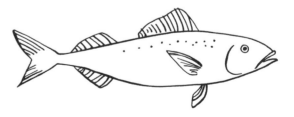

Olive Oil-Poached Sablefish

Traditionally, seafood is poached in court bouillon, a delicate broth made from herbs and vegetables. Here olive oil replaces court bouillon to lend additional flavor and juiciness to the sablefish. This recipe also works nicely with Pacific cod or catfish.

SERVES 4

4 (4- to 6-ounce) sablefish fillets, skins on
Sea salt, to taste
Freshly ground black pepper, to taste
2 garlic cloves, thinly sliced
1 1/4 cups olive oil
6 to 8 Picholine or other green olives, sliced

Preheat the oven to 250°F.

Generously season the sablefish fillets with salt and pepper. Place the fillets in a large, shallow baking dish, scatter the garlic slices over them, and add the olive oil. Place the baking dish in the oven and poach, uncovered, for 25 minutes until fork-tender and opaque. At this point scatter the sliced olives over the fish and then bake for another 10 to 15 minutes. The fillets will be opaque and tender when finished. You can also give the fish a quick poke with an instant-read thermometer; if the internal temperature has reached around 135°F, your fish is done. Allow the fish to rest for 5 minutes before serving.

 *Salmon*

No matter where you travel in North America, you can expect to find salmon on menus and in markets. One of the most familiar fish around, salmon possesses a storied history on this continent. At one time Native Americans of the Pacific Northwest believed that, if the salmon disappeared, their tribes would perish. As a result, they took measures and performed rituals to ensure that nothing would offend the fish's spirit. Centuries later, American canneries thrived on a seemingly endless supply of salmon.

Due to overfishing and habitat pollution, though, by the early twentieth century salmon had all but disappeared from the dinner table. To combat this loss, salmon farms were established. Now most of what we see in markets is farmed in the Americas and Scandinavia. Debate continues over which are better: farmed salmon that are fattier, juicier, but detrimental to the ecosystem or wild salmon that are firmer, stronger flavored, but less prevalent.

Wild salmon come from the northern waters of the northern hemisphere. Born in freshwater, the pale pink- to ruby red–fleshed fish swim out to sea where they spend much of their life. They later leave their saltwater environments and return to their home rivers to spawn. Fishermen catch them there, at the mouths of the rivers.

There are six common species of salmon in North America. From the East comes Atlantic, and from the Pacific West come chinook (or king), coho (or silver), sockeye (or red), pink (or humpback), and chum. When choosing salmon, consider the species being sold and how you plan to cook it. Sockeye (red), coho (silver), chum and pink (humpback) all posess good eco-ratings. Although chinook is another sound environmental choice, it is rarely seen in markets. Poorly farmed and high in contaminats, Atlantic salmon possesses the worst eco-rating and should be avoided. See the sidebar Know Your Salmon (opposite page), for descriptions of and environmental recommendations for each fish.

While you will come across wild Pacific salmon at your local market, you won't ever see wild Atlantic salmon there. Wild Atlantic is an endangered species and cannot be commercially fished. If you see Atlantic salmon at markets or on restaurant menus, those fish have been farmed and are not an environmentally sound choice.

Sold whole and as steaks and fillets, salmon can be prepared almost any way. It's lovely when roasted in butter or grilled with a grind of salt and pepper. Its succulent flesh shines when smoked or preserved in salt and made into gravlax. It likewise responds beautifully to baking, braising, broiling, marinating, pan-frying, poaching, sautéing, searing, and steaming. It also is served raw in sashimi and tartares.

Salmon goes well with a vast array of foods. Asparagus, fava and flageolet beans, carrots, lentils, mushrooms, potatoes, tomatoes, and watercress make great accompaniments. Similarly, flat-leaf parsley, tarragon, thyme, chives, black pepper, garlic, shallots, onions, lemons, lime, butter, heavy cream, oil, mustard, and dry white or red wine magnify the unique flavor of this fish.

KNOW YOUR SALMON

There are six common species of salmon. Five come from the Pacific. The sixth is farmed in the Atlantic. The following descriptions will help to determine which fish to pick for your dinner table.

Atlantic: Farmed Atlantic's pinkish-orange flesh looks marbled and is, obviously, quite fatty. Thanks to this fat, Atlantic is moist and mildly flavored. This makes it particularly perfect for smoking, salt-curing, grilling, broiling, baking, or roasting, in addition to the other, aforementioned techniques. Although it can grow to 18 pounds, it usually ranges between four and six pounds in weight. Because it freezes well, Atlantic salmon is available year-round. Regrettably, due to high PCB levels and the negative environmental impact of its aquaculture, farmed Atlantic salmon is a fish that consumers should avoid.

Chinook or king: Pacific chinook or king salmon boasts a red, fatty, moist flesh and a buttery taste. Like Atlantic salmon, it responds well to a host of cooking methods. While it can top the scales at fifty pounds, most often chinook averages around fifteen pounds. Because it accounts for only 1 percent of Alaska's catch, it is not a fish that you'll encounter often. Chinook usually stays on the West Coast, where it appears on the menus of high-end restaurants. Chinook is one of the eco-friendliest salmons.

Sockeye or red: This scarlet red–fleshed fish competes with its wild cousin chinook for best flavor. Rich and firm-textured, it does particularly well when marinated and grilled. It ranges in weight from four to ten pounds. Although it frequently appears in canned form, sockeye can be purchased fresh when in season and frozen when not. Sockeye is another eco-sound salmon.

Coho or silver: Another Pacific species, coho has a fairly high fat content and moderately firm, velvety, coral-colored meat. In the wild it can weigh up to ten pounds, but when farmed in floating pens, it weighs at most around three pounds. Fresh, wild coho is in season in the fall. Similar to chinook and sockeye, coho is a safe seafood option.

Chum: Lower in fat than the salmon cited above, Pacific chum has orange, mild-flavored flesh. Due to its reduced fat content, chum doesn't respond well to broiling or grilling. Ranging between six to twelve pounds, it can be found year-round, fresh, frozen, or canned. Chum is an environmentally good choice.

Pink or humpback: Lean, dry, and slightly bitter, Pacific pink is best suited for mixtures, such as salmon cakes, loaves, or croquettes. It weighs between two and six pounds and is most commonly sold frozen or canned. Similar to chum, the price for pink is quite low and its eco-rating is quite good.

Great Gravlax

Often confused with smoked salmon, gravlax is raw salmon preserved in a mixture of salt, sugar, and dill. In medieval times fishermen salted their freshly caught salmon, wrapped them in birch bark, and then buried them in the ground to protect the fish from ravenous animals. These burials provided the cured salmon with its name, a shortened form of gravad lax, meaning "buried salmon." Adapted from the cookbook *Very Swedish*, this recipe is delicious atop dark rye, multigrain, or sourdough bread, bagels, or poached eggs.

MAKES ABOUT 2 POUNDS

For the gravlax:

$1/2$ cup sugar

$1/3$ cup iodized salt

1 tablespoon coarsely ground white pepper

$2^1/4$ pounds salmon fillet, deboned but with the skin intact

3 bunches fresh dill, chopped

For the sauce:

1 tablespoon yellow mustard

1 tablespoon Dijon mustard

1 tablespoon sugar

2 tablespoons red wine vinegar

$1/2$ cup grapeseed oil

$1/4$ cup finely chopped dill

TO MAKE THE GRAVLAX, mix together the sugar, salt, and pepper and massage the mixture into both sides of the salmon. Rub the dill on the meat (not skin) side. Place the fish in a plastic bag and seal it. Put the bag on a plate and place a heavy cutting board on top of it. If your cutting board is too light, weight it down with a cookbook or two.

Allow the fish to rest at room temperature for 2 hours. After 2 hours have passed, remove the cutting board and refrigerate the salmon for 24 to 48 hours, turning it 3 to 4 times during this period.

TO MAKE THE SAUCE, mix together the mustards, sugar, and vinegar in a medium bowl. Drizzle in the oil while whisking vigorously to emulsify the sauce. Stir in the chopped dill.

Remove the fish from the refrigerator. Scrape and rinse off the seasonings. Thinly slice the salmon as needed and serve cold with sweet mustard sauce on the side. Gravlax will keep for 4 to 5 days in the refrigerator.

Smoked Salmon-Avocado-Tomato Tartare

During medieval times the Tartars, a Turko-Mongol tribe from Central Asia, invented this eponymous dish. To make the tough, low-quality horse meat and beef that they ate more digestible, the Tartars shredded it with a knife and devoured it raw. Over the years tartare evolved into a dish of finely diced, high-quality, raw beef, seafood, fruit, or vegetables.

I've served the following tartare as an appetizer, first course, and side dish. It's a fast and tasty way to showcase smoked salmon. If you want to smoke your own salmon, refer to the steps in the sidebar Smokin' on page 102.

SERVES 4 TO 6

4 tomatoes, seeded and diced
1 cup red onion, diced
2 avocados, diced
¼ cup chopped fresh parsley
Freshly squeezed juice of 1 lemon
1 cup (approximately 6 ounces) smoked salmon, cut into small strips
Freshly ground white pepper, to taste

Place the tomatoes, onion, avocado, and parsley in a medium bowl and drizzle the lemon juice over top. Add the smoked salmon and a dash of white pepper. Stir to combine. Taste for seasoning and add more pepper if necessary. Cover with plastic wrap, pressing down on the surface to expel all of the air, and refrigerate for a minimum of 2 hours and up to 5 hours. Serve chilled.

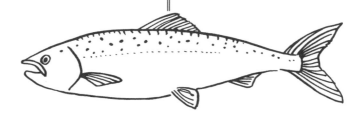

Seven Spice Salmon

For this recipe you'll need to buy a side of salmon weighing about three pounds. The skin should be left on, but the pin bones should be removed before cooking.

SERVES 6 TO 8

1 teaspoon fennel seeds, toasted
1 star anise pod, toasted
2 teaspoons onion powder
1 teaspoon red peppercorns
$\frac{1}{2}$ teaspoon sea salt
$\frac{1}{2}$ teaspoon ground cumin
$\frac{1}{2}$ teaspoon sweet paprika
$\frac{1}{4}$ teaspoon ground nutmeg
$\frac{1}{4}$ cup grapeseed oil
1 tablespoon olive oil
1 side of salmon (about 3 pounds),
    with skin on and pin bones removed

Using a mortar and pestle, grind together the fennel seeds, star anise, onion powder, peppercorns, salt, cumin, paprika, and nutmeg. Add the grapeseed oil and whisk until well combined.

Coat a baking tray with the olive oil. Place the salmon on it, skin side down, and brush the marinade over the salmon. Allow the fish to marinate for 20 to 30 minutes at room temperature.

Preheat the broiler on high. Place the baking tray on the rack closest to the broiler and cook until an instant-read thermometer inserted in the thickest part of the fish registers 135°F, about 15 minutes. Remove from the oven and allow the fish to rest for 5 to 10 minutes before serving.

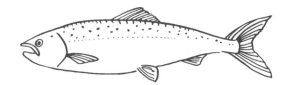

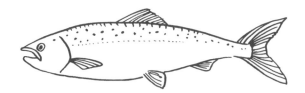

Sesame-Crusted Salmon with Sweet Tamarind Sauce

Because sesame seeds originate in sub-Saharan Africa and tamarind trees grow throughout the tropics of Africa and South Asia, I tend to think of this sesame-crusted salmon as my pan-African–inspired meal. You can also use this recipe with char.

SERVES 4

2 tablespoons tamarind paste

2 tablespoons boiling water

1 tablespoon freshly squeezed lime juice

1 tablespoon plus $1/4$ teaspoon sugar

Sea salt, to taste

$1/4$ cup sesame seeds

3 tablespoons olive oil

4 (4- to 6-ounce) salmon fillets, skins on

1 egg white, lightly beaten

In a small bowl mix together the tamarind paste, water, lime juice, sugar, and salt, stirring until the tamarind paste has dissolved completely into the liquids. Place the sesame seeds in a flat, shallow dish.

Heat the olive oil in a non-stick frying pan over medium heat. As the oil is heating, whisk together the egg white and 1 teaspoon of water and brush the mixture over the skinless side of the salmon fillets. Dredge the skinless side of each fillet in the sesame seeds and then place the fillets, seed side down, in the frying pan. Cook until golden, about 5 minutes. Turn the fillets with tongs and cook on the skin side until just done. The fish should be pale pink and tender. Depending on the thickness of the salmon, this could be anywhere from 2 to 4 minutes.

Place the fillets skin side down on 4 dinner plates. Drizzle the sweet tamarind sauce over top of each. Serve immediately.

SWEETLY TART TAMARIND PASTE

Tamarind paste comes from the brown, sweetly sour pulp of the tamarind pod. This concentrated paste flavors chutneys, stews, sauces, and drinks in North African, Indian, and Asian cuisines. It also appears in the English condiment Worcestershire sauce.

You can buy tamarind paste and five- to eight-inch-long tamarind pods in African and Asian markets, health food stores, and some supermarkets.

Swordfish

With its massive body, sail-like dorsal fin, and sword-like snout, swordfish is one tough fish. During classical times this formidable fish was rumored to have thrust its sword deep into the sides of boats, often with disastrous results. It still uses this sword as a weapon, flinging it about to kill or stun smaller fish, which it then eats. Once its feasting is finished, the cocky swordfish lounges on the ocean's surface. Here is where fishermen harpoon or trap the nervy fish, as it dawdles about.

Found in temperate and tropical waters worldwide, swordfish grows to about thirteen feet long and can weigh over one thousand pounds. Usually it falls between fifty and two hundred pounds. Its firm, moist, oily flesh ranges from pinkish-orange to ivory; when cooked, the meat turns off-white. Because its flesh is so beefy in texture and taste, it has become a favorite among meat enthusiasts, as well as those who limit their meat consumption for health reasons. In fact, during the 1980s swordfish was considered the heart-healthy dining choice.

Swordfish is usually cut and sold as steaks. However, smaller fish may be beheaded, gutted, and sold in logs or chunks. Look for firm, shiny flesh that smells good, has tightly swirled meat, and is at least one inch thick. Avoid swordfish with dull, discolored, or browning skin or loose, gaping flesh. You can refrigerate steaks for up to two days and chunks for up to three days.

Due to its firmness, swordfish responds well to almost any cooking method. This includes baking, broiling, grilling, marinating, and sautéing. In Turkey it's smoked, while in North America we tend to grill the fatty meat. No matter what technique that you choose, be sure to not to overcook swordfish; it dries out easily.

Swordfish has an affinity for such foods as capers, olives, chile peppers, corn, red onions, lemons, limes, tomatoes, and anchovies. It also goes well with olive oil, red wine vinegar, and white wine.

Note that, due to its high mercury levels and bycatch of sea turtles, birds, and sharks, swordfish is not a sound seafood choice for health- or eco-conscious consumers.

Swordfish Tacos

Tuna, tilapia, catfish, and Pacific cod can all stand in for swordfish in this dish. You can also grill the fish instead of broiling it.

SERVES 6

3 tablespoons extra-virgin olive oil, divided

1$1/2$ pounds swordfish steaks

$1/2$ teaspoon kosher salt, plus more to taste

Freshly ground black pepper, to taste

6 soft white corn tortillas

2 ripe tomatoes, diced

3 scallions, whites and 1 inch of greens diced

1 green bell pepper, diced

1 avocado, diced

Freshly squeezed juice of 1 lime

$1/8$ teaspoon cayenne pepper

Preheat the oven broiler on high. Lightly grease a baking sheet with 1 tablespoon of the olive oil.

Brush both sides of the swordfish steaks with 1 tablespoon olive oil. Season them with salt and pepper. Place the steaks on the greased baking sheet and put the sheet on the middle oven rack, about 6 inches from the broiler. Broil the steaks on one side until they develop golden hues on top, 4 to 6 minutes. Turn the steaks over and broil until tender and just cooked through, about 4 minutes. Remove from the oven and allow the fish to rest for a minute or so.

Meanwhile, warm the tortillas in the oven or microwave. As they're warming, toss together the tomatoes, scallions, pepper, avocado, lime juice, the $1/2$ teaspoon salt, cayenne, and the remaining tablespoon of olive oil in a small bowl.

Slice the swordfish steaks into pieces and divide them among the tortillas. Top each with the salsa and serve.

Lime-Marinated Swordfish Kebabs

Tuna or mackerel makes a pleasant substitute for swordfish in these kebabs. The kebabs go well with Tomato-Onion-Cucumber Salad (page 223), Warm Summer Corn Salad (page 228), or Chilled Red Lentils (page 230).

SERVES 4

Grated zest of 2 limes

$1/3$ cup freshly squeezed lime juice

$1/4$ cup olive oil

1 teaspoon sea salt

$1/4$ teaspoon freshly ground white pepper

$1^{1}/_{2}$ pounds swordfish steaks, cut into $1^{1}/_{2}$-inch chunks

In a medium bowl, whisk together the lime zest and juice, oil, salt, and pepper. Place the swordfish cubes in the marinade and toss to coat. Refrigerate the fish for 1 hour. If using wooden or bamboo skewers, soak them in water for 30 minutes.

Preheat your grill on high.

Thread the fish onto skewers and lay the kebabs on the preheated grill. Grill until just cooked through, about 5 minutes, brushing the marinade over the kebabs as they cook and turning so that they cook evenly. Serve on or off the skewers.

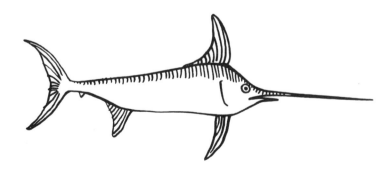

Tuna

Whenever I order a tuna sandwich in a deli, café, or restaurant, I can expect it to contain flaked tuna spooned from a can. In the U.S. tuna remains the most popular canned fish. A lesser-known fact is that fresh tuna makes quite a remarkable meal. It's blessed with fatty and firm, flaky and tender flesh and a savory, full-bodied flavor that differentiates it from all other seafood. It is similar to swordfish in that respect—its beefy taste wins over the most ardent meat eaters. As a matter of fact, darker tuna can stand in for beef in recipes. Light tuna can replace chicken or veal.

There are more than fifty species of tuna. Consumers are most familiar with five—albacore, blue fin, yellow fin, bonito, and skipjack. (See the sidebar Talking Tuna, page 116, for details and eco-recommendations about each.) No matter what the species, this fish travels at high speeds in dense, oceanic schools. It ranges in weight from six to more than a thousand pounds, and its flesh varies in color from pinkish white to scarlet red. Migratory and warm-blooded, tuna is a member of the mackerel family.

Due to its tough, almost inedible skin, tuna is usually sold skinless and as steaks. Occasionally, you may encounter fillets. Unquestionably, you'll find countless cans of precooked tuna packed in olive oil or water. All can be purchased year-round. Depending on the variety, fresh tuna will only be available from late spring to early fall. When buying fresh tuna, skip those fish that look dry, are uneven in color, or have brown spots. Avoid any that give off unpleasant odors. As tuna spoils quickly, refrigerate it in a container of crushed ice for up to one day.

Tuna does well when braised, broiled, grilled, poached, sautéed, seared, steamed, and stir-fried. It has long been consumed raw in sushi, carpaccio, and tartares. It marries nicely with a myriad of flavors and foods, including anchovies, avocados, chile peppers, chives, cilantro, cucumbers, garlic, ginger, lemon, lime, onions, parsley, pepper, scallions, sesame oil and seeds, soy sauce, thyme, tomatoes, vinegar, and wasabi.

Although over fifty varieties of tuna exist, Americans tend to cook with only five of them—albacore, bluefin, bonito, skipjack, and yellowfin. While tuna vary in size and color, they all come from the ocean where they're caught primarily with long lines and purse nets. Unfortunately, these modes have a moderately high level of marine mammal bycatch, making tuna an environmentally unfriendly food. If you can, buy pole-caught tuna, which have been obtained in an eco-safe manner.

Albacore: Fatty and with the lightest-colored flesh, albacore bears a strong resemblance to veal. Its soft, mild meat makes it an inappropriate choice for sushi, carpaccio, or tartare, but it is put to good use canned. This fish grows quickly and may reach sixty pounds. Pole-caught albacore from the North American Pacific is among the eco-best tuna available.

Bluefin: The fattiest of the tunas, bluefin possesses firm, red, beef-like flesh when raw and a dense, rich flavor when cooked. It's often seared or served raw in sushi, ceviche, or tartare. A whopper of a fish, bluefin tunas can weigh more than a thousand pounds. Unfortunately, due to its high levels of PCBs and mercury, bluefin ranks as an "eco-worst" seafood choice.

Bonito: Moderately high in fat, bonito is the strongest-tasting tuna. It is often dried and used in Japanese dishes. A smaller fish, it typically weighs around twenty-five pounds. In its pole-caught form bonito is an environmentally sound fish choice.

Skipjack: While this smallish tuna also goes by the names Arctic bonito, oceanic bonito, and aku, it gets the moniker "skipjack" for its tendency to skip up and out of the water. It has a pinkish, flavorful flesh that's similar to yellowfin. Another fast-grower, it can get as heavy as forty pounds but usually only reaches six or eight. Like bonito, when pole-caught, skipjack is an eco-friendly option.

Yellowfin: Exhibiting pale pink flesh and a taste bolder than albacore, yellowfin's flavor reminds most consumers of swordfish. It grows quickly and can weigh up to three hundred pounds. Unfortunately, like bluefin, it contains high levels of mercury. If you're eating yellowfin, make sure that it's pole-caught in the U.S. Otherwise it's best to avoid this fish.

Chilled Tuna and White Beans

Canned tuna rarely gets the respect it deserves. People drench it in mayonnaise and slap it between slices of white bread or drown it in noodles and canned mushroom soup. Here, I give the fish its due with a simple dressing of olive oil and lemon juice. Serve this as a light main course on a steamy summer day.

SERVES 4

$^1/_3$ cup olive oil

Grated zest of 1 lemon

$^1/_4$ cup freshly squeezed lemon juice

$^1/_4$ teaspoon sea salt

$^1/_2$ teaspoon freshly ground white pepper

1 celery stalk, diced

1 small green bell pepper, diced

1 tablespoon minced shallot

2 (15-ounce) cans Great Northern or
  other white beans, rinsed and drained

2 (5-ounce) cans solid, pole-caught albacore
  tuna
  in water, drained

$^1/_3$ cup feta cheese, crumbled

In a small bowl, whisk together the oil, lemon zest and juice, salt, and pepper.

In a large bowl, toss together the celery, bell pepper, shallot, white beans, and half of the dressing. Add the tuna and toss lightly to combine. Refrigerate the mixture and remaining dressing for 30 minutes or until ready to serve.

To serve, divide the chilled tuna and white beans between four plates. Whisk the dressing together again and pour equal amounts of it over the tuna-bean combo. Sprinkle 1 tablespoon of crumbled feta over each plate. Serve.

Supper Club Tuna Salad

Appropriately enough, I first had this salad for supper at Jason Hafer's house. A long-time pescetarian and skilled home cook, Jason created this stellar dish as a tribute to—and substitute for—all the steak salads that, as a child, he and his father would make on Sunday afternoons. Recipe courtesy of Jason Hafer.

SERVES 4

4 (4- to 6-ounce) tuna steaks,
  each about 1-inch thick

For the marinade:
$1/2$ cup soy sauce
1 tablespoon chopped onion
2 chopped garlic cloves
$1/2$ teaspoon sugar
$1/2$ teaspoon ground ginger
$1/3$ cup extra-virgin olive oil

For the caramelized onions:
1 tablespoon unsalted butter
1 tablespoon extra-virgin olive oil
1 medium onion, thinly sliced
$1/2$ teaspoon sea salt
$1/2$ teaspoon sugar

For the dressing:
$1/2$ cup balsamic vinegar
2 garlic cloves, chopped
1 teaspoon Dijon mustard
1 teaspoon freshly squeezed lemon juice
$1/2$ teaspoon freshly ground black pepper
$1/4$ teaspoon sea salt
$3/4$ cup extra-virgin olive oil

For the salad:
1 head iceberg lettuce, quartered
Capers, rinsed and drained, to taste
1 to 2 tablespoons grapeseed or olive oil
Handful of roughly chopped kalamata olives
$1/4$ cup crumbled feta or blue cheese

Place the tuna steaks on a shallow platter or baking dish.

TO MAKE THE MARINADE, combine all the marinade ingredients, except for the oil, in a mixing bowl. Stir to combine and then whisk in the oil.

Pour the marinade over the tuna steaks. Refrigerate and allow the tuna to marinate for at least 1 hour.

TO MAKE THE CARAMELIZED ONIONS, while the fish steaks are marinating, heat the butter and oil in a medium frying pan over medium-high heat. Once the butter is melted, add the onions and cook, stirring, for about one minute. Add the salt and sugar and stir to coat the onions.

Reduce the heat to medium-low. Continue to cook, stirring occasionally, until the onions are soft and dark brown, 35 to 45 minutes. If the onions start to stick, you may need to reduce the heat to low during this period. Remove the pan from the heat and set aside.

TO MAKE THE DRESSING, combine all the ingredients for the dressing, except for the oil, in a mixing bowl and stir together. Slowly pour in the oil, whisking until the ingredients have emulsified. Note that the dressing can be made ahead of time and refrigerated until needed.

TO ASSEMBLE THE SALAD, place the quartered iceberg wedges on dinner plates or in a wide salad bowl. Sparsely sprinkle with capers. If working ahead of time, store the plated wedges in the refrigerator.

WHEN READY TO COOK THE TUNA, heat a cast-iron skillet over high heat. Once the pan is hot (first wisp of smoke), pour in enough grapeseed or olive oil to coat the pan. Place the tuna steaks in the pan and cook for 2 to 3 minutes per side, until medium rare, or seared on the outside but still pink inside. Ultimately, your cooking time depends, more or less, on your guests' preferences for doneness.

Drizzle a little bit of dressing over the iceberg wedges and add the caramelized onions. Place the tuna steaks on top of the wedges, and drizzle a little more dressing over top. Finish with kalamata olives and feta or blue cheese, depending on taste. If tomatoes are in season, slice a few fresh tomatoes and serve them alongside.

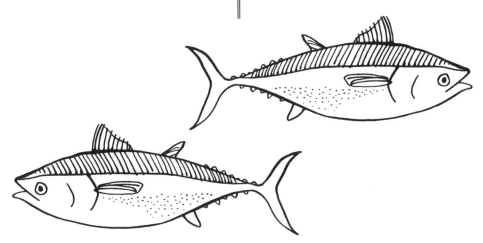

Dive Bar Tuna Delight

One of the high points of my Upper

West Side New York City neighborhood is my proximity to Amsterdam Avenue and the Dive Bar. Contrary to its name, this is not a dive but rather a bar that serves exceptionally wholesome, frequently creative food. Among my longstanding Dive Bar favorites is the Mary Ryan club sandwich. Featuring sliced avocado, tomato, and sprouts perched atop a thick, medium-rare tuna steak, the Mary Ryan puts all other tuna sandwiches to shame. With a nod to Dive Bar owner Lee Seinfeld, I offer my take on this delightful sandwich. You can find wasabi powder in the Asian section of supermarkets and online from such purveyors as Kalustyan's.

SERVES 4

4 (4- to 6-ounce) tuna steaks, each
   about 1-inch thick
1 to 2 tablespoons olive oil
$1/2$ teaspoon kosher salt, plus more to taste
Freshly ground black pepper, to taste
$1^1/2$ teaspoons wasabi powder
$1^1/2$ teaspoons whole milk, at room temperature
$1/3$ cup good-quality mayonnaise
8 slices seeded rye or multigrain bread,
   lightly toasted

$1/2$ cup alfalfa sprouts
2 avocados, sliced
1 large, ripe tomato, sliced

Preheat your grill on high.

Brush the tuna steaks with the olive oil and season with salt and pepper.

In a small bowl, whisk together the wasabi powder and milk. Add the mayonnaise, stirring until smooth and well combined. Cover and refrigerate until ready to use.

Place the tuna steaks on the preheated grill, cover, and reduce the temperature to medium-high. Cook for 3 minutes, then flip the steaks and cooking on the other side for an additional 2 to 3 minutes, until the center is just slightly pink. Remove the steaks from the grill and cover to keep warm.

To assemble the sandwiches, spread equal amounts of wasabi mayonnaise on 4 slices of toasted bread. Lay equal amounts of sprouts, avocado slices, and tomato on top of the mayonnaise-coated bread and then add a tuna steak to each sandwich. Cover with a plain slice of toast, cut the sandwich in half, and skewer each half with a toothpick to hold together. Serve immediately.

Firm, Flavorful Fish

Firm, flavorful fish are an eclectic and fascinating bunch. Among them are a fish that croaks like a frog, one that looks like a monstrous sea creature, and another that resembles a stunning work of art. Two from the group—mahi mahi and striped bass—rank as important sport fish while another, char, is one of the environmentally safest farmed fish around.

The dissimilarities don't end here. These fish may live in cold, temperate, or tropical regions, or lakes, rivers, or oceans. They range in weight from one to two hundred pounds and in length from twelve inches to six feet. Their skin varies in color from iridescent silver to red or blue-green. Their flesh ranges from stark white to deep red when raw. When cooked, they could be bright white or deep pink.

What the fish in this chapter share in common are texture and taste. They have firm flesh that, while moist, is not terribly fatty. The flesh itself is blessed with a sweet savoriness that satisfies seafood lovers and caters to those who abhor fishy fish.

Flexible and flavorful, these fish perform well with most cooking techniques. You can bake, broil, grill, pan- or deep-fry, poach, roast, sauté, sear, or steam them with great success. In the case of char and croaker, you can even smoke the fish (page 102).

While none of these fish are particularly oily, they remain quite perishable. You should refrigerate whole fish in crushed ice for a maximum of two days. Most fillets and steaks should likewise be stored in ice in the refrigerator for up to two days.

Char

At one time I had to pound the pavement in search of char. Today, however, this northern freshwater fish has become a staple of many seafood shops and restaurants. Related to trout and bearing a strong physical resemblance to salmon, char has bright, silvery skin and pale pink to ruby red flesh. Its flavor is reminiscent of mild salmon or bold trout. When cooking, I treat it as I would either of those fish.

Several varieties of char exist. Of these, you'll most often find Arctic char in markets and on menus. The name Arctic char is a bit of a misnomer. This fish comes not from the North Pole but from lakes in North America, Great Britain, and Iceland.

The char that I purchase has been raised on land in tanks. This method of aquaculture releases little pollution or parasites, making farmed char a sound seafood choice. For the same reason it is also a good alternative to farmed Atlantic salmon, whose aquaculture pollutes waters and contains a large amount of toxins.

Farmed char is available year-round in markets. Wild char is found in limited quantities in the fall. Whether farmed or wild, the fish is sold whole and as fillets and steaks.

When selecting char, look for clear, silvery skin and firm, unblemished, pink-to-red flesh. The fish should smell clean and fresh. Once you've purchased your fish, keep it under crushed ice in the refrigerator for up to two days.

Char responds nicely to baking, broiling, braising, grilling, pan-frying, poaching, and cold- or hot-smoking. It has an affinity for such ingredients as basil, butter, chervil, chives, cream, curry, ginger, lemon, mushrooms, parsley, rosemary, sesame, shallots, tarragon, and white wine.

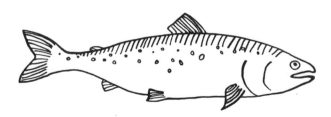

Sautéed Char with Mushrooms

This light yet earthy dish can also be made with salmon or trout. To manage the amount of liquid in the sauté, don't wash the mushrooms in water. Instead wipe them off with a damp dishcloth or paper towel.

Serve with Haricot Verts (page 229) or Sweet Peas (page 227).

SERVES 4

2 tablespoons unsalted butter

2 tablespoons olive oil, divided

2 garlic cloves, minced

3 ounces shiitake mushrooms, stems discarded and caps sliced

4 ounces cremini mushrooms, stems discarded and caps sliced

8 ounces portobello mushrooms, diced

$1/2$ teaspoon sea salt, plus more for seasoning

$1/2$ teaspoon freshly ground black pepper, plus more for seasoning

$1/4$ teaspoon ground nutmeg

4 (4 to 6-ounce) char fillets, skin on

3 tablespoons chopped flat-leaf parsley

Heat the butter and 1 tablespoon of the olive oil in a large frying or sauté pan over medium-high heat. Add the garlic and mushrooms and sauté until the mushrooms have softened and begun to release their liquid, about 3 minutes. Reduce the heat to medium; add the salt, pepper, and nutmeg, and sauté until the mushrooms have browned, 4 to 7 minutes. Transfer the mushrooms to a bowl, cover, and set aside.

Pour the remaining tablespoon of olive oil into the pan over medium-high.

As the oil heats, season the char with the salt and pepper. Place the fillets in the pan, skin side down, and cook until lightly browned, about 3 minutes. Flip the fillets and cook on the other side until browned and opaque, 3 to 5 minutes.

Return the mushrooms to the pan and toss to reheat, 1 minute. Place the char on a serving platter. Spread the mushrooms and chopped parsley over the top. Serve immediately.

Cedar Planked Char

Since at least the early 1800s Native Americans have grilled whole salmon, shad, and other fish on hunks of oak, alder, and cedar. For them, these planks were the means of cooking over an open fire. Now, though, most cooks use wood planks to add flavor, retain moisture, and stop the fish from falling apart on or sticking to the grill.

For this recipe you'll need two cedar grilling planks that have soaked in water for a minimum of 30 minutes.

SERVES 6

Grated zest and juice of 1 large orange

$^1/_2$-inch piece fresh ginger, peeled and
  minced (about 1 tablespoon)

$^1/_4$ cup honey

1 tablespoon olive oil

6 (4- to 6-ounce) char fillets, skin on

Sea salt, to taste

Freshly ground black pepper, to taste

4 to 6 small scallions, whites and 1-inch
  of greens sliced

In a small saucepan over medium-high heat, whisk together the orange juice and zest, ginger, and honey. Cook, whisking frequently, until the juice reduces and thickens, about 10 minutes. Remove from the heat, whisk in the olive oil, and set aside to cool slightly.

Set up your grill for indirect grilling (see Grilling Indirectly, opposite page).

Preheat the grill on high.

Season the char with salt and pepper. Brush the cooled orange glaze over the fillets and allow them to marinate for 15 to 20 minutes.

Place the fillets skin side down on the planks. Lay the planks on the grill, away from the hot coals, and cover. If using a gas grill, reduce the heat to medium high.

Grill until the fish is opaque and sizzling and the flesh flakes when tested with a fork. Depending on the thickness of your fillets, this could take anywhere from 15 to 30 minutes. Scatter the scallions over the char and serve immediately from the planks.

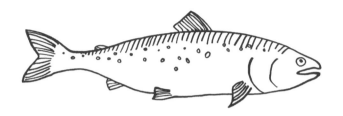

GRILLING INDIRECTLY

Indirect grilling is a bit like smoking. With a charcoal grill you light the fire as you normally would, but, once the coals are hot, you push the pile of briquettes over to one side. You then put a small pan on the other side under the rack; this pan will collect any food drippings.

If you're using a gas grill, flip on the burners on the far left and right, leaving the center burner turned off. You won't need to add a drip pan, since that is a built-in feature of a gas grill.

Place your seafood on the part of the grate that is farthest away from the heat. If using a charcoal grill, lay your food directly over the drip pan. If using a gas grill, the food rests in the center.

Cover and cook at a temperature between 300°F and 400°F. If your grill doesn't have a built-in thermometer, you can monitor the cooking temperature with an oven thermometer.

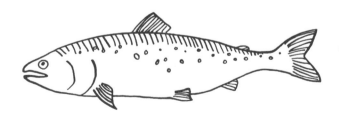

Croaker

If you've ever heard a croaker croak, you'll have to agree that this fish is aptly named. A member of the same family as drum (a larger fish that makes a drumming sound), the petite croaker is known for the loud bellowing noise that it creates with its air bladder. It's especially noisy during mating season.

Although roughly 270 species of croaker and drum exist, only three croakers make it to markets—Atlantic, white, and spot. Atlantic croaker is caught from Cape Cod to the Gulf of Mexico and has golden-silver skin. White croaker resides in the North Pacific, from British Columbia to Mexico, and has brownish-silver skin with yellowish-white fins. As its name indicates, spot croaker has a dark blotch right behind its gill. All three species have lean, white, firm meat. Small in size, these guys average one pound in weight and reach a maximum of two feet in length.

Due to its diminutive proportions croaker is usually sold whole, with or without its head. When purchasing croaker, look for red gills and bright, unbruised skin. The fish should smell sweet and not fishy. Once you get the fish home, store it on ice in the refrigerator for up to two days. Fillets will keep for one day in ice.

Often cooks will dust croaker with cornmeal and then deep- or pan-fry it. However, this fish can be prepared using a wealth of techniques and flavors. I've found that small croaker does best when grilled or broiled as well as pan- or deep-fried. One-pounders respond well to those techniques and to baking, sautéing, searing, smoking, and steaming. Recipes for butterfish, cod, and porgy can also be used for croaker.

Croaker works well with cilantro, ginger, onions, tomatoes, paprika, sesame seeds, cornmeal, bacon, soy sauce, and white wine.

Fast-growing but with raised PCB levels, Atlantic croaker is considered an "eco-okay" fish. Look for croaker that hasn't been caught by trawler for an environmentally friendlier choice.

Breadcrumb-Crusted Croaker

This recipe uses whole wheat bread- crumbs, herbs, and spices for a lively variation on the usual cornmeal-dusted croaker. You can also put this coating on catfish fillets. Serve with Warm Summer Corn Salad (page 228) or Ratatouille (page 231) and a squeeze of lemon juice.

SERVES 4

1 large egg
2 tablespoons skim milk
1 cup plain whole wheat breadcrumbs
1½ teaspoons chopped fresh rosemary
1½ teaspoons chopped fresh basil
½ teaspoon garlic powder
1 teaspoon freshly ground black pepper, divided
1 teaspoon sea salt, divided
2 tablespoons olive oil
4 (1-pound) whole croakers, gutted, scaled, and rinsed
Lemon wedges, for serving

In a medium bowl whisk together the egg and milk. In a separate bowl toss together the breadcrumbs, rosemary, basil, garlic powder, and half of the pepper and salt.

Season the insides of the croaker with the remaining salt and pepper.

Dip each fish into the egg mixture and then into the breadcrumbs.

Heat the olive oil in a large, nonstick frying pan over medium-high heat.

Fry the fish until the skin is golden brown, about 4 minutes. Turn the croakers over and cook on the other side until the skin has browned and the flesh is white and cooked through, 3 to 5 minutes. Serve hot with lemon wedges.

Barbecued Croaker Salad

I slather barbecue sauce over pretty much anything. Yet I do find that firm, flavorful fish such as croaker pair exceptionally well with this sweetly piquant condiment. The muscovado sugar gives the sauce a richer, deeper flavor than raw or brown sugar. You can also use this recipe with meaty, oily fish such as salmon and with more delicate seafood such as catfish, sea bass, and barramundi.

SERVES 4

For the barbecue sauce:

$1/4$ cup tomato paste

$1/4$ cup white wine vinegar

$1/4$ cup firmly packed muscovado sugar

2 tablespoons honey

1 teaspoon freshly squeezed lemon juice

1 teaspoon yellow mustard

1 teaspoon onion powder

$1/2$ teaspoon freshly ground black pepper

$1/4$ teaspoon garlic powder

Pinch of cayenne pepper

1 garlic clove, minced

For the salad:

3 tablespoon extra-virgin olive oil, divided

4 (4 to 6-ounce) croaker fillets

Sea salt, to taste

Freshly ground black pepper, to taste

1 tablespoon balsamic vinegar

4 firmly packed cups (about $4^1/2$ ounces) fresh baby spinach

8 ounces sugar snap peas, ends trimmed

2 large scallions, whites and 1-inch greens sliced

1 large tomato, diced

2 tablespoons pine nuts, toasted

TO MAKE THE BARBECUE SAUCE, in a small saucepan over medium heat whisk together $3/4$ cup of water with the tomato paste, vinegar, muscovado sugar, honey, lemon juice, mustard, onion powder, black pepper, garlic powder, cayenne, and garlic. Bring the ingredients to a boil, reduce the heat to low, and allow the sauce to simmer, stirring frequently, until thick and fragrant, 20 to 30 minutes. Remove the pan from the heat and let the sauce cool to room temperature. You will have roughly $3/4$ cup thick barbecue sauce when finished.

TO MAKE THE SALAD, preheat the oven to 425°F. Spread 1 tablespoon of the olive oil over the bottom of a shallow baking dish.

Season the croaker fillets with salt and pepper and place them in the greased dish. Using $1/4$ cup barbecue sauce, brush generous amounts of sauce over the tops and sides of the fillets.

Bake, uncovered, for 15 to 20 minutes, spreading more sauce over the fish halfway through the cooking time. When finished, the fillets will flake when probed with a fork.

Whisk together the vinegar and remaining 2 tablespoons of olive oil and toss with the spinach, peas, scallions, tomato, and pine nuts. Distribute the salad evenly on four dinner plates. Lay a fillet in the center of each salad and spread additional barbecue sauce over the fillets, if desired. Serve immediately.

Halibut

The biggest of all the flatfish, halibut occasionally gets mistaken for an array of odd objects, such as kelp beds, rotting rafts, and overturned boats. I'm willing to bet that it's even been called a sea monster. Although that may sound far-fetched, it's not at all surprising when you consider this fast-moving fish's size: halibut can grow up to nine feet long and weigh more than six hundred pounds. So ravenous is its appetite that it's been known to eat birds' eggs that have fallen into the ocean. Sometimes it gobbles up adult birds, too.

The forked-tailed, greenish-brown halibut lives on the bottom of the North Atlantic and Pacific Oceans. Its preference for cold waters causes it to grow slower and bigger than other flatfish. Unfortunately, because of its slow growth rate, it has been overfished in the Atlantic. Halibut aquaculture does exist, but it is hampered by the enormous amounts of food required by the fish.

Halibut has lean, white meat with few bones. Its larger cousin, known as whale halibut, has a coarser texture than smaller halibut. Also known as chicken halibut, the smaller, finer-fleshed fish weighs from two to ten pounds.

When shopping for halibut, look for small fish with white, glistening flesh and a sea-like smell. Stay away from browning, dried out, yellowing, or gaping meat. Also, if available, opt for Pacific halibut, which has not been overfished.

Halibut is sold whole and as steaks and fillets. You can keep fillets and steaks for two days in ice in the refrigerator. Whole fish will last for three days. Halibut can also be refrozen, since it retains moisture well.

You can bake, broil, grill, poach, roast, sauté, sear, or steam halibut. Just remember that, in order to maintain their shape, steaks should be cooked with the skin on.

Halibut couples well with such foods as almonds, artichokes, asparagus, mushrooms, potatoes, scallions, shallots, and tomatoes. It also goes nicely with basil, butter, capers, chervil, chives, dill, fennel, mustard, flat-leaf parsley, and rosemary. Liquids such as lemon juice, lime juice, white wine, and balsamic, sherry, and wine vinegars can also jazz up its flavor.

Sadly, in terms of eco-friendly seafood, Atlantic halibut is one of the worst choices. This is due to its depleted population. Pacific halibut from Alaska or Canada is a better option because fishing conditions there are both safe and sustainable. Likewise, pollutants are lower in the northern Pacific waters, so people can safely consume four meals of Pacific halibut each month. If you can't track down Pacific halibut, substitute U.S. hook-and-line–caught haddock or Atlantic pollock from Norway.

Braised Halibut with Shallot-Herb Butter

Braising helps to retain halibut's succulence. You can also poach the fish in a saucepan with $2^{1}/_{2}$ cups chicken stock for 10 to 12 minutes and then dress it with shallot-herb butter. Both braised and poached halibut go well with Haricot Verts (page 229), Wild Rice-Mushroom Pilaf (page 232), or Parmesan Polenta (page 237).

SERVES 4

6 tablespoons unsalted butter,
    at room temperature, divided
1 medium shallot, minced
1 tablespoon minced fresh flat-leaf parsley
$^{1}/_{2}$ tablespoon minced fresh rosemary
$^{1}/_{2}$ teaspoon kosher salt, plus more to taste
Pinch of freshly ground white pepper
2 tablespoons olive oil
$1^{1}/_{2}$ pounds Pacific halibut steaks or fillets
Freshly ground black pepper, to taste
1 cup chicken stock

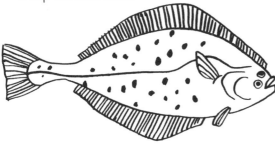

Melt 1 teaspoon of the butter in a large sauté pan over medium heat. Add the shallot and sauté for 1 minute, until slightly soft and aromatic. Remove the pan from the heat. Spoon the shallot into a bowl with the remaining butter. Add the parsley, rosemary, $^{1}/_{2}$ teaspoon kosher salt, and white pepper and mash with a fork until well combined.

Return the pan to the stove, and heat the olive oil over medium-high heat.

Pat the halibut dry and then season with salt and pepper. Place the fish, skin sides up, in the pan and sear until the flesh starts to brown slightly, 2 to 3 minutes. Turn the fillets over and cook on the skin side for 1 minute until the skin starts to color slightly.

Remove the fish from the pan and cover to keep warm.

Pour the stock into the sauté pan and bring to a boil. Return the halibut to the pan, cover, and reduce the heat to low. Braise until cooked through and flaky, 5 to 8 minutes.

Remove the halibut and place it on a platter. Spread equal amounts of shallot-herb butter over the fish and serve immediately.

Halibut Cassoulet

A slow-cooked classic from the

Languedoc region of France, cassoulet is a light, flavorful, one-pot wonder. Although many variations exist, the two basic components are white beans and pork. This version, which features halibut and a smidgen of salt cod, goes beautifully with hunks of crusty French bread.

SERVES 6

4 tablespoons olive oil, divided

$1\frac{1}{2}$ pounds skinless Pacific halibut steaks or fillets, cut into 1-inch chunks

1 (6-ounce) salt cod fillet, soaked in 3 changes of cold water for 24 hours and then cut into $\frac{1}{2}$-inch chunks

2 ounces smoked bacon, diced

1 medium leek, whites and $\frac{1}{2}$-inch of greens chopped

1 large carrot, chopped

4 garlic cloves, chopped

1 small yellow onion, chopped

$\frac{1}{2}$ teaspoon sea salt

3 ripe tomatoes, seeded and chopped

1 tablespoon tomato paste

1 bay leaf

$\frac{1}{4}$ cup dry red wine

$1\frac{1}{2}$ cups chicken or fish stock (see page 158 for fish stock)

1 (15-ounce) can cannellini beans, drained and rinsed

Freshly ground black pepper, to taste

Handful of fresh flat-leaf parsley, chopped, for serving

Preheat the oven to 350°F.

In a medium Dutch oven or oven-safe sauté pan heat 2 tablespoons of the olive oil over medium-high heat. Add the halibut and salt cod and cook for 2 minutes. Stir in the diced bacon and cook for an additional 2 minutes. Remove the fish and bacon from the pan and cover to keep warm.

Heat the remaining 2 tablespoons of olive oil in the pan over medium-high heat. Add the leek, carrot, garlic, onion, and salt and sauté until softened, 3 to 5 minutes.

Add the tomatoes, tomato paste, bay leaf, and red wine and stir to combine. Reduce the heat to medium and simmer for 5 minutes or until the tomatoes have softened. Pour in the stock and bring to a boil. Cook for another 5 minutes, stirring occasionally, until the flavors are well combined.

Remove the pan from the heat. Pluck out the bay leaf and stir in the fish, bacon, and cannellini beans. Season generously with pepper.

Transfer the cassoulet to the oven and bake, uncovered, until a crust forms on top, 35 to 40 minutes. Serve hot, sprinkled with the fresh parsley.

Mahi Mahi

At one time the powerful, fast-growing mahi mahi went by the name "dolphin fish." Due to its dolphin-like habit of swimming alongside boats in the ocean. The confusion between the marine mammal and the fish resulted in consumer outrage—"I'm not about to eat Flipper!" This, in turn, prompted fishermen and seafood suppliers to start using the Hawaiian name, mahi mahi, for the fish. Meaning "strong-strong" in Hawaiian, the mighty mahi mahi resides primarily in the southern Atlantic and Caribbean. It can also be found, though, in warm waters throughout the world.

Sporting iridescent blue-green and gold skin and a body-length dorsal fin, mahi mahi is a particularly handsome fish. Popular with fishermen, this magnificent creature can grow up to five feet long and weigh up to forty-five pounds. At markets it usually weighs between three and six pounds. It has firm, moist, sweet meat that makes a fitting substitute for swordfish.

When buying mahi mahi, look for bright, light-colored, firm flesh. Dark, streaky meat means that you've found an old fish.

Mahi mahi is usually sold in fillets. These can be refrigerated for up to two days. Prior to cooking or, at the very least, to eating, you should remove its tough skin.

Although its season varies depending upon the region, the freshest mahi mahi generally is available in the summertime. This is ideal as mahi mahi performs fantastically on the grill. It doesn't require much more than a squeeze of lemon or lime juice, or melted butter and a dash of salt and pepper to achieve a delicious meal.

Along with grilling, mahi mahi responds well to broiling, baking, sautéing, steaming, and stir-frying. It has an affinity for such foods as avocado, cabbage, onion, shallot, scallion, tomato, and tropical fruits such as mango and kiwi. It is compatible with such herbs and spices as cilantro, dill, juniper berry, mustard, oregano, sesame, thyme, and white pepper.

Overall mahi mahi is an eco-friendly and safe seafood choice. It has only moderate levels of mercury and can therefore be consumed several times per month. It also grows quickly and has a thriving population. When purchasing, choose mahi mahi caught in the U.S. by troll or pole. These methods have the least amount of marine bycatch.

Jamaican Jerk Mahi Mahi

Although the blend of ingredients varies from cook to cook, Jamaican jerk typically contains thyme, chiles, garlic, and onion. Some cooks rub their dry mixture directly onto meat, poultry, or fish. Others whisk in a liquid, such as olive oil or citrus juice, and use the jerk as a marinade.

Although in this recipe I pan-fry the mahi mahi, it can also be grilled. To prevent the fish from sticking to or falling apart on the grill, lay the fillets on a sheet of lightly oiled foil.

SERVES 4

3 jalapeño peppers, halved and seeded
4 garlic cloves, halved
1 small white onion, quartered
1 tablespoon plus 1 teaspoon firmly
  packed light brown sugar
1 tablespoon dried thyme
1 tablespoon ground allspice
1 teaspoon ground nutmeg
1 teaspoon ground cloves
1 teaspoon freshly ground black pepper
1 teaspoon sea salt

$^1/_2$ teaspoon ground cinnamon
2 tablespoons white wine vinegar
2 tablespoons soy sauce
4 (6-ounce) mahi mahi fillets, skinned
2 tablespoons olive oil

Place the jalapeños, garlic, and onion in the bowl of a food processor or blender and pulse several times to mince the ingredients. Add the brown sugar, thyme, allspice, nutmeg, cloves, pepper, salt, cinnamon, vinegar, and soy sauce and process until well combined, 1 to 2 minutes.

Spread a thick layer of the jerk marinade in a long shallow bowl or platter. Place the fish fillets on top of the marinade. Brush the remaining jerk over the sides and tops, making sure that each fillet is coated completely. Cover and refrigerate for a maximum of 30 minutes.

Heat the oil in a nonstick frying pan over medium heat. Working in batches if necessary, place the fillets in the heated pan, cover, and cook on one side until lightly browned, 4 minutes. Turn the fish over and cook on the other side until firm and browned, 3 to 4 minutes. Serve immediately.

Tropical Mahi Mahi

In this recipe, moist fillets are coated with a light pineapple sauce and then broiled until golden. You can find canned cream of coconut in the international section of grocery stores and in Latin American and Asian markets.

SERVES 4

1 tablespoon grapeseed oil
1 small shallot, minced
$\frac{1}{2}$ cup canned pineapple juice
3 tablespoons canned cream of coconut
1 teaspoon sugar
4 (6-ounce) mahi mahi fillets, skins on
Sea salt, to taste
Freshly ground black pepper, to taste
$\frac{2}{3}$ cup canned crushed pineapple, drained
1 kiwi, diced
1 teaspoon freshly squeezed lime juice
2 tablespoons fresh chopped cilantro

Preheat the oven broiler on high. Line a rimmed baking sheet with aluminum foil and then grease with the oil.

In a small saucepan over medium-low heat combine the shallot, pineapple juice, cream of coconut, and sugar. Simmer for 5 minutes, stirring occasionally, until the sauce thickens.

Season the mahi mahi fillets with salt and pepper. Lay the fillets skin side down on the lined baking sheet and spread half of the pineapple sauce over the fish.

Place the baking sheet on the rack closest to the broiler and broil for 6 to 8 minutes, until the fillets are golden and cooked through. As the fillets are broiling, toss together the pineapple, kiwi, lime juice, and cilantro.

Plate the fillets with the pineapple-kiwi salsa. Pour the remaining sauce over the fillets and serve immediately.

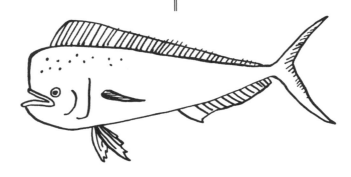

Monkfish

With its bumpy skin, enormous mouth filled with spiky teeth, and monstrously large, flat head adorned with spiny filaments, monkfish has to be one of the homeliest fish in the ocean. Consequentially, it is also one of the tastiest. Known as "poor man's lobster," this hermit-like, deepwater fish possesses a sweet, firm, white meat that is indeed quite similar to and a good substitute for lobster.

Monkfish gets its name from its reclusive nature. This flatfish lives in isolation at the bottom of ocean. Found around the globe but particularly in the North Atlantic, it survives by capturing and eating other fish and shellfish. Wiggling the long, luminescent threads that protrude from its head, it entices the curious to its massive mouth. The mouth gapes open, the fish get swallowed, and the monkfish continues on, growing as large as six feet long and two hundred pounds in weight.

You won't see a two hundred-pound monkfish in markets. In fact, you probably won't find a whole monkfish for sale anywhere. What you will encounter is a one- to four-pound, benign-looking tail. According to the late British food writer Jane Grigson, purveyors first started selling only filleted monkfish tails because they worried customers would be too repulsed to purchase a whole fish.

As with other fish, you should avoid monkfish that give off strong odors or look discolored, blemished, or dry. Occasionally the tail will have a blue-gray membrane covering it. This should be removed before cooking.

Monkfish can be braised, broiled, grilled, poached, roasted, or sautéed. It's also a lovely addition to soups and stews. Its sweet, lobster-like flavor makes it a good companion for coriander, paprika, parsley, saffron, shallots, garlic, onions, fennel, cabbage, potatoes, tomatoes, lemon, bacon, butter, and dry white wine.

Thanks to its unattractiveness, monkfish was once considered suitable only for cats and cat food. Opinions changed, and monkfish hit its stride in American markets in the 1980s. By the mid-nineties it was in short supply on the East Coast. Its population has since rebounded, but monkfish still has no definite eco-recommendations. It does, however, contain moderate levels of mercury, so it's best to consume it in moderation.

Bouillabaisse

Long associated with the French
seaside city of Marseille, bouillabaisse is the most
famous of all the Mediterranean seafood stews. This
soup came about when French fishermen started tossing their least worthwhile seafood into cauldrons.
Along with the unmarketable fish, a generous dose of
olive oil, and water, they dropped onions, garlic, tomatoes, and parsley into their cooking pots. Simmered
and then ladled into bowls and eaten with slices of
grilled or crusty bread, aromatic bouillabaisse satisfied
the French fishermen in even the bitterest weather.

Bouillabaisse demands a wide assortment of
seafood. Firm-fleshed fish that can be eaten in
chunks (such as monkfish, red snapper, and striped
bass), delicate fish that disintegrate and create a
sumptuous broth (such as sole), and inexpensive
shellfish all find their way into the stew pot.

SERVES 6

2 tablespoons extra-virgin olive oil
1 large leek, whites only, finely chopped
1 celery stalk, finely chopped
1 small fennel bulb, quartered, cored, and finely
   chopped
1 medium white onion, chopped
$3/4$ teaspoon sea salt

1 bay leaf
$1/2$ teaspoon saffron threads
$1/2$ teaspoon freshly ground black pepper
$1^1/2$ teaspoons dried basil
6 garlic cloves, finely chopped
$1/2$ cup dry white wine
1 tablespoon tomato paste
1 (14.5-ounce) can chopped tomatoes
   with their juices
$5^1/2$ cups vegetable stock
1 pound monkfish, cut into 1-inch pieces
1 pound sole, flounder, or halibut,
   cut into 1-inch pieces
1 pound littleneck clams, scrubbed
$1/2$ pound mussels, debearded
$1/2$ pound bay scallops
$1/2$ cup fresh flat-leaf parsley, chopped

Heat the oil in a large stockpot over medium-high
heat. Add the leek, celery, fennel, and onion, sprinkle
the salt over top, and sauté the vegetables until softened but not browned, 5 minutes.

Add the bay leaf, saffron, black pepper, basil, and
garlic and sauté for 2 minutes.

Add the white wine, tomato paste, tomatoes, and
vegetable stock. Cook for 10 to 15 minutes, until the
vegetables have softened completely and the soup

has become very aromatic. Taste and add more salt and pepper, if needed.

Remove the bay leaf from the pot and add the monkfish and sole. Simmer for 2 minutes before adding the clams, mussels, and scallops. Cover the pot and simmer for 5 to 8 minutes, shaking the pot periodically so that the seafood cooks evenly. Uncover and remove any unopened mussels and clams. Stir in the chopped parsley and ladle the bouillabaisse into bowls. Serve immediately.

Saffron and Cinnamon-Scented Monkfish Kebabs

I first had these aromatic kebabs

in the Moroccan seaside town of Essaouira. When I returned home, I spent hours trying to recreate this heavenly repast. When I can't eat monkfish kebabs near a windswept, North African beach, with the tangy smell of the sea mingling with the heady scents of cinnamon and saffron, I can still enjoy the rich flavors and memories that the dish evokes.

You can serve these monkfish kebabs alongside couscous and Moroccan Carrots (page 224) or Mango-Tomato Salsa (page 223).

SERVES 4

$^2/_3$ cup plain Greek yogurt
1 teaspoon ground cinnamon
$^1/_2$ teaspoon saffron threads
$^1/_2$ teaspoon ground cumin
$^1/_2$ teaspoon freshly ground black pepper
$^1/_2$ teaspoon sea salt

Juice and grated zest of 1 small orange
$1^1/_2$ pounds monkfish fillet, cut into $1^1/_2$-inch cubes

In a small bowl mix together the yogurt, cinnamon, saffron, cumin, pepper, salt, and orange zest and juice.

Place the monkfish cubes in a large bowl. Add the marinade and toss so that the fish is completely coated. Cover and refrigerate for 1 hour.

When you're ready to cook the kebabs, preheat your grill on high.

Using either metal skewers or bamboo skewers that have soaked in water, thread three to four pieces of monkfish onto each skewer. Be sure to leave at least a $^1/_2$-inch of space between each cube and also to reserve the marinade for basting.

Place the kebabs on the grill and cook for 7 to 9 minutes, basting and turning them 2 or 3 times to make sure they cook evenly. When finished, they will be firm and golden brown.

Remove the kebabs from the grill and serve.

Snapper

Yet another unusual member of the diverse group of firm, flavorful fish, snapper gets its name from its snapping jaws and teeth. Within this mouth-snapping family there are approximately 250 species. Among these are the wildly popular but grossly overfished red snapper, and the eco-friendlier lane, mutton, and yellowtail snapper.

Depending on the species, snapper can weigh as little as one or as many as thirty-five pounds. It can grow up to three feet in length. While the overall coloring varies, its scales typically have a reddish hue. In the case of red snapper, the fish progresses from silvery pink around the belly to deep rose on top. No matter which species, snapper has firm, lean, tasty meat. In fact, it's considered one of the best-flavored white fish.

Snapper is available year-round. Small fish are sold whole, while larger ones are marketed as steaks and fillets. A whole fish should have red gills, bright eyes, and bruise-free flesh. Fillets and steaks should have a slight pink tinge and appear firm and glistening. Overall the fish should look and smell good.

Whole snapper keeps for two days in the refrigerator. Fillets can be stored for one day. Cover both with crushed ice before refrigerating.

Snapper's firm, delicious flesh does well with all cooking methods. It partners with such foods as bell and chile peppers, leeks, garlic, shallots, onions, potatoes, lemon, tomatoes, and dry white wine. Herbs such as bay leaves, chives, parsley and thyme also enhance its pleasant taste.

Despite all of its selling points, snapper is not fish that we should eat regularly. All commonly consumed species possess elevated mercury levels and shouldn't be eaten more than three times a month. They also cause significant amounts of bycatch. Additionally, red snapper has been greatly overfished and, as a result, is in low supply. Safer, wiser alternatives to snapper include mahi mahi and farmed striped bass.

Salt Baked Snapper

Any whole, firm fish can be used in the recipe. When salt baked, the fish becomes tender, juicy, and flavorful. Plan on one pound of fish per person.

SERVES 2

4 pounds coarse sea or kosher salt, plus
    more as needed

2 pounds whole lane snapper or other firm fish,
    gutted, rinsed, and patted dry

Ground black pepper, to taste

2 large sprigs fresh rosemary

Preheat the oven to 400°F.

On a large baking sheet make a 1-inch-deep bed of salt. Place the fish in the center of the bed. Season the interior of the fish with black pepper and stuff in the rosemary sprigs.

Pour enough salt over top to cover and form a thick, solid mound over the fish. No skin should be visible.

Bake the fish for 40 minutes, checking the internal temperature with an instant-read thermometer to ensure that it has reached 137°F before removing it from the oven.

Using a knife and fork, crack open and peel back the salt crust and skin. If the skin doesn't peel off, use your fork and knife to remove it.

Lift pieces of fish off the bone, then flip the fish over. Remove the skin, remove the rest of the fish from the bones, and serve immediately.

SALTY LIKE THE SEA?

My first taste of whole fish baked in salt was at a seaside restaurant in sunny Cascais, Portugal. On that memorable evening the server wheeled over a dining cart weighted down by a white dome of coarse sea salt. After he slid the cart into place, he thwacked the saline mound with the butt of a bread knife. Cracking it open, he peeled back the crust, revealing a steaming hot fish. When the fish was uncovered, he skinned and filleted it, and doled out our dinner tableside.

One look at the piles of caked salt on his cart and I assumed that this entree would taste as salty as the sea. Instead, the soft, juicy fish lacked any hint of over-saltiness. The salt had acted not as a seasoning but as an insulator, keeping in moisture and producing a luscious, flavorful meal.

Steamed Ginger-Sesame Snapper

In Vietnam steaming is one of the main methods of preparing seafood. Using either a commercial steamer or a small, mesh tray placed inside a lidded pot, a cook quickly steams the fish in its own juices and a smidgen of water. Once it's fork-tender, the fish is served family-style from the pot. That is how I first tried the juicy and flavorful Steamed Ginger-Sesame Snapper—spooned out of a large, metal steamer and shared with my husband, his step-father, and a family friend in a waterfront restaurant in Can Tho, Vietnam.

Although I prefer bamboo steamer baskets, you can also use baskets made from metal or silicone. Just make sure that the device is large enough to hold the fillets without overcrowding them. In addition to snapper, mahi mahi or monkfish would work well in this recipe.

SERVES 4

1-inch piece fresh ginger, peeled and grated
   (about 2 tablespoons)
2 tablespoons sesame oil
2 tablespoons freshly squeezed lime juice

2 tablespoons plus 2 teaspoons honey
$1/2$ teaspoon fish sauce
4 (6-ounce) snapper fillets, skins on
Sea salt, to taste
Freshly ground white pepper, to taste
2 tablespoons sesame seeds, toasted

In a small bowl whisk together the ginger, sesame oil, lime juice, honey, and fish sauce. Measure out 1 tablespoon of ginger-sesame sauce; you will use this to marinate the fish. Set the rest aside.

Season the snapper fillets with salt and pepper. Lightly brush the 1 tablespoon of sauce over the skinless side of the fillets. Cover and refrigerate for 1 to 2 hours.

Fill a large, wide pot with $1^{1}/_{2}$-inches of water. Place the steamer basket over the water and bring to a boil.

Place the marinated fillets skin side down in the basket. Cover and steam the fish for 8 to 10 minutes. The snapper will be firm and white when cooked through.

Remove the fillets and dress them with the sesame-ginger sauce and toasted sesame seeds. Serve immediately.

Striped Bass

Since colonial times Americans have prized the moist and sweet striped bass Back then, the fish grew in abundance, weighing as much as one hundred pounds and growing as big as six feet in length. As often is the case with highly popular fish, people overfished it and its wild population dwindled. Today most striped bass are farm-raised on the East Coast, and, as a result, they are much smaller and milder than what our ancestors caught in the wild.

Named for its black, horizontal stripes, wild striped bass can be found along the Atlantic coastline from Canada to Florida. Similar to salmon, they are anadromous fish, leaving the ocean to spawn in freshwater. Their strength and feisty nature have made them coveted sport fish. In fact, fishermen often rank them as one of the best game fish in the world.

The striped bass that you see at markets is usually farmed. Sold whole and as steaks and fillets, its flesh is firm and pinkish. Whole striped bass should have bright red gills; fillets and steaks should be moist and uniform in color. Avoid any bass that looks bruised, browned, or dry. At home, refrigerate the fish in crushed ice for up to two days.

Versatile and eco-friendly, American-sourced farmed striped bass can replace meaty as well as milder fish in recipes; this includes salmon, cod, halibut, and sea bass. In terms of cooking, it performs well when baked, braised, broiled, deep-fried, grilled, roasted, poached, sautéed, seared, or steamed. It fancies such ingredients as flat-leaf parsley, thyme, garlic, scallions, pearl and red onions, potatoes, oranges, and black pepper. It also goes with butter, lemon juice, Champagne, sherry, and red wine vinegar.

Chermoula-Coated Striped Bass

Countless recipes exist for the North African condiment chermoula. All begin with a mixture of cilantro, parsley, garlic, lemon juice, and olive oil. Depending upon who's in the kitchen, these recipes could go on to include ginger, red pepper oil, saffron, paprika, cayenne, and/or vinegar. The end result is used as a marinade for white-fleshed fish and as a cold sauce for fried fish and shellfish. Multipurpose chermoula enlivens any firm fish. It also dresses up vegetables and plain couscous. Couscous and Moroccan Carrots (page 224) are excellent sides for Chermoula-Coated Striped Bass.

If you don't have a fish basket, grill the fish on an oiled piece of foil to ensure that it doesn't stick to the grill.

SERVES 4

6 garlic cloves, quartered
$1^1/_2$ teaspoons crushed red pepper flakes
1 teaspoon ground cumin
1 teaspoon sea salt
$1/_2$ teaspoon sweet paprika
Generous handful of fresh cilantro, stems removed
Handful of fresh flat-leaf parsley, stems removed
Freshly squeezed juice of $1^1/_2$ lemons
$2^1/_2$ tablespoons olive oil
Freshly ground black pepper, to taste
2 tablespoons grapeseed oil
1 ($1^1/_2$-pound) striped bass fillet, skin on

Preheat a grill on high.

Place the garlic, red pepper flakes, cumin, salt, paprika, cilantro, parsley, lemon juice, olive oil, and black pepper in the bowl of a food processor. Pulse the ingredients together until a paste forms, 1 to 2 minutes. Alternatively, you can use a mortar and pestle, mashing the garlic together with the red pepper flakes, cumin, salt, paprika, cilantro, parsley, and black pepper. Add the olive oil and lemon juice right before using. You will end up with roughly $1/_3$ cup of chermoula.

Drizzle the grapeseed oil over the striped bass. Place the fillet in a fish basket and lay it on the grill. Cover and grill for 5 minutes or until the skin has browned. Flip the fish and grill for an additional 5 to 7 minutes, until the skin has browned and the meat is firm, white, and juicy.

Remove the fillet from the basket, coat the top with the chermoula, and serve.

FIRM, FLAVORFUL FISH

Angkor-Style Striped Bass

Amok trey **is a traditional Cambodian** cooking technique that results in a highly succulent, flavorful dish. The "amok" refers to the steaming of fish, chicken, or tofu in banana leaves woven into a basket. If, like me, you're a disaster at making baskets, you can steam the fish in 6-ounce, oven-safe ramekins.

In the Angkor region of Siem Reap, Cambodia, where I learned to make this dish, cooks use locally caught snakehead fish. Striped bass or any other firm, white-fleshed fish works equally well. You can find galangal root and morinda or noni leaves in the produce section of Asian markets. Jars of minced galangal root are sold in the Asian section of most supermarkets. The morinda leaf gives this dish a slightly woody flavor, while the galangal root adds a citrusy, mustardy spiciness.

A distinctly Cambodian or Khmer flavoring, kroeung normally consists of fresh lemongrass, galangal root, turmeric, kaffir lime leaves, and garlic. After pounding the ingredients together with a mortar and pestle, cooks use the chunky, aromatic paste to season stir fries, soups, curries, and amok trey.

SERVES 4

For the kroeung or paste:

2 garlic cloves, chopped

1 tablespoon chopped lemongrass

1 tablespoon minced galangal root

1-inch piece fresh ginger, peeled and roughly chopped (about 2 tablespoons)

1 teaspoon sea salt

$^1/_2$ teaspoon ground turmeric

For the fish:

$^3/_4$ cup well-shaken canned coconut milk, plus more for serving

1 morinda or noni leaf, chopped

2 tablespoons fish sauce

2 teaspoons sugar

2 large eggs, whisked

$^1/_2$ teaspoon sea salt

$^1/_4$ teaspoon freshly ground black pepper

12 ounces striped bass fillets, skinned and thinly sliced

$^1/_2$ small red bell pepper, thinly sliced

3 to 4 cups steamed rice, for serving

Fill a large, wide pot with $1^1/_2$-inches of water. Place a steamer basket in the pot and bring the water to a boil.

TO MAKE THE KROENG, using a mortar and pestle, pulverize the garlic, lemongrass, galangal root, ginger, salt, and turmeric until you have a thick paste.

It will make about $1/3$ cup. Spoon $2^1/_2$ tablespoons of the kroeung into a large bowl. Cover and refrigerate the rest for future use.

TO MAKE THE FISH, add the coconut milk, morinda leaf, fish sauce, sugar, eggs, salt, and black pepper to the $2^1/_2$ tablespoons of kroeung and mix the ingredients together until well combined. Add the fish and stir gently to coat.

Spoon the mixture into 6 to 8 small, oven-safe ramekins or banana leaf baskets, filling each about two-thirds full. Place them in the steamer basket, cover, and allow the fish to steam for roughly 15 minutes. When finished, the fish will feel firm and appear white and cooked through.

Carefully remove the ramekins or baskets from the steamer. Garnish the top of each with slices of red pepper and a drizzle of coconut milk. Serve hot with steamed rice.

BANANA LEAF BASKET WEAVING

Believe me. Basket weaving is much harder than people claim. However, if you want to prepare a truly authentic amok trey, you've got to have banana leaf baskets.

To make the baskets, you'll need 4 large banana leaves and 2 to 3 dozen toothpicks. Begin by filling a large bowl with lukewarm water. Wipe off the banana leaves with a clean, damp cloth and then soak them in the water for 10 minutes. This will soften them and make them easier to use.

Dry the leaves and place them on a clean work surface. Using a sharp knife, slice the leaves into 5-inch squares. For each basket stack 2 squares with a straight side facing you. Place 2 more leaf squares—turned clockwise 45 degrees—on top of the other two.

Fold the squares inward $1/_2$-inch on one side and secure the fold with a toothpick. Repeat this for the other three sides. When finished, you should end up with a small basket. Repeat with the remaining squares.

1. **2.** **3.**

Pearl Onion, Orange, and Thyme-Stuffed Striped Bass

Perhaps it's the presence of seasonal oranges and yellow pearl onions, but I always prepare this stuffed, whole striped bass for fall gatherings. In keeping with the autumnal theme, I serve it with Golden Brown Cauliflower (page 233) and Crispy Rosemary Potatoes (page 236).

SERVES 4

1 (4-pound) whole striped bass, gutted and rinsed
2 tablespoons olive oil
Sea salt, to taste
Freshly ground black pepper, to taste
10 to 12 yellow pearl onions, halved
1 small orange, scrubbed and thinly sliced
4 to 5 sprigs fresh thyme

Preheat the oven to 500°F. Line a baking sheet with foil.

Rinse and dry the striped bass. Brush the interior and exterior of the fish with the olive oil. Season the inside with salt and black pepper, and fill it with the halved onions, orange slices, and thyme.

Lay the fish on the baking sheet and slip the sheet in the oven. Roast until firm to the touch and moist and white in appearance, 20 to 22 minutes. Remove and let the fish rest for 5 minutes.

To serve, peel back the skin with a knife. Using either a knife or fork and spatula, lift off portions of the fish from the bone on each side of the fish and place them on a serving platter. Discard the orange slices, and scatter the pearl onions onto the platter. Serve immediately.

Mild, White-Fleshed Fish

When I come across a recipe calling for white fish, I reach for the subjects of this chapter. Mild, white-fleshed fish consist of such memorable creatures as the whiskered catfish and toad-like turbot. This category also includes such popular but overfished favorites as cod, grouper, and orange roughy.

Versatility is what attracts people to this group. Not only can these fish be cooked in a wealth of ways, but they can also stand in for each other in recipes. Can't find sea bass? Use porgy, grouper, or any other white fish. It's that easy.

Mild, white-fleshed fish do well with almost every cooking technique. You can bake, braise, broil, pan-fry, deep-fry, stir-fry, poach, roast, sauté, sear, or steam them. They enliven soups, stews, and chowders and make delicious gratins and tagines. They partner with a range of ingredients but can also stand on their own with minimal seasonings.

In spite of their shared flavor, texture, and color, these fish remain fairly diverse. Some thrive in cold waters. Others prefer the tropics. One grows in abundance while several have been fished almost to extinction. They can weigh as little as one pound or as much as six hundred pounds. They can be plump, smooth-skinned, and brightly colored or flat, warty, and dull-looking. Nonetheless they share many important characteristics that make them perfect for almost any dish.

Catfish

With a flattened head and eight long, whisker-like barbels (feelers) scattered around its nose and mouth, the catfish lives up to its name. When I look at this guy, I think of both feline and fish. While a few members of its family prefer saltwater, this low-fat fish primarily lives in the freshwaters of Europe, Asia, North America, and the Amazon.

Out of the two thousand catfish species worldwide, North America has twenty-eight. Among the North American varieties channel catfish is the most commercially important. Fast growing and highly sustainable, channel is farmed in Canada and the American South. So safe and successful is its aquaculture that it has become America's most commonly farmed fish. It is also one of the country's eco-best seafoods.

Unlike farmed salmon, which tends to have an insipid flavor, farmed catfish is favored over wild. Farmed lacks the muddy taste of its wild brethren. Mild and inexpensive, catfish is available year-round.

Catfish is typically sold in seasoned and unseasoned fillets, but whole fish are periodically available. When selecting either, look for off-white to white, iridescent flesh. It should smell sweet and fresh and not earthy. Because its tough skin is inedible, either take it off yourself or ask your fishmonger to remove the skin.

You can store seasoned catfish fillets for up to two days in ice in the refrigerator. Boneless, skinless, unseasoned fillets will keep for one day.

In terms of preparation, catfish is highly flexible. You can bake, broil, fry, grill, poach, sauté, stir-fry, or steam it. Its delicately sweet meat works well with celery, green chiles, red pepper, scallions, garlic, onion, lemon, tomato, paprika, pecans, sesame, soy sauce, and vinegar. Catfish is common in Southern cooking and marries nicely with Cajun seasonings. You'll often see cornmeal-dusted, fried catfish served with hush puppies in Southern-style restaurants.

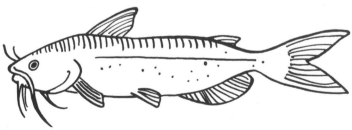

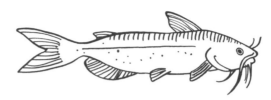

Chunky Catfish Stew

Similar to soups, stews were created to stretch small portions of meat or fish into bigger meals. Simmered with vegetables and a touch of stock or water, the slow-cooked meat or fish becomes moist, tender, and packed with flavor. This savory stew is certainly no different. Pair this delicious, filling dish with warm cornbread.

SERVES 4

2 tablespoons olive oil

1 small yellow onion, diced

2 celery stalks, diced

2 garlic cloves, minced

1 pound red bliss potatoes, cut into 1-inch cubes

1 large red bell pepper, chopped

1 cup frozen or fresh corn

$^3/_4$ teaspoon sea salt

$^1/_2$ teaspoon freshly ground black pepper

$^1/_2$ teaspoon sweet paprika

$^1/_2$ teaspoon dried basil

1 teaspoon dried oregano

5 cups chicken stock

1 pound catfish fillets, skinned and cut into 1-inch chunks

Heat the olive oil in a large stockpot over medium heat. Add the onion, celery, and garlic and sauté for 3 to 5 minutes or until the vegetables become soft and slightly translucent.

Add the potatoes and red pepper and sauté for 2 minutes.

Turn the heat up to medium-high. Add the corn, salt, pepper, paprika, basil, oregano, and stock and bring to a boil. Allow the ingredients to bubble away, uncovered, for 15 to 18 minutes, until the flavors have melded together and the stock has reduced by about one-third.

Add the catfish and cook for 5 to 7 minutes; the fish will be flaky and cooked through. Taste and adjust the seasonings. Serve immediately.

Catfish Curry

Derived from the ancient Tamil word kari, meaning "sauce," curry has become synonymous with a spicy, yellowish, Indian stew. Yet, not every curry is yellow or a stew. In its purest sense, curry is a spiced sauce for meat, fish, or vegetables. Catfish curry is a combination of these two meanings—a spicy, saucy, stew-like dish.

You can purchase garam masala and black mustard seeds at gourmet and Indian markets and online from such purveyors as Kalustyan's and Penzeys Spices. Depending upon your preference for hot foods, use up to two jalapeño peppers in this curry.

SERVES 4

2 tablespoons olive oil
$^1/_2$ teaspoon black mustard seeds
$^1/_4$ teaspoon cumin seeds
$^1/_2$ small white onion, chopped
2 teaspoons garam masala
2 medium tomatoes, diced
1 to 2 jalapeño peppers, seeds removed and sliced
$^1/_2$ teaspoon freshly ground black pepper, plus more for seasoning the fish
$^1/_2$ teaspoon sea salt, plus more for seasoning the fish
Freshly squeezed juice of 1 lime
$^1/_2$ cup chopped fresh cilantro
1 pound catfish fillets, skinned

Heat the oil in a large frying or sauté pan over medium heat. Add the mustard seeds, cumin seeds, and onion and sauté for 3 to 5 minutes, until the onion begins to soften and the spices release their aromas. Add the garam masala, tomatoes, jalapeños, salt, and pepper and cook for 2 to 3 minutes, until just softened. Add the lime juice and cilantro and stir to combine.

Season the catfish with salt and pepper.

Move the curry to the side of the pan and add the fillets. Cover them with the curry and cover the pan with a lid. Simmer for 5 to 8 minutes, until the fish is white and flakes easily. Place the fillets and sauce on a serving platter and serve immediately.

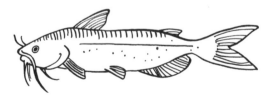

Catfish Puff Pie

Catfish puff pie comes directly from my stable of comfort foods. Tuck into this ethereal potpie on bad days or blustery nights, and you'll feel happy and toasty in no time.

SERVES 4

2 tablespoons olive oil

1 tablespoon unsalted butter

1 small yellow onion, diced

1 celery stalk, chopped

3 garlic cloves, minced

1 carrot, diced

1 russet potato, peeled and cubed

1$^{1}/_{4}$ pound catfish fillets, skinned and cut into 1-inch chunks

1 teaspoon sea salt

1 teaspoon freshly ground black pepper

1 teaspoon dried thyme

$^{1}/_{4}$ teaspoon sweet paprika

1 cup chicken stock

$^{1}/_{4}$ cup heavy cream, at room temperature

2 to 3 tablespoons unbleached all-purpose flour

1 sheet frozen puff pastry, defrosted

Preheat the oven to 400°F. Grease a shallow, 1$^{1}/_{2}$- or 2-quart baking dish.

Heat the olive oil and butter in a 12-inch frying or sauté pan heat over medium heat. Add the onion and celery and sauté until slightly soft and aromatic, 3 minutes.

Add the garlic, carrot, and potatoes and sauté for 5 minutes, until the potatoes are opaque and the garlic is golden in color.

Increase the heat to medium-high. Add the catfish, salt, black pepper, thyme, and paprika. Cook for 2 minutes, then flip the fish chunks over and cook for another minute.

Pour in the chicken stock and stir to combine. Bring the ingredients to a boil and allow the filling to bubble away until the sauce has thickened, 5 to 8 minutes. Add the cream and stir to combine. At this point, taste and adjust the seasonings.

Spoon the filling into the greased baking dish.

Dust a rolling pin and work surface with 2 to 3 tablespoons flour. Lay the puff pastry on your work surface and roll it out so that it is big enough to stretch just over the edge of your baking dish. Lay the pastry over the catfish filling and trim off anything that droops over the rim of the dish.

Bake until the crust is golden and puffed up and the filling is bubbling, 15 to 18 minutes. Serve warm.

Cod

Ask what my very first seafood dinner was, and I'd have to say with some chagrin, "Fish sticks made from cod." I'm not surprised that cod—albeit minced and breaded cod—was my introduction to seafood, for it is one of history's most prevalent and important fish. Found in the North Atlantic and Pacific Oceans, this mild, lean, saltwater fish has fed natives, explorers, and colonists for over a thousand years. Entire regions, including New England, have been supported by it. At least one community, Cape Cod, was named for it. So coveted is this fish that wars have even been fought over it.

Why cod? Quite simply, it's the perfect white fish. From drying to deep-frying you can do almost anything to it. It freezes and cooks well, holding its shape and texture under most conditions. Nearly all of the torpedo-shaped fish, including its tongue and cheeks, is eaten. Even its liver gets put to good use in the health supplement cod liver oil.

At one time the North Atlantic teemed with this fish. Unfortunately, cod's utility led to overfishing. This, in turn, resulted in extremely depleted populations. Add to this the facts that cod fishing trawlers decimate marine habitats and collect considerable bycatch and you can see why cod, specifically North Atlantic cod, ranks as one of the eco-worst seafood choices.

Should you crave cod, look for Pacific or Alaskan. These are fished in a sustainable manner and have healthier populations. You can likewise request line-caught cod. This method of fishing doesn't harm the marine environment.

When selecting cod steaks or fillets, pick those with moist, white, clean-smelling meat. If the skin has been left on, remove it before cooking. You can also purchase whole cod and salt-dried cod, known as bacalhau. Note that salt-dried cod must be soaked in several changes of cold water before cooking. This reconstitutes it and also diminishes its saltiness.

Cod responds well to a host of cooking methods. These include baking, boiling, broiling, deep- and pan-frying, poaching, roasting, salting, sautéing, and steaming. It goes with such foods as anchovies, arugula, bacon, beans, carrots, celery, mushrooms, onions, red bliss potatoes, salt pork, shallots, and tomatoes. It likewise pairs with such seasonings as basil, capers, cayenne, dill, lemon juice, mustard, saffron, and thyme. It gets an additional boost from dry white wine and balsamic, Champagne, red wine, sherry, tarragon, and white wine vinegars.

In recipes calling for cod, you can substitute catfish, hook- and line-caught haddock, and Pacific halibut. In truth any mild, firm, white fish can stand in just fine.

Tagine of Cod

If you don't own a conical terra cotta cooker, you can use a Dutch oven to make this recipe. If you cannot find Pacific cod, substitute any other firm, white fish. This tagine is seasoned with chermoula, a Moroccan spice-and-herb mixture (page 143). Serve over plain couscous.

SERVES 8

3 pounds Pacific cod fillets, skinned and
   cut into small chunks
5 tablespoons chermoula (see page 143)
4 tablespoons olive oil
3 large russet potatoes, peeled and thinly sliced
2 large green bell peppers, cut into strips
2 tablespoons tomato paste
3/4 cup warm water, plus more as needed
1 pint cherry tomatoes
5 garlic cloves, thinly sliced
Sea salt, to taste
Freshly ground black pepper, to taste
Handful of kalamata olives
4 cups steamed couscous, for serving

Place the chucks of fish in a large bowl. Spread the chermoula over the fish and toss to coat evenly. Cover and refrigerate for 1 hour.

Heat the olive oil in a tagine or Dutch oven over medium heat. Add the potatoes and cook, stirring frequently, until softened, 5 minutes.

Add the peppers. Cover and cook for another 5 minutes, frequently checking and stirring the vegetables so that they don't brown or stick to the pan.

Mix together the tomato paste and water. Pour the mixture over the potatoes and peppers. Add the cherry tomatoes and garlic and then lay the cod on top of the vegetables. Add the salt and pepper to the tagine. Stir to combine. If the sauce appears too thick, add water, as needed. You want it to be smooth and pourable, not dry and dense.

Cover and cook the stew for 15 minutes, or until the fish flakes easily when probed with a fork. Add the kalamata olives. Simmer for another 3 minutes, or until the olives have softened. Serve hot over steamed couscous.

Beer-Battered Cod

Fish and chips are the quintessential British meal, one that this Anglophile invariably orders at least once during any U.K. journey. Oddly enough, one of my best fish 'n' chips feasts happened not in Great Britain but in the Republic of Ireland, at Dublin's luxurious Fitzwilliam Hotel. So delicious was the crisp crust that enveloped the perfectly fried fillet of cod that I requested and later adapted the Fitzwilliam's recipe. The following is my take on this timeless dish.

In Great Britain fish 'n' chips frequently appear with a side of mushy peas. With this in mind I serve beer-battered cod alongside Sweet Peas (page 227) and Parsnip Chips (page 234).

SERVES 6

4 cups unbleached all-purpose flour, sifted
1 tablespoon baking powder
1/2 teaspoon baking soda
2 tablespoons cornstarch
1 teaspoon garlic powder
1/2 teaspoon onion powder
1/4 teaspoon sweet paprika
3 large eggs
1 1/2 cups skim milk
1 cup premium lager beer, such as Harp or Smithwick's

Sea salt, to taste
Freshly ground black pepper, to taste
6 (6-ounce) Pacific cod fillets, skinned
1/3 cup grapeseed oil, plus more as needed for frying

In a medium bowl whisk together the flour, baking powder, baking soda, cornstarch, garlic powder, onion powder, and paprika. Set aside.

In a separate bowl beat together the milk and eggs. Add the beer and stir to combine. Slowly add the flour mixture to the egg mixture, stirring until blended.

Season the cod fillets with salt and pepper.

Heat the oil in a small frying or sauté pan over high heat. You should have between 1/4 and 1/2 inch of oil in your pan. When the oil starts to shimmer, it's time to fry the fish.

Dip a seasoned cod fillet into the beer batter, coating it completely. Using tongs, gently lower the fish into the hot oil. Fry on one side until golden, 3 to 4 minutes. Flip the fillet over and cook on the other side until golden and crispy, 3 to 4 minutes. Remove the cod from the pan, place it on a stack of clean paper towels, and cover. Repeat with the remaining fillets, adding more oil as needed. Serve immediately.

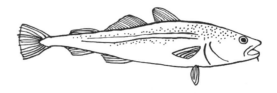

Grouper

I think of grouper as one of the loners of the marine world. Solitary and predatory, it hangs out on its own in the shallow, rocky waters of the Atlantic Ocean and the Gulf of Mexico. Rather than chasing after prey, the large, stout grouper lies in wait among rocks and in caves. When an unsuspecting fish swims by, this crafty omnivore opens its massive mouth and swallows the fish whole. Far from choosy, it consumes everything from small shellfish to octopus. Yet, in spite of its vast and indiscriminating diet, grouper maintains a subtle and slightly sweet flavor.

A member of the sea bass family, grouper can grow to weigh more than six hundred pounds. Its market size, though, falls between five and fifteen pounds.

Grouper is usually sold skinned and filleted, but whole fish and steaks are occasionally available. Fillets should be pure white and have a mild seawater scent. Whole grouper should be unbruised and firm looking. The fish keeps for up to two days on crushed ice in the refrigerator.

Although grouper is a fairly lean fish, it manages to maintain its moistness even when overcooked. This characteristic makes it quite popular with culinary novices who tend to overcook fish. Its versatility also wins it innumerable fans. Grouper can be braised, baked, fried, grilled, roasted, sautéed, steamed, and stir-fried. It's also delicious in soups and stews.

Grouper's smooth flavor couples well with butter, garlic, lemon juice, sesame oil, flat-leaf parsley, white pepper, poultry and pork stocks, and red and white wine. It also joins perfectly with such ingredients as mangoes, onions, olives, papaya, pineapple, passion fruit, and tomatoes. It has a special liking for Caribbean flavorings and spices.

As lovely as grouper can be, it's not the most eco-friendly seafood choice. Thanks to overfishing and elevated levels of mercury, it's actually considered one of the "eco-worst" fish. Unless you can find red or black grouper from the Gulf of Mexico, skip this fish. You can substitute sea bass in recipes calling for grouper.

Souper Grouper

Quick and easy to make, this dish makes for a filling starter as well as a satisfying main course. If you prefer a creamier soup, add $1/4$ to $1/2$ cup light cream, along with the tomatoes, right before serving. As in all grouper recipes, you can substitute sea bass or other firm, mild, white fish.

SERVES 4

2 tablespoons extra-virgin olive oil

1 large yellow onion, diced

$1/2$ teaspoon sea salt

4 garlic cloves, minced

1 teaspoon dried marjoram

$1/2$ teaspoon dried tarragon

$1/2$ teaspoon ground white pepper

4 cups chicken stock

$1/4$ cup dry white wine

$3/4$ cup ditalini or other small pasta

$1^{1}/2$ pounds grouper fillets, skinned and cut into 1-inch chunks

1 medium tomato, seeded and diced

Heat the oil in a small stockpot over medium heat. Add the onion and sprinkle the salt over top. Sauté for 5 minutes or until softened.

Add the garlic, marjoram, tarragon, and white pepper and sauté until the garlic has softened but is not yet brown, 1 to 2 minutes.

Pour in the chicken stock and white wine. Raise the temperature to high and bring the stock to a boil. Once the liquid begins to boil, add the pasta and the grouper. Reduce the heat to medium, cover, and simmer for 5 to 8 minutes, until the pasta and fish are just cooked.

Add the tomatoes and simmer for 1 minute. Stir, taste, and adjust seasonings before serving.

Caribbean Stir-Fry

If you don't own a wok, use a heavy-
bottomed sauté or frying pan. The key is to keep the
oil hot and to cook the food quickly in it. Serve this
with steamed rice. You can also make this stir-fry with
sea bass or mahi mahi.

SERVES 4

1 tablespoon firmly packed light brown sugar
1 tablespoon reduced-sodium soy sauce
3 tablespoons canned pineapple juice
1 1/2 pounds grouper fillets, skinned
   and cut into 1-inch-long pieces
Sea salt, to taste
Freshly ground black pepper, to taste
1 passion fruit
2 tablespoons peanut oil, divided
1/2 small red onion, sliced
1 cup canned cubed pineapple, drained
1 small papaya, diced
1/2 cup chopped fresh cilantro

In a small bowl, whisk together the brown sugar, soy
sauce, and pineapple juice.

Season the grouper with salt and pepper. Place it in
a shallow dish and pour the sauce over it. Cover and
marinate for 15 minutes at room temperature.

Meanwhile, cut the passion fruit in half. Using a
spoon, scoop out the seeds; avoid taking the bitter
white pith with them. Discard the skins. Place the
seeds in a small bowl and set aside.

Heat 1 tablespoon of the peanut oil in a wok or
heavy-bottomed sauté pan over high heat. When the
oil starts to shimmer and almost smoke, it's ready.

Remove the fish from marinade and discard the liquid. Add the grouper to the wok.

Gently stir-fry until the pieces have begun to whiten,
1 minute. Remove the fish from the wok and cover.

Drain off any liquid that's accumulated in the wok.
Add the remaining tablespoon of oil and heat on high.

Place the onion, pineapple, and papaya in the wok
and stir-fry until just softened, 1 minute.

Return the grouper to the wok and stir-fry until firm
and white, 3 to 4 minutes.

Remove the wok from the heat. Mix in the fresh
cilantro. Spoon the stir-fry into a serving bowl.
Sprinkle the passion fruit seeds over the top. Serve
immediately.

Ocean Perch

Ocean perch is an inexpensive, all-purpose fish. Available year-round, it can be used in any recipe calling for white-fleshed fish. Ocean perch hails from the Atlantic and Arctic Oceans but its close relative, Pacific rockfish, sometimes goes by the same name. Both Pacific rockfish and ocean perch possess gorgeous, rose-colored skin and lean, mild, firm white meat.

At one time ocean perch was an important deep-water fish, one that thrived in the Atlantic and Arctic. Today its numbers have dropped dramatically, pushing it into the overfished category. As a result, the ocean perch that you purchase may instead be Pacific rockfish. When caught by hook and line in British Columbia and Alaska, Pacific rockfish is an eco-okay food choice. Otherwise, neither rockfish nor ocean perch is a sound seafood option.

Whole perch generally weigh between one to two pounds. Most often they are sold as in skin-on fillets. You can, however, find skinless fillets and whole fish.

When selecting fillets, look for minimal gaping and clean, white flesh. The gills of a whole perch should be a clear pinkish-red. Avoid browning, graying, or bad-smelling fish. Frozen ocean perch will keep for about six months. Fresh will keep for two days in the refrigerator.

With the exception of smoking, perch responds nicely to all cooking techniques. It goes with such foods as avocado, garlic, lemon, mushrooms, onions, oranges, scallions, shallots, and tomatoes. Its mild flavor also teams up with basil, butter, chives, cilantro, dill, sesame, soy sauce, tarragon, and dry white wine.

GET YOUR FISH STOCK!

Fish stock is one of those ingredients that you don't easily find in supermarkets. In many instances you may have to make your own. Luckily, this is easy to do.

Take $1^3/_4$ to 2 pounds of shells, skins, and bones, along with a quartered onion, 2 chopped celery stalks, one chopped carrot, one chopped leek, and a teaspoon of sea salt, and place them in a large saucepan. Add 4 to 6 cups of water and bring the ingredients to boil. Reduce the heat to medium and simmer for 20 to 25 minutes. Strain the stock, discarding the solids.

If you don't have seafood scraps on hand, you can always ask your fishmonger for 1 pound of trimmings—heads, skeletons, skins, and shells. Rinse them well before using.

Ocean Perch Gratin

The perch in this satisfying gratin

can be replaced with catfish, mahi mahi, or salmon.

SERVES 4

4 tablespoons unsalted butter, divided

1/2 cup unbleached all-purpose flour

2 3/4 cups fish stock (see page 158)

1 tablespoon dry sherry

1 teaspoon sea salt, divided

1/2 teaspoon ground black pepper, divided

1/4 cup heavy cream

1 cup grated Parmesan cheese, divided

1/2 cup plain white breadcrumbs

2 tablespoons chopped fresh flat-leaf parsley

1 small shallot, minced

4 ounces cremini mushrooms, stems discarded
and caps sliced

1 pound line-caught ocean perch fillets, skinned
and cut into 1/2-inch cubes

1/2 pound small (36-45 count) shrimp, shells
removed and halved

Preheat the oven to 400°F. Grease a 2-quart baking
dish.

In a medium saucepan melt 2 tablespoons of butter
over medium heat. When the butter begins to foam,
whisk in the flour and stir until a smooth paste forms.

Slowly pour in the fish stock, stirring constantly to
get rid of any lumps. Once the stock has been incorporated and begins to thicken, add the sherry and
half of the salt and pepper. Stirring constantly, allow
the liquid to simmer for 3 to 4 minutes before adding
the cream. Stir to combine, remove the pan from the
heat, and sprinkle in half of the Parmesan cheese.
Stir again to combine.

In a small bowl, mix the remaining Parmesan
cheese with the breadcrumbs and parsley.

In a small frying pan melt the remaining 2 tablespoons of butter over medium heat. Add the shallot
and mushrooms and sauté until the vegetables have
softened, 2 to 3 minutes. Add the perch, shrimp, and
remaining salt and pepper. Sauté until the perch
appears white and the shrimp begin to turn pink, 2
minutes. At this point spoon the fish and vegetables
into the greased baking dish.

Pour the creamy sauce over the perch, shrimp, mushrooms, and shallots. Smooth out the top of the gratin
and then spread the Parmesan-breadcrumb mixture
over the top. Bake until the gratin bubbles and the
topping turns golden brown, 15 to 18 minutes. Serve
immediately.

Red, White, and Green Perch

Colorful and succulent, this festive dish can also be made with catfish or Pacific cod. Serve it alongside Garlic Mashed Potatoes (page 238) or Parmesan Polenta (page 237).

You can purchase garlic paste at gourmet, Mediterranean, and Asian food shops as well as online from such specialty food vendors as Kalustyan's.

SERVES 4

³/₄ cup canned diced tomatoes, drained
¹/₂ cup plain panko breadcrumbs
¹/₄ cup fresh flat-leaf parsley, chopped
3 tablespoons blanched almonds, chopped
¹/₂ teaspoon sea salt
¹/₂ teaspoon freshly ground black pepper
1¹/₂ teaspoons garlic paste
2 tablespoons olive oil
4 (4- to 6-ounce) ocean perch fillets, skins on

Preheat the oven to 450°F. Grease a shallow baking dish and set aside.

In a small bowl, mix together the tomatoes, breadcrumbs, parsley, almonds, salt, and pepper.

In another bowl, whisk together the garlic paste and olive oil.

Lay the fillets skin side down in the baking dish and brush the garlicky oil over each. Spread the tomato topping over the fillets.

Bake, uncovered, until the fillets are opaque and tender and the topping has browned slightly, 10 to 12 minutes. Serve immediately.

Orange Roughy

With its orange skin, big, round head, and spiky fins, orange roughy reminds me of an oversized, rough 'n' tumble goldfish. In its native country of New Zealand, though, folks once referred to it as "slimehead," alluding to the fish's slippery, mucus-filled head. In reaction to a diminishing demand for this unfortunately nicknamed fish, smart marketers changed the name of the reddish-orange creature to orange roughy. The rest, as the saying goes, is history.

Orange roughy can be found in the cold waters of New Zealand and Australia. Because it grows at an extremely slow rate, it's highly vulnerable to overfishing. Thus, it's not a particularly wise fish to eat.

Nonetheless, many do consume orange roughy. Introduced as a substitute for cod, this low-fat fish has been popular with Americans since the 1980s.

Orange roughly is almost always sold in fillets. If buying this fish, pick fillets that appear bright pearly white. Darker meat means lower quality. There should be no gaping, brown, or gray spots, and no bad smell. If you buy fillets with the skin on, remember to take off the inedible, orange band beneath the skin before cooking. Store the fish on ice in the refrigerator for no longer than two days.

Orange roughy can be baked, broiled, poached, sautéed, or steamed. Its moist, subtle meat takes to such bold ingredients as basil, chiles, chives, curry, ginger, rice wine, sesame, and soy sauce. It also combines nicely with bell pepper, butter, lemon, lime, mango, orange, papaya, pineapple, and tomato.

Because it possesses high levels of mercury and has a dwindling population, orange roughy is considered to be an unsound seafood choice. Use catfish, Pacific cod, or another firm, white-fleshed fish instead.

Paprika Orange Roughy

Baked orange roughy is the Friday night dish of my childhood. Ordered at my parents' favorite Italian restaurant, the paprika-coated fish was invariably served with a sour cream–loaded baked potato and side of string beans. With a nod to the fish Fridays of my youth, I pair Paprika Orange Roughy with Haricot Verts (page 229) and Crispy Rosemary Potatoes (page 236).

You can also make this dish with catfish, Pacific cod, or tilapia.

SERVES 4

4 (4 to 6-ounce) orange roughy fillets, skins and orange bands removed
Sea salt, to taste
Freshly ground black pepper, to taste
Freshly squeezed juice of 1 lemon
1 tablespoon sweet paprika
1 teaspoon garlic powder
¼ teaspoon onion powder
2 tablespoons unsalted butter, cut into chunks

Preheat the oven to 450°F. Grease the bottom of a medium baking dish.

Season both sides of the fillets with salt and pepper and place them in the baking dish. Pour the lemon juice over the fillets.

In a small bowl stir together the paprika, garlic powder, and onion powder. Sprinkle the seasoning over the fillets and then dot the fillets with the butter.

Bake, uncovered, until the fish becomes firm and can be flaked with a fork, 12 to 15 minutes. Serve immediately.

Indian Spiced Orange Roughy

Here, orange roughy is marinated in a mixture of such traditional Indian spices as cardamom, coriander seeds, and turmeric. You can replace orange roughy with catfish, Pacific cod, or mahi mahi.

SERVES 4

2 garlic cloves, roughly chopped

1 teaspoon ground cardamom

1 teaspoon coriander seeds, toasted

1 teaspoon sea salt

1/2 teaspoon black peppercorns

1/4 teaspoon ground turmeric

1/4 teaspoon hot paprika

1/8 teaspoon ground cumin

2 tablespoons olive oil

Grated zest of 1 orange

1/4 cup freshly squeezed orange juice

4 (4- to 6-ounce) orange roughy fillets, skins and orange bands removed

With a mortar and pestle mash together the garlic, cardamom, coriander seeds, salt, peppercorns, turmeric, paprika, and cumin to form a thick paste.

Stir in the olive oil and orange zest.

Spread the marinade over the orange roughy, cover, and refrigerate for 45 minutes.

Preheat the oven to 450°F.

Grease a large baking dish. Place the marinated fillets in the dish and drizzle the orange juice over each. Bake, uncovered, until the fish becomes firm and can be flaked with a fork, 12 to 15 minutes. Serve immediately.

Pollock

Because its name applies to more than one species, I find pollock to be a rather troublesome fish. Atlantic pollock is a mild, somewhat oily, European favorite. Pacific pollock is blander, drier, and coarser than its Atlantic relation. Yet both are labeled and sold as plain old pollock.

Found year-round, pollock is what Americans use in processed fish sticks. It also masquerades as the imitation crab meat known as surimi.

In the U.S., fishermen harvest Pacific pollock with factory trawlers and process the fish onboard. As a result, you'll rarely find whole pollock at markets. Instead this fish is usually sold in fillets, which are similar to cod in appearance and should be white and moist. They should not have any hint of browning or odd odors.

Pollock fillets keep for one day on ice in the refrigerator. If you happen across a whole fish, it will last for two days on ice in the fridge. Should you find a dark strip, known as the fat line, running through the center of your pollock, remove it before cooking.

Pollock can be baked, braised, broiled, deep- or pan-fried, sautéed, or steamed. It performs nicely in pies as well as in soups and stews. Its slightly sweet taste is enhanced by such foods as bell and jalapeño peppers, cilantro, cumin, garlic, lemon, lime, onion, shallot, sour cream, tarragon, and tomato.

Atlantic pollock from Norway, which is typically caught by purse seines or gillnets, is the best environmental choice. The heavy harvesting of Pacific pollock has resulted in a gradual decline in its population. If you cannot find Norwegian Atlantic pollock, substitute Pacific cod or hook- and-line-caught haddock.

Pollock Fingers

Think of these as upscale fish sticks for adults. You can serve them as a substantial appetizer or as a main with Parsnip Chips (page 234) or Garlic Mashed Potatoes (page 238) and Sweet Peas (page 227).

SERVES 4

¹/₃ cup cornmeal

²/₃ cup buttery cracker crumbs
(about 16 crushed crackers)

1 teaspoon onion powder

1 teaspoon dried parsley

¹/₄ teaspoon freshly ground white pepper

1 large egg

1¹/₄ pounds Atlantic pollock fillets, skins and
fat lines removed

Sea salt, to taste

Freshly ground black pepper, to taste

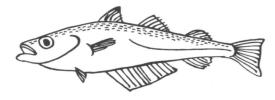

Preheat the oven to 425°F. Grease a large baking sheet.

In a large bowl, mix together the cornmeal, cracker crumbs, onion powder, parsley, and white pepper. In a small bowl, beat the egg with 1 tablespoon of water.

If the dark fat line hasn't been removed from the pollock fillets, do so now. Otherwise, lay the fillets on a flat work surface with the wider side facing you. Using a chef's knife, slice off the short (tail) end and trim any uneven ends on each fillet. Cut each fillet into 1-inch-wide and 2- to 3-inch long strips. The number of strips that you get from the fillets will vary according to the length and width of the fish.

Season the strips with salt and black pepper.

Dredge each pollock strip into the egg mixture and then into the cornmeal-cracker topping, coating the fish completely. Lay the pollock sticks on the greased baking sheet, leaving 1 inch of space between them.

Bake for 5 minutes, then flip the fish and bake for an additional 4 to 6 minutes. When finished, the coating will be light brown and crisp. Serve immediately.

Hazelnut Pesto Pollock

This bright, zesty dish features one of my favorite seasonal treats, fresh basil. For a truly summery meal, serve this alongside Tomato-Onion-Cucumber Salad (page 223). For a heartier meal pair with Parmesan Polenta (page 237).

SERVES 4

¹⁄₄ cup blanched hazelnuts

2 cups fresh basil leaves

2 garlic cloves

¹⁄₃ cup grated Romano cheese

¹⁄₂ cup extra-virgin olive oil

2 tablespoons peanut oil

1 pound Atlantic pollock fillets, skins and
    fat lines removed

Sea salt, to taste

Freshly ground black pepper, to taste

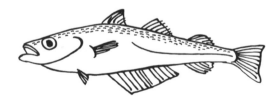

Chop the hazelnuts in the bowl of a food processor or blender by pulsing 3 to 4 times. Add the basil, garlic, and Romano cheese and pulse until combined. With the food processor or blender running on low, slowly pour in the olive oil. Scrape down the sides of bowl and pulse once or twice. You should end up with a smooth pesto.

Heat the peanut oil in a 12-inch, nonstick sauté or frying pan over medium-high heat. Season the pollock fillets with salt and pepper.

Cook the fillets until they have turned opaque and slightly golden on one side, 2 to 3 minutes. Flip the fish and spread a thin layer of pesto over the cooked side of each fillet. Reserve the remaining pesto to use as additional tableside topping for the fish or as a spread for bread.

Cook until the pollock becomes flaky and slightly browned, 3 to 4 minutes. Place the fish on a platter and serve immediately.

Porgy

Some people know this sweet, low-fat fish as porgy. Others refer to it as sea bream. A few outliers dub it scup. No matter what you call this saltwater fish, it falls into the category of mild, white-fleshed fish.

There are at least thirty different species in the porgy family. Preferring warmer waters, some reside in the Western Atlantic Ocean and Caribbean Sea. Though they can weigh as much as twenty pounds, most weigh only between one and three pounds.

Because porgy has numerous small bones, it's quite difficult to fillet. Baking and roasting will soften the bones in whole porgy. However, if you want to avoid that extra bit of crunch, ask your fishmonger to debone and fillet the fish for you.

When purchasing porgy, look for shiny, bright scales and clear, white flesh. It should smell fresh and not display any unpleasant odors or colors. Store porgy in the refrigerator, surrounded by crushed ice, for up to two days.

Porgy can be baked, braised, broiled, grilled, poached, or sautéed. It goes with such foods as anchovies, celery, fennel, lemon, onion, potatoes, scallions, shallots, and tomatoes. It also joins successfully with basil, bay leaves, parsley, saffron, thyme, and white wine. Low in contaminants, U.S. wild-caught porgy ranks as an ecologically neutral seafood choice.

Porgy Pie

While there's no question that home- made dough tastes better, I do use a store-bought, frozen crust for this pie. It saves time and also allows the porgy filling to be the true star of the dish.

SERVES 6

2 tablespoons unsalted butter

1 small celery stalk, minced

1 small carrot, diced

1/2 small white onion, diced

1 large russet potato, peeled, halved, and thinly sliced

1/2 teaspoon sea salt

1 1/2 teaspoons dried thyme

1 teaspoon freshly ground black pepper

1 bay leaf

3/4 cup chicken stock

1 1/2 pounds porgy fillets, skinned and cut into 1-inch chunks

1 (2-ounce) can anchovies, drained and chopped

2 tablespoons heavy cream

1 (9-inch) frozen piecrust, defrosted

Preheat the oven to 350°F. Grease a 9-inch pie pan with butter.

In a medium frying or sauté pan melt the butter on medium. Add the celery, carrot, onion, and potato and sprinkle the salt over top.

Sauté until the vegetables are softened but not browned, 4 to 6 minutes. Add the thyme, black pepper, bay leaf, and chicken stock, stir, and bring to a simmer. Cook for 3 minutes before adding the porgy and anchovies.

Raise the heat to medium-high and cook, stirring occasionally, for 4 minutes. The porgy will be somewhat flaky and almost cooked through.

At this point remove and discard the bay leaf and add the cream. Stir to combine and simmer for 1 minute.

Spoon the hot filling into the greased pie pan and smooth it out so that the fish is evenly distributed. Lay the piecrust over the top and cut off any excess dough hanging over the edge of the pan.

With your thumb and forefingers, crimp the edges of the dough so that you have a textured rim on the crust. Using a sharp knife, make four small slashes in the top of the crust.

Bake for 20 to 30 minutes, until the crust is golden-brown and the filling is bubbling. Cool slightly, about 10 minutes, before cutting the pie into six pieces. Serve warm.

Garlic Porgy

This is my riff on the classic French chicken dish *Poulet aux Quarante Gousses d'Ail* that uses forty cloves of garlic. So as not to overwhelm the mild porgy, I've reduced the number of cloves to fifteen.

SERVES 4

1¹/₂ pounds porgy fillets, skins removed
¹/₂ teaspoon sea salt
¹/₂ teaspoon freshly ground white pepper
²/₃ cup extra-virgin olive oil
¹/₂ cup dry white wine
2 small sprigs of fresh rosemary
15 garlic cloves, peeled
2 tablespoons chopped fresh basil, for serving

Preheat the oven to 400°F.

Season the fish with the salt and pepper. Place the seasoned fillets in a 2-quart baking dish. Add the olive oil, white wine, rosemary, and garlic.

Bake the fillets for 20 to 25 minutes, basting the fish periodically, until they are opaque, tender, and flaky.

Place the fillets on a large serving platter. Scatter the garlic cloves and chopped basil around and on the fish. Serve immediately.

Sea Bass

Europeans have treasured sea bass since Roman times. It's no wonder why. This mild, firm-fleshed, North Atlantic fish has delicious-tasting skin, few bones, and a gentle flavor reminiscent of shellfish. Delightful when cooked whole, it holds its shape well and makes a beautiful offering for a buffet table.

Also known as black sea bass or rock bass, this bottom-feeder possesses a plump body, charcoal to black skin, and firm, white meat. When sold whole, it weighs between one and three pounds, with a maximum length of three feet.

When purchasing sea bass, look for bright eyes, deep coloring, red gills, and a sweet smell. If it doesn't look almost alive, skip it.

Sea bass is usually sold whole. Because the dorsal fin is quite sharp, I always ask my fishmonger to remove it for me. That way, I won't have to worry about nicking myself.

When shopping for this fish, I avoid precut fillets as these might not come from true sea bass. Branzino, which is a Mediterranean relation, sometimes masquerades as sea bass. I also steer clear of Chilean sea bass. This is not actually sea bass but instead the meaty Patagonian toothfish. Renamed for marketing purposes, Chilean sea bass is grossly overfished and not a sound seafood choice.

You can bake, braise, broil, deep- or pan-fry, grill, roast, poach, sauté, or steam sea bass. You can also make stir-fries and ceviche with it. It partners with such foods as bacon, bell peppers, butter, carrots, leeks, lemon, lime, mushrooms, onions, potatoes, shallots, shrimp, spinach, and tomatoes. Its mild taste is also compatible with bay leaves, butter, chervil, cilantro, coriander, garlic, marjoram, mint, flat-leaf parsley, ground pepper, sesame seeds, soy sauce, thyme, and vinegar.

Line-caught sea bass is considered an okay seafood choice. It has moderate levels of mercury and PCBs, and in the southern Atlantic Ocean, it remains overfished. Possible alternatives for sea bass are porgy and catfish.

Sea Bass Ceviche

Whenever I mention my love of ceviche, I often hear in response, "Eeew! You eat raw fish?" Frequently misunderstood, this Latin American specialty does include uncooked fish, but when marinated in lime or lemon juice, the raw fish is essentially cooked by the citric acids of the juice.

When making ceviche, be sure to use the freshest sea bass possible. This will ensure the best-tasting dish.

SERVES 4

1¼ pounds sea bass fillets, skinned and cut into ½-inch cubes

1 cup freshly squeezed lime juice (from 1 dozen small limes)

1 teaspoon kosher salt

2 tablespoons extra-virgin olive oil

½ small red onion, thinly sliced

¼ cup chopped fresh cilantro

1 tablespoon chopped fresh mint

Freshly ground black pepper, to taste

In a medium bowl toss together the sea bass, lime juice, salt, and olive oil. Cover and refrigerate for 2 hours, stirring periodically.

Add the onion, cilantro, and mint to the fish. Toss to combine. Cover and refrigerate, stirring occasionally, until the fish becomes completely white and opaque, about 1½ hours. Season with black pepper and serve.

Sea Bass Satay

A specialty of Indonesia, Thailand, and Malaysia, satay consists of thin strips of marinated meat, poultry, or fish that have been threaded onto bamboo skewers and grilled or broiled. Although usually accompanied by a light peanut sauce, this scrumptious satay needs no other adornments.

SERVES 4

2 tablespoons miso paste

2 tablespoons sugar

1 tablespoon hot water

1 small shallot, minced

$1/2$ teaspoon crushed red pepper

3 tablespoons freshly squeezed lime juice

$1/4$ cup reduced-sodium soy sauce

1 pound sea bass fillets, skinned and
    sliced into 2-inch strips

In a medium bowl whisk together the miso paste, sugar, and hot water until the miso and sugar have dissolved. Add the shallot, red pepper flakes, lime juice, and soy sauce and whisk to combine.

Pour one third of the marinade into a shallow baking dish. Add the sea bass strips and then pour another third of the marinade over the strips, reserving the last third to dress the cooked satay. Toss the strips to ensure they're completely coated. Cover and refrigerate the fish for at least 1 hour.

Preheat the oven broiler on high. Line a baking sheet with tin foil.

Thread the marinated fish onto metal or bamboo skewers. (Note that if you are using bamboo or wood skewers, you must soak them in water for 30 minutes before skewering the fish with them. Otherwise, when exposed to the heat, they could catch on fire.)

Lay the skewers on the lined baking sheet and place them on the rack closest to the broiler. Broil until the flesh whitens and starts to brown, 2 to 3 minutes. Turn the skewers over and broil for another 1 to 2 minutes, until the fish flakes when probed with a fork.

Place the skewers on a platter and drizzle the reserved marinade over the satay. Serve immediately.

Turbot

Whenever I see a whole turbot, I think of a toad. **This large, almost circular** flatfish has brown, scale-free, bumpy skin and a small, squashed head reminiscent of the aforementioned amphibian. Unlike the toad, though, the turbot fish lives on the bottom of the Atlantic Ocean and the Mediterranean and Black Seas.

The global population of turbot is low, and it's lean, snow white meat is highly prized, placing it in the category of expensive, special occasion seafood. In Europe it's known as "royalty fish." Cooks there pair it with luxurious sauces and serve it from oblong, fish-shaped pans known as turbutières.

Turbot can weigh as much as thirty pounds, though they generally range between three and six pounds at markets. They are sold year-round as whole fish, steaks, and fillets.

When selecting turbot, look for firm, shiny, white flesh. Fillets should smell sweet and not have any gaping or browning. As with sea bass, precut and frozen fillets may not truly come from turbot. When I want fillets, I either fillet the fish myself, or I ask my fishmonger to fillet it for me. Whole turbot keeps for two days in the refrigerator, while fillets will keep for one day.

Traditionally, turbot is poached in milk to maintain its pristine whiteness. However, you can also bake, broil, grill, roast, sauté, or steam this fish. Its pleasantly sweet meat goes with such ingredients as artichoke, bay leaf, basil, brandy, chives, crayfish, cream, lemon, lobster, mushrooms, flat-leaf parsley, shallot, tarragon, thyme, and tomatoes.

At this time there are no environmental recommendations for turbot, but since it is such a costly fish with a limited population, you'd be wise to leave it for rare occasions. You can always replace turbot with catfish and Pacific halibut in recipes.

Seasonal Simmered Turbot

This light dish features a combination of fresh, spring ingredients. The earthy tang of mushrooms, shallots, and herbs all complement the mild sweetness of turbot.

SERVES 4

1 tablespoon olive oil

4 ounces white mushrooms, stems discarded and caps sliced

1 small zucchini, diced

1 large carrot, diced

1 large shallot, minced

1 tablespoon chopped fresh thyme

1¹/₂ pounds turbot steaks or fillets, skins removed

¹/₂ teaspoon sea salt

¹/₄ teaspoon freshly ground black pepper

1 cup chicken stock, warmed

1 tablespoon brandy

1 bay leaf

1 tablespoon unsalted butter, cut into chunks

2 to 3 chives, chopped

Preheat the oven to 450°F. Grease a 3-quart baking dish with butter.

Heat the olive oil in a medium frying or sauté pan over medium heat. Add the mushrooms, zucchini, carrot, and shallot and sauté until the vegetables are warmed through and slightly softened, 4 minutes. Remove from the heat, add the thyme, and stir to combine.

Generously season the turbot with salt and pepper and place in the baking dish. Pour the chicken stock and brandy over the fish and add the bay leaf.

Spoon equal amounts of the vegetable mixture over the top of each steak or fillet. Dot each with a chunk or two of butter.

Cover the dish and bake for 17 to 20 minutes. When finished cooking, the fish will be opaque, tender, and white. Remove the bay leaf. Sprinkle the chopped chives over the fish and serve immediately.

Tarragon Turbot

If sweet, aromatic tarragon isn't one of your favorite herbs, you can substitute fresh basil in this dish.

SERVES 4

1 tablespoon olive oil

6 sprigs fresh tarragon

4 tablespoons unsalted butter, softened

1 teaspoon dry sherry

$1/2$ teaspoon freshly ground black pepper, plus more for seasoning

Sea salt, to taste

1 whole (4 to 5-pound) turbot, gutted, rinsed, and dried

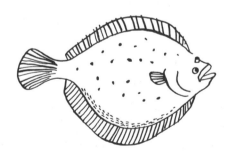

Preheat the oven to 450°F.

Tear off a sheet of aluminum foil large enough to fold over and cover the turbot completely, and place it on top of a baking sheet. Coat the top of the foil with the oil.

Remove and mince the leaves of 1 to 2 tarragon stems; you should end up with 1 heaping tablespoon of minced tarragon. Using a fork, mix together the minced tarragon, butter, sherry, and $1/2$ teaspoon black pepper.

Season the inside of the turbot with salt and pepper. Spread equal amounts of tarragon butter and the remaining tarragon sprigs inside the fish.

Place the turbot in the center of the foil and fold the edges over so that the fish is completely covered. Bake until the meat is opaque, white, and tender, 20 to 25 minutes. Allow the turbot to rest for 5 minutes before removing the foil and serving.

Delicate, Flaky Delights

The fish in this chapter have everything going for them. Think I'm exagger-ating? Consider their light, subtle flavors that sneak up on and then bowl you over. Then there's their succulent, melt-in-your-mouth flesh that leaves you hungry for more. They respond to a wealth of techniques. Plus, you can easily determine when they're finished cooking; if they turn opaque and flake when probed with a fork, they're ready to be eaten.

Although the members of this group share many outstanding characteristics, they do differ from one another in several respects. The first of these is habitat; barramundi, tilapia, and trout, thrive in fresh water, while flounder, haddock, and sole are ocean dwellers.

Then there's sustainability. A few of these fish, such as barramundi and trout, are highly sustainable while one fish, haddock, has seen its population dwindle severely. Yet another member, tilapia, ranks as the most regularly farmed fish in the world. These fish also vary in physical features. Several possess pristine white flesh while one ranges in color from pinkish-white to red. Most are round fish, though flatfish such as sole and flounder also qualify as delicate, flaky delights.

In spite of their differences these fish remain a pleasure to cook and an even greater pleasure to eat.

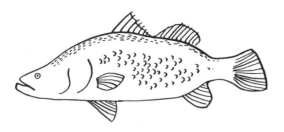

Barramundi

Whenever I'm in need of a tender, flaky fish, my first thought is of barramundi. Native to Australia, this fast-growing, freshwater fish possesses a mild, buttery taste and soft, succulent texture that can't be beat. Now raised in Massachusetts in enclosed, recirculating tanks, it also qualifies as environmentally sound seafood.

The silver-skinned, long-bodied barramundi ranges in weight from ten to more than one hundred pounds and can grow as long as three feet. At markets a barramundi usually weighs about twelve pounds and is sold whole and as fillets and steaks.

To choose good-quality barramundi, look for bright, clean skin and firm, white flesh. Barramundi spoils quickly so don't leave it in the refrigerator for more than a day.

Barramundi's sweet meat, edible skin, and culinary flexibility make it a widely popular fish. Whole barramundi can be grilled, baked, roasted, or steamed. Fillets and steaks are ideal for pan-frying, sautéing, and broiling. The fish's gentle flavor suits ingredients like arugula, bok choy, brown sugar, cilantro, garlic, lime, scallion, shallot, and soy sauce.

Remember to purchase barramundi farmed in the U.S. Those from the Indo-Pacific tend to be raised in pens prone to leakage, which can spread pollutants and disease to the surrounding environs.

Banana Leaf Barramundi

Banana leaves plays multiple roles in Asian and Southeast Asian cooking. They can perform as a plate, steamer basket, grill pan, moisture retainer, or flavor infuser. Here, they act as both a taste enhancer and grilling device.

If you prefer a little less heat in your food, reduce the amount of curry paste by half. You can find both red curry paste and banana leaves in Asian and Caribbean markets and in some gourmet shops.

SERVES 4

4 large banana leaves

1/2 teaspoon freshly ground red or black pepper, plus more for seasoning

1 tablespoon firmly packed muscovado sugar

2 tablespoons red curry paste

2 1/2 tablespoons freshly squeezed lime juice

3 tablespoons canned unsweetened coconut milk

1 garlic clove, sliced

4 (6-ounce) barramundi steaks or fillets, skins removed

4 scallions, white parts and 1 inch of the greens chopped

4 firmly packed cups (about 4 1/2 ounces) arugula

1 tablespoon good-quality balsamic vinegar, plus more as needed

Preheat a grill on high.

Wipe off the banana leaves with a clean dry cloth, and then soak them in warm water for 10 minutes. This will soften them and make them easier to fold.

In a small bowl, whisk together the ground pepper, sugar, curry paste, lime juice, coconut milk, and garlic.

Remove the banana leaves from the water. Wipe both sides with a clean, dry cloth before placing them on a clean, flat work surface.

Lay a fish fillet in the center of each banana leaf. Generously brush the top and sides of the fish with the red curry sauce. Sprinkle a few scallions over the top of each fillet and then fold over the edges of the banana leaves. You should end up with packets that look like legal or letter-sized envelopes.

Place the fish packets fold side down on the grill. Cover and grill for 5 to 7 minutes on one side. Flip the barramundi over and grill on the other side for 3 to 5 minutes or until a toothpick inserted in the center of the leaf-covered fish enters with no resistance. If using an instant-read thermometer, wait until the fish registers 135°F.

Remove the packets from the grill and allow the fish to rest, still wrapped, for 5 minutes. The internal temperature should ultimately be 137°F.

Toss the arugula with balsamic vinegar, adding more if the greens seem too dry. Distribute the dressed arugula on four dinner plates. Remove the barramundi from the banana leaves and place a fillet on each mound of greens. Serve immediately.

Miso-Glazed Barramundi

Here you have the yin and yang of flavors with the bold, piquant glaze balancing out the mild, buttery barramundi. If your local market doesn't carry barramundi, you can substitute char, sea bass, or tilapia in this recipe.

SERVES 4

1 pound barramundi fillets, skins on
$1/4$ cup miso paste
2 tablespoons hot water
3 tablespoons plain rice vinegar
2 tablespoons soy sauce
2 tablespoons firmly packed light brown sugar
1 tablespoon peanut oil
2 scallions, whites and 1-inch of greens minced

Lay the barramundi in a medium, shallow baking dish.

In a small bowl, whisk together the miso paste and hot water. Add the vinegar, soy sauce, and brown sugar and whisk until well combined. Pour the marinade over the fillets, cover, and refrigerate for at least 45 minutes and up to 2 hours.

To cook the fish, heat the oil in a large, nonstick frying pan over medium heat. Once the oil starts to shimmer, place the fillets skin side down in the pan.

Cook on one side until the skin browns and the flesh becomes white, 2 to 3 minutes. Flip the fish over and cook on the other side for another 2 to 3 minutes, or until you can easily flake the flesh with a fork.

Place the fillets on a serving platter and sprinkle the minced scallions over top. Serve warm.

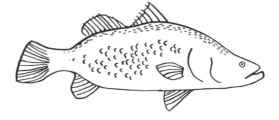

Barramundi Pilaf

Pilaf, rice that is cooked in meat or poultry stock, is a Middle Eastern specialty. This particular pilaf features the Moroccan spice blend *ras el hanout*, which you will find at gourmet and specialty food shops and online from such purveyors as Kalustyan's.If you can't track down barramundi, substitute smoked haddock, smoked or fresh trout, or fresh salmon or char.

SERVES 6

4 tablespoons olive oil, divided
2 garlic cloves, minced
$^1/_2$ small red onion, diced
1 large yellow or orange bell pepper, diced
1 small zucchini, diced
1 teaspoon *ras el hanout* spice blend
2 cups uncooked basmati rice, rinsed
$1^1/_4$ teaspoons sea salt, plus more for seasoning
$^1/_4$ teaspoon freshly ground black pepper, plus more for seasoning
$2^1/_2$ cups chicken stock
$^1/_4$ cup slivered almonds, toasted and roughly chopped
1 pound barramundi fillets, skinned
3 tablespoons chopped fresh flat-leaf parsley
Freshly squeezed juice of $^1/_2$ lemon

Heat 2 tablespoons of the olive oil in a large saucepan over medium-high heat. Add the garlic, onion, bell pepper, and zucchini and sauté until the vegetables are slightly soft and golden, 1 to 2 minutes. At this point add the *ras el hanout*, rice, $1^1/_4$ teaspoons salt, and $^1/_4$ teaspoon black pepper and stir to coat.

Pour in the stock, raise the temperature to high, and bring the stock to a boil. Stir and then cover with a tight-fitting lid, reducing the heat to medium-low and simmering until all the liquid has been absorbed. Depending on the size of your saucepan, this could be anywhere from 8 to 15 minutes.

Fluff the rice with a fork, add the nuts, and toss to combine. Cover the rice again to keep it warm.

Heat the remaining 2 tablespoons of oil in a large frying pan over medium-high heat. Season the barramundi with salt and pepper and then place the fillets in the pan, working in batches if necessary.

Cook on one side until browned, 3 to 4 minutes. Flip over the fillets and cook for 2 minutes longer, or until fish is cooked through and flakes easily when probed with a fork. Remove the cooked fillets from the pan and place them on a cutting board.

Using a fork, flake the barramundi into chunks and add them to the saucepan with the rice. Add the parsley and toss to combine. Taste and adjust seasonings if necessary. Sprinkle the lemon juice over the top and serve immediately.

Flounder

When I ask for flounder at a supermarket or restaurant, I could be getting the flatfish known as flounder, but I could also receive another member of the flounder family such as yellow tail, California halibut, plaice, or lemon sole. No matter which variety lands on my dinner plate, though, I know I'll be enjoying one fine fish.

A true flatfish, flounder swims on its side and its eyes are located on its top. Ranging in color from gray to reddish brown, a flounder's skin tends to match the ocean environment in which it lives. Just as the ocean floor may have a smattering of pebbles and debris, these fish have dark spots scattered over their bodies.

Located primarily in northern waters, flounder normally grow to about twelve inches in length. A few, though, may reach as long as two feet. At markets you'll find whole flounder that weigh between one and five pounds. The fish is sold whole and as fillets.

A good flounder will have glossy skin and a fresh scent. As always, if it smells funky, walk on by.

Whole flounder can be grilled, broiled, baked, or steamed. Fillets can be baked, pan-fried, poached, steamed, or stuffed, rolled, and baked. The delicate composition of flounder fillets makes them less than ideal for grilling or stir-frying because they either stick to or fall apart on the grill or pan. Due to its leanness you shouldn't overcook flounder. If you do, you'll end up with a bone-dry dinner. As soon as the flesh turns opaque, it's done cooking.

Famous for its fragile texture and subtly sweet taste, flounder appreciates such fuller-bodied foods as almonds, bell peppers, Gruyère and Parmesan cheeses, lemon, mushrooms, pasta, peas, spinach, tomatoes, and zucchini. It also gets a boost from butter, chervil, chives, coconut milk, dill, fennel, flat-leaf parsley, shallots, tarragon, and white wine. In terms of sustainability and consumer safety U.S. Pacific wild-caught flounder ranks as an eco-okay choice. Avoid all the others.

Creamy Pasta with Flounder and Peas

Think of this as flounder fettuccini

alfredo. If you don't have access to flounder, use sole or catfish.

SERVES 4

$1^1/_2$ cups fresh or frozen peas

2 teaspoons sea salt, plus more for seasoning

1 pound fettuccini pasta

2 tablespoons olive oil

1 pound Pacific flounder fillets, skins removed

Freshly ground black pepper, to taste

1 cup whole milk, heated

$^3/_4$ cup grated Parmesan cheese

$^1/_4$ cup grated Romano cheese

1 garlic clove, crushed

$^1/_2$ teaspoon freshly ground white pepper

$^1/_8$ teaspoon ground nutmeg

Bring a medium saucepan filled with water to a boil. Add the peas and cook until just tender. Depending on whether you're using fresh or frozen peas, this could take between 4 to 7 minutes. Remove from heat, drain and set aside.

Bring a stockpot of water and 2 teaspoons salt to a boil. Add the pasta to the water and cook according to the package instructions.

As the pasta is cooking, heat the olive oil in a large, nonstick frying pan over medium heat. Season the flounder on both sides with salt and black pepper.

Cook the flounder until its edges have turned white, 3 minutes. Turn the fish over and cook on the other side until it becomes stark white, 2 to 3 minutes. Transfer the fish to a plate, flake it into small chunks with a fork, and cover to keep warm.

In a small saucepan over medium-low heat, whisk together the heated milk, Parmesan and Romano cheeses, garlic, white pepper, and nutmeg. Allow the ingredients to simmer for 3 to 5 minutes, stirring occasionally, until hot and well combined.

Drain the pasta and return it to the stockpot. Remove the garlic clove from the cheese sauce. Pour the sauce over the pasta and toss to combine. Drain and add the peas along with the flaked flounder. Gently toss to combine. Serve immediately.

Flounder Braciole

I grew up in a largely Italian-Ameri-can community where foods such as the stuffed and rolled meat dish known as braciole were as commonplace as hamburgers and apple pie. With a nod to my hometown dining experiences I offer my seafood take on that dish. Here, flounder fillets stand in for the thin strips of steak found in traditional braciole.

SERVES 4

2 tablespoons olive oil, divided

$^1\!/_2$ small white onion, chopped

1 cup plain white breadcrumbs

$^1\!/_2$ cup chopped flat-leaf parsley

1 teaspoon dried oregano

$^1\!/_2$ teaspoon sea salt, plus more for seasoning

Grated zest of 1 lemon

4 (5 to 6-ounce) Pacific flounder fillets,
   skins removed

2 tablespoons unsalted butter, cut into small pieces

Freshly ground black pepper, to taste

$^1\!/_2$ cup chicken stock, warmed

Preheat the oven to 350°F. Grease a 2-quart baking dish.

Heat 1 tablespoon of the olive oil in a small frying or sauté pan over medium heat. Add the onion and sauté until soft and translucent but not browned, 4 minutes.

In a small bowl, toss together the cooked onion, breadcrumbs, parsley, oregano, $^1\!/_2$ teaspoon salt, lemon zest, and the remaining tablespoon of olive oil.

Place the fillets on a flat work surface and spread 2 to 3 tablespoons stuffing over each. Dot the stuffing with a few pieces of butter.

Starting at the thinner, narrower end of each fillet, roll the fish up and secure with a toothpick. Place the rolled fillets in the greased baking dish. Season to taste with salt and pepper.

If you have any butter pieces leftover, place them on top of the fillets and pour the chicken stock over top. Bake, uncovered, until the flounder turns opaque and flakes easily when probed with a fork, 18 to 20 minutes. Serve immediately.

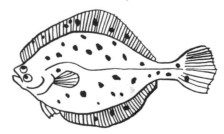

Haddock

Whenever I see haddock at markets, memories of fish and chips dinners spring to mind. For decades this tender, flaky, white fish has competed with cod as the most popular filling for that quintessential British dish. Considering its ambrosial flavor and smooth consistency, haddock seems almost too good to be featured in breaded and deep-fried foods. Yet, as I learned in Scotland and the North of England, where this fish reigns supreme, deep-fried haddock makes for one tasty meal.

The dark, brown- to gray-skinned haddock lives along the seafloor of the North Atlantic. Similar in appearance to cod, it differentiates itself by being smaller. It also has a distinct, black thumbprint and black lateral line over its pectoral fin that cod does not possess.

Generally, haddock is sold in skin-on fillets. When raw, these fillets should appear bright white, moist, and firm. They should have little to no gaping and should smell fresh. Along with these characteristics, I look for haddock that has been line-caught and, therefore, has been fished in a sustainable manner.

Haddock is wonderful when baked, broiled, deep- and pan-fried, poached, roasted, or sautéed. It's lovely in soups, chowders, and pies. It also can be dried or smoked. The latter is especially popular in Scotland and France, where the term "haddock" refers solely to smoked haddock.

Haddock favors an assortment of foods and flavors. Bacon, eggs, onions, potatoes, scallions, and shallots all dress up its moderately sweet taste. Butter, chervil, chives, cream, parsley, and thyme also enhance its flavor.

Until very recently haddock's population had been greatly depleted. As a result, you should consider using another tender, white fish. If you do go with haddock, stick with U.S. line-caught fish, which is a sound seafood choice.

Smoked Haddock Frittata

Frittatas are Italy's take on omelets.
Served hot or cold, open-faced, and in slices, they are delicious at breakfast, lunch, or dinner.

You can substitute smoked trout, or sablefish in this dish.

SERVES 4

1¹⁄₂ teaspoons olive oil
¹⁄₂ small yellow onion, chopped
¹⁄₄ teaspoon sea salt
5 large eggs
1 egg white
¹⁄₄ teaspoon freshly ground black pepper
¹⁄₄ teaspoon dried chervil
¹⁄₄ teaspoon dried oregano
1 ounce goat cheese, crumbled
3¹⁄₂ ounces smoked haddock, flaked

Preheat the oven broiler on high.

Heat the oil in a 10-inch, nonstick, oven-safe frying or sauté pan over medium. Add the onion and salt and sauté until just softened, 3 minutes.

In a large bowl, whisk together the eggs, egg white, black pepper, chervil, and oregano. Add the goat cheese and haddock and gently stir to combine.

Pour the egg mixture into the pan and swirl to distribute the ingredients.

Cook for 5 minutes, or until the eggs have set on the bottom and sides and begin to set on top. Place the pan in the oven on the rack closest to the broiler. Broil for 2 to 3 minutes, until the frittata is puffed up and browning. Remove from the oven and slice into 4 pieces. Serve hot.

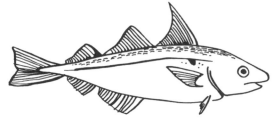

Haddock Couscous

You can find Moroccan, dry-cured, black olives online and in gourmet and ethnic grocery stores. If you can't track them down, don't substitute generic canned black olives; the taste is completely different. Instead, leave out the olives and add sea salt, to taste.

SERVES 6

2 cups vegetable stock

1^1/$_2$ cups uncooked Israeli couscous

^{1}/$_4$ cup freshly squeezed lemon juice

^{1}/$_4$ cup plus 2 tablespoons extra-virgin olive oil, divided

^{1}/$_2$ teaspoon ground cumin

Pinch of cayenne pepper

1 pound U.S. line-caught haddock fillets, skins removed

Sea salt, to taste

Freshly ground black pepper, to taste

3 scallions, white parts and 1 inch of greens sliced

1 small cucumber, peeled, seeded, and diced

1 cup drained canned chickpeas

^{3}/$_4$ cup (about 13) grape tomatoes, cut into quarters

3 tablespoons diced Moroccan dry-cured black olives

In a large, nonstick saucepan bring the vegetable stock to a boil. Add the couscous and stir to combine. Cover and allow the couscous to simmer until tender and fluffy, 8 to 10 minutes.

In a small bowl whisk together the lemon juice, ^{1}/$_4$ cup of olive oil, cumin, and cayenne. Set aside.

Heat the remaining 2 tablespoons of olive oil in 12-inch frying or sauté pan over medium heat.

Season the haddock fillets with salt and pepper. Cook until the flesh turns white on the bottom and edges, 3 to 4 minutes. Flip the fillets and cook for another 2 to 3 minutes; when finished, the fish will be stark white in color and will flake easily when probed with a fork.

Remove the fish from the pan and place it on a cutting board. Using a fork, flake the fillets into bite-sized pieces. Cover to keep warm.

Fluff the couscous with a fork. Add the scallions, cucumber, chickpeas, tomatoes, and olives and toss to combine. Add the flaked haddock and drizzle the lemony oil over top. Toss again to combine and serve immediately.

Fish Plaki

Fish Plaki comes courtesy of my childhood friend Dr. Nikoleta Kolovos and her mother Vasiliki Kolovos. Here's the tale behind this Greek classic, in Nickie's words: "The first time that I brought my future husband home to meet my parents, my mom made this recipe. Little did I know that he didn't like fish . . . so he ate it really quickly. My mother, assuming this to be a sign of hunger and enjoyment, promptly served him another helping, which he ate as well. He didn't tell me he didn't like fish until the ride home. I then realized that things might be getting serious between us."

In Greek cooking plaki refers to foods that are spread out and cooked in a baking dish. You can substitute Pacific cod for the haddock in this recipe.

SERVES 4

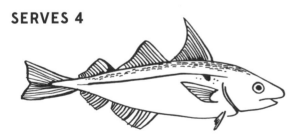

$1\frac{1}{4}$ pounds U.S. line-caught haddock fillets, skins removed

1 (14.5-ounce) can chopped tomatoes, drained

1 cup fresh flat-leaf parsley, chopped

$\frac{1}{2}$ small white or yellow onion, chopped

4 garlic cloves, chopped

Freshly squeezed juice of $1\frac{1}{2}$ lemons

2 tablespoons olive oil

1 teaspoon dried oregano

$\frac{1}{4}$ teaspoon freshly ground black pepper

Sea salt, to taste

Preheat the oven to 350°F.

Place the fish in a medium baking dish. Mix all the other ingredients together in a bowl and then pour over the fish.

Bake, uncovered, until much of the liquid has cooked down and the fish is white and flaky, 25 to 30 minutes. Serve immediately.

Sole

I **love a fish with a good story, and sole has several of them. The ancient**
Romans supposedly loved this delicate flatfish so much that they dubbed it *solea Jovi*, or "Jupiter's sandal," after the king of their gods, Jupiter. Its present name reputedly comes from the old French term *sole*, which refers to the foot. Both monikers reference the fish's flattened, foot-like appearance.

In the U.S. we incorrectly refer to several fish, including a flounder species known as petrale and lemon sole, as sole. True sole comes from European coastal waters, from the Mediterranean to the south of Norway. Oval in shape, it grows up to twenty inches long and generally weighs between one and six and a half pounds.

Sole has either gray or light brown skin with a white belly. The skin itself feels sticky to the touch. Its meat is firm, fine, and subtle in flavor.

Good-quality sole will look moist, smell sweet, and show no signs of browning or drying. To ensure that you're purchasing true sole, select a whole fish and ask your fishmonger to fillet it for you.

Though many cooks say that sole tastes best two to three days after being caught, this fish will not keep longer than two days in the refrigerator.

Before cooking sole, you should remove the skin. You can then bake, broil, pan-fry, poach, sauté, or steam it.

An abundance of famous sole recipes exist including *sole Marguery*, *sole meunière*, *sole Veronique*, and *sole almondine*. Beyond these classics, sole takes to such ingredients as cayenne, chive, lemon, white and morel mushrooms, flat-leaf parsley, shallot, spinach, tarragon, tomato, and dry white wine. Pacific, wild-caught sole rates as an "eco-okay" fish.

Picholine-Caper Sole

Here, tart Picholine olives and briny capers add a little kick to the French classic sole meunière. Serve this with Golden Brown Cauliflower (page 233) or Parmesan Polenta (page 237).

SERVES 4

2 tablespoons unsalted butter
1 tablespoon olive oil
¼ cup unbleached all-purpose flour
4 (4 to 6-ounce) Pacific sole fillets, skins on
Sea salt, to taste
Freshly ground black pepper, to taste
¼ cup (12 to 16) green Picholine olives, halved
1½ tablespoon capers, rinsed
2 tablespoons freshly squeezed lemon juice

Heat the butter and oil in a large nonstick frying or sauté pan over medium heat. Spread the flour onto a small plate.

Season the fillets with salt and pepper. Dredge the sole through the flour, coating both sides.

Lay the fish skin side down in the pan and cook for 3 minutes, until the skin browns and the flesh begins to turn white around the edges. Flip the fish over and add the olives and capers, swirling them around the pan. Cook for 2 to 3 minutes, or until the sole is flaky and cooked through. Place the fish on a serving platter and cover to keep warm.

Add the lemon juice to the hot pan and swirl the ingredients around to blend. Pour the olive-caper sauce over the fish and serve immediately.

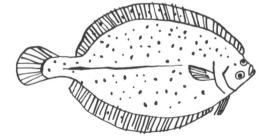

Parmesan-Coated Sole

An exquisite Parmesan cheese crust adds a bit of crunch to tender sole. You can also use this recipe with catfish, flounder, and haddock.

Because I find that visual cues for doneness aren't as helpful when working with coated or breaded seafood, I often rely upon an instant-read thermometer to confirm when the fish is done. Since fish will continue to cook after being removed from the oven, I take it out once its internal temperature reaches around 135°F. I then allow the fish to rest for a few minutes. When ready, its temperature will be 137°F.

SERVES 4

$1/2$ cup grated Parmesan cheese
$1/3$ cup plus 1 tablespoon plain panko breadcrumbs
$1/4$ teaspoon freshly ground white pepper
Pinch of sweet paprika
4 (6-ounce) sole fillets, skins removed
Sea salt, to taste
Freshly ground black pepper, to taste
2 egg whites

Preheat the oven to 425°F. Generously grease a 2-quart baking dish with butter.

On a large plate mix together the Parmesan cheese, breadcrumbs, white pepper, and paprika.

Season the sole fillets with salt and black pepper.

In a small bowl whisk together the egg whites and 1 tablespoon of cold water.

Using a pastry or barbecue brush, brush the egg whites over each fillet and then dredge it through the cheese mixture, pressing firmly to make a thick coating on the fish. Lay the coated fillets in the greased baking dish.

Bake, uncovered, for 12 to 15 minutes. The coating should be crusty and light brown in color and an instant-read thermometer inserted into the fillets should read 135°F. Remove and allow the fish to rest for 2 to 3 minutes. Serve hot.

Tilapia

When I hear "tilapia," I envision the low-fat, farm-raised fish that is ever-present in supermarkets and restaurants. Yet, there's far more to this freshwater fish than its frequent appearance on menus. Originating in East Africa and Asia, tilapia has been an important food source for centuries. Thanks to its abilities to survive in both fresh and salt waters and to grow rapidly, it has become the most commonly farmed fish worldwide. Abundant supplies have resulted in moderate prices, making this mild herbivore a great buy.

Also known as St. Peter's fish, tilapia may be green or red in color. It can grow as long as twenty inches and as heavy as fourteen pounds. At markets I usually see tilapia weighing between ten to twenty ounces. This fish is available whole and as fillets.

Before purchasing tilapia, check to see where it has been raised. The American West and Southwest have the safest aquaculture practices; they grow the fish in closed tanks with minimal risk of pollution or escapes and are considered "eco-best". Farmed tilapia from Latin America isn't as environmentally friendly, and tilapia from Asia should be avoided altogether.

Once you've determined your fish's source, make sure that it looks healthy. The flesh should be pinkish-white and somewhat firm. The skin should be bruise-free and shiny. Whole fish or fillets should smell clean and sweet and not muddy. Tilapia sometimes takes on a swampy taste, so if it smells earthy, it'll taste even earthier.

You can refrigerate on ice whole and filleted tilapia for two days. Defrost frozen tilapia overnight in your refrigerator.

Whole tilapia turns out best when stuffed and baked, broiled, or grilled. Fillets do well when braised, broiled, pan-fried, sautéed, or steamed. Tilapia's subtle taste gets a lift from such ingredients as almonds, dill, lemon, lime, mustard, olives, orange, pistachios, red onion, shallots, tarragon, thyme, tomatoes, walnuts, and white wine. If your market is out of tilapia, you can replace it with porgy or sea bass in recipes.

Warm Potato and Tilapia Salad

This light yet satisfying salad can also be made with trout or two (9-ounce) cans of solid white pole-caught albacore tuna.

SERVES 4

2 tablespoons grapeseed oil, divided

$1/2$ small red onion, thinly sliced

1 pound U.S. farmed-raised tilapia fillets, skins removed

Sea salt, to taste

Freshly ground black pepper, to taste

$1^1/2$ pounds baby red potatoes, boiled until just tender and cut in half

$1/2$ pound green beans, parboiled for 3 minutes and cut into 1-inch sticks

8 grape tomatoes, quartered

2 tablespoons Dijon mustard

2 tablespoons red wine vinegar

$1/2$ cup olive oil

Pinch of sugar

Heat 1 tablespoon of the grapeseed oil in a large frying pan over medium heat. Add the onion to the pan and sauté until softened but not opaque or browned, 1 to 2 minutes. Place the onion in a large bowl and set aside.

Add the remaining grapeseed oil to the pan and heat over medium-high.

Season the fillets with salt and pepper and place in the pan. Cook on one side until the fish has turned white, 3 minutes. Turn the fillets over and cook on the other side until golden and flaky, 2 to 3 minutes. Remove the fish from the pan.

Using a knife or fork, break the tilapia fillets into bite-size chunks. Add them to the onions and toss them together in the bowl with the potatoes, beans, and tomatoes.

In a separate bowl, whisk together the mustard, vinegar, olive oil, and sugar. Taste the dressing and add salt and black pepper as needed. Pour the dressing over the fish and vegetables and gently toss to combine. Serve immediately.

Tilapia Patties with Dijon-Caper Mayo

As a kid growing up in a landlocked city outside of Pittsburgh, I ended up eating quite a bit of canned fish. Canned tuna casseroles and canned salmon patties and loaves were mainstays of my mother's dinner repertoire. The following tilapia patties hark back to those long-ago family meals.

On days when I'm feeling a bit homesick, I replace the tilapia with three (5-ounce) cans of Alaskan wild pink salmon. With a dash of nostalgia and a quick stir, I have a beloved Patricia Hunt specialty, salmon patties.

SERVES 4 TO 6

1 pound U.S. farmed-raised tilapia fillets, skins removed, cut into chunks

1 large egg, lightly beaten

1 cup plain white breadcrumbs

$1/2$ small yellow onion, diced

1 small green bell pepper, diced

$1^1/4$ teaspoons Worcestershire sauce

1 teaspoon dried dill weed

$1/2$ teaspoon sea salt

$1/2$ teaspoon freshly ground black pepper

1 tablespoon olive oil

$1/4$ cup good-quality mayonnaise

1 tablespoon Dijon mustard

3 capers, rinsed and minced

Place the fillets in the bowl of a food processor and pulse several times until minced.

In a medium bowl, mix together the minced tilapia, egg, breadcrumbs, onion, green pepper, Worcestershire sauce, dill, salt, and pepper.

Using your hands, make 4 to 6 equal-sized patties, each about $1/2$ inch thick. Flatten them slightly with the palm of your hand.

Heat the olive oil in a large, nonstick frying pan over medium heat.

As the oil is heating, in a small bowl, mix together the mayonnaise, Dijon, and capers. Set aside.

Place the tilapia patties in the pan, cover, and cook until browned on one side, 3 minutes. Flip over the patties, cover again, and cook for another 2 to 3 minutes. When finished, the patties will be golden-brown and firm to the touch. Place a dollop of the Dijon-caper mayo on each and serve immediately.

Mediterranean Tilapia Packets

Here tilapia's gentle taste gets a boost from the fresh, vibrant flavors of the Mediterranean. You can also make this dish with Pacific halibut.

SERVES 4

2 tablespoons olive oil, divided

2 tablespoons tomato paste

2 tablespoons hot water

4 oil-packed sun-dried tomatoes, patted dry and thinly sliced

1 tablespoon chopped fresh rosemary

1½ tablespoons chopped fresh basil

½ teaspoon sea salt, plus more for seasoning

½ teaspoon freshly ground pepper, plus more for seasoning

10 to 12 kalamata olives, pitted and halved

4 (6-ounce) U.S. farmed-raised tilapia fillets, skins removed

Preheat the oven to 375°F.

Tear off 4 large sheets of aluminum foil, each big enough to cover and enclose a tilapia fillet.

In a small bowl, whisk 1 tablespoon of the olive oil with the tomato paste and hot water until well-combined. Add the sun-dried tomatoes, rosemary, and basil and stir together.

Brush the center of the foil sheets with olive oil. Season the tilapia with salt and pepper. Place a fillet in the center of each sheet and spread equal amounts of tomato topping over each fillet. Add 2 to 3 olives per packet.

Fold the long sides of the foil inward until they touch and then crimp the sides together. Do the same with the short ends of the foil.

Lay the packets seam side up on a baking sheet. Bake for 20 to 25 minutes, until the fish flakes when probed with a fork. Serve immediately.

Trout

Every now and then a much-loved fish turns out to also be a sound seafood choice. Such is the case with trout. This beautiful, robust fish is the oldest example of successful aquaculture in America. It is also one of the country's eco-friendliest.

A relative of salmon, trout can be found on every continent except Antarctica. Depending upon the species (see Know Your Trout, below, for species and sustainability information), the fish ranges in color from silvery green to coppery brown and with red, orange, or brown spots scattered over its skin. Influenced by diet and habitat, its delicate flesh ranges from creamy white to red in color. In terms of size, trout can weigh up to fifty pounds in the wild. When farm-raised it weighs only between eight and sixteen ounces.

Trout is sold whole and as fillets. Look for shiny skin, bright eyes, moist flesh, and a fresh smell. Whole trout should have a layer of transparent slime over it; the more slime, the better and fresher the fish. Whole trout will have more flavor than boned fillets.

KNOW YOUR TROUT

Brown: Freshwater brown trout's population has been depleted through overfishing, habitat destruction, and pollution. As a result, it is not an environmentally sound seafood choice.

Rainbow: Rainbow trout started out in the rivers and streams of the American West. Today it's primarily farm-raised in the U.S. If you find wild rainbow trout, it will have white flesh. Farm-raised rainbow trout will have pink flesh. Both have silvery green bodies and a pinkish stripe along their sides. For the "eco-best" choice, purchase U.S. farm-raised rainbow trout.

Sea or salmon trout: This is brown trout that has abandoned its freshwater habitat for the salty sea. For the same reasons as freshwater brown trout, sea trout should be avoided.

Steelhead: This is a rainbow trout that has migrated to the ocean. Highly prized by fishermen and cooks alike, it possesses a fine flake, subtle taste, and moderate amount of fat. Treat steelhead as you would salmon. Note that, because wild steelhead populations have become threatened and farmed steelheads possess the same downsides as farmed Atlantic salmon, steelhead only ranks as an "eco-okay" choice.

Trout can be baked, broiled, grilled, poached, smoked, steamed, or sautéed. Its nutty taste marries well with almond, apple, bacon, carrot, celery, mint, orange, pine nut, scallion, shallot, tarragon, thyme, tomato, and walnut. It is also enlivened by cider, lemon juice, and wine. Relatively inexpensive and an eco-friendly fish, you can enjoy U.S.-farmed trout as often as you like.

Trout, Spinach, and Watercress Salad

If you can't find watercress, substi-tute arugula or Belgian endive and add an extra dash of freshly ground black pepper. You can also make this salad with grilled char or tuna.

SERVES 4

$1/2$ teaspoon sugar

$3/4$ teaspoon freshly ground black pepper, plus more for seasoning.

1 teaspoon sea salt, plus more for seasoning

2 teaspoons Dijon mustard

1 small shallot, minced

$1/4$ cup cider vinegar

$1/3$ cup plus 2 tablespoons olive oil

$1/2$ cup sliced almonds, toasted

2 cups (1 bunch) firmly packed watercress

3 firmly packed cups (about $3^1/2$ ounces) baby spinach

1 pound U.S. farm-raised rainbow trout fillets, skin on

2 ounces goat cheese, crumbled

In a small bowl whisk together the sugar, black pepper, salt, mustard, shallot, vinegar, and $1/3$ cup of the olive oil.

In a large bowl, toss together the almonds, watercress, and spinach. Add half of the dressing and toss again. Distribute the salad among four dinner plates.

Heat the remaining 2 tablespoons of oil in a nonstick frying pan over medium-high heat.

Season the trout with salt and pepper and lay it skin side down in the pan. Cook for 2 to 3 minutes, until the skin has browned. Flip over the fillets and cook on the other side until the flesh turns opaque, another 2 to 3 minutes.

Place a fillet in the center of each salad. Sprinkle equal amounts of goat cheese onto the salads and drizzle over the remaining dressing. Serve immediately.

Smoked Trout-Topped Potato Pancakes

A variation on the traditional smoked salmon and caviar blini, potato pancakes with smoked trout provide yet another scrumptious way to consume this fish. Here the yeast and buckwheat flour in the blini have been replaced with baking soda and potatoes. Though they are hearty enough to be a main course, smoked trout–topped potato pancakes also make a great appetizer. If serving as hors d'oeuvres, use two tablespoons of batter per pancake.

SERVES 6

2 teaspoons sea salt
2 pounds russet potatoes, peeled
1 tablespoon salted butter
1 cup skim milk
1 1/2 cups unbleached all-purpose flour, sifted
1 teaspoon baking soda
1 cup buttermilk, at room temperature
Freshly ground black pepper, to taste
1 tablespoon unsalted butter, plus more as needed
10 ounces smoked trout, sliced
Reduced-fat sour cream (optional)
2 tablespoons chopped chives (optional)

Bring a small stockpot filled with water and 2 teaspoons salt to a boil.

Cut half of the potatoes into chunks. Boil the chunks in salted water until tender, 7 to 10 minutes. Drain and mash the cooked potatoes with the salted butter and milk. Set aside.

Using a box grater, grate the remaining pound of potatoes into a bowl. Strain or squeeze the liquid from the grated potatoes, then add them, along with the flour, baking soda, and buttermilk, to the mashed potatoes. Stir well to combine. Sprinkle in the black pepper and stir again.

Melt 1 tablespoon of unsalted butter in a large, nonstick skillet over medium heat.

Using a 1/4 cup measuring cup or a small ladle, add 2 to 3 pancakes to the frying pan, leaving at least an inch between each.

Fry until the batter has bubbled and appears slightly dry, 3 to 5 minutes. Flip the pancakes over and cook on the other side until browned, another 3 minutes. Remove and cover to keep warm.

Continue cooking the pancakes in batches, adding more butter to the pan as needed.

Place the pancakes on a serving platter. Top each with a slice or two of smoked trout, dollop of sour cream, and a dusting of chopped chives, if desired. Serve warm.

Pecan-Crusted Trout

This earthy preparation pairs nicely with Roasted Chestnut-Garlic Brussels Sprouts (page 235), Haricot Verts (page 229), or Ratatouille (page 231).

SERVES 4

1 teaspoon kosher salt

$^1/_2$ teaspoon freshly ground white pepper

Pinch of ground nutmeg

$1^1/_4$ cup pecans, toasted and finely chopped

$^1/_4$ cup unbleached all-purpose flour

1 large egg

1 tablespoon unsalted butter

1 tablespoon olive oil

4 (6-ounce) U.S. farm-raised rainbow trout fillets, skins on

Sea salt, to taste

Freshly ground black pepper, to taste

On a large plate mix together the kosher salt, white pepper, nutmeg, and chopped pecans. Spread the flour on a separate plate. In a small bowl whisk together the egg and 1 tablespoon of water. Set aside.

Season the trout fillets with sea salt and black pepper and then dredge them through the flour. Dip the skinless side of each fillet into the whisked egg, and then press it into the chopped pecans, making sure the nuts adhere to the fish.

Heat the butter and olive oil in a large, nonstick frying pan over medium-high heat.

Lay the fillets pecan side down in the heated pan. Cook until the crust is crisp, about 3 minutes. Gently turn the fillets over without disturbing the pecan topping and cook until the skin has browned and the flesh is flaky and opaque when probed with a fork, 2 to 3 minutes. Remove and serve immediately.

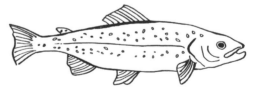

Chapter 8

Fabulous, Sometimes Forgotten Seafood

Every now and then I get into a rut with cooking. To pull me out of this slump, I look to a pool of fantastic yet often overlooked seafood. Exotic univalves, sea snails, and cephalopods drag me out of my groove and put some excitement back into my kitchen.

This group contains an assortment of unusual creatures—a mollusk smart enough to twist open jars and daring enough to crawl out of its aquarium; a fish that spends years drifting at sea, searching for the proper coastline to call home; the cephalopod that shoots ink; and the gastropod that resides in a gorgeous, spiral shell. At times the marine life from this group almost seems too interesting to eat.

Sweet abalone and whelk, along with the mildly nutty squid and rich, somewhat lobster-like octopus, are a part of this bunch. There is also the full-bodied eel, which possesses an ethereal flavor unlike any other fish.

In spite of unique and delectable tastes, this category often gets overlooked, due, in part, to appearance. As open-minded as I try to be, I must admit that the multiappendaged octopus and squid and the serpent-like eel are weird-looking, if not downright alarming.

Looks aside, there's also the issue of preparation. Cleaning, much less grappling with, eight- to ten-armed seafood or preparing muscular-footed mollusks such as abalone can be intimidating. However, once you move past looks and pick up a few cleaning tips, you're on your way to enjoying some incredible seafood.

Abalone

I put abalone in a category of luxurious foods to indulge in on rare occasions. This exquisite mollusk has a single, ear-shaped, iridescent shell, the inside of which is used to produce mother-of-pearl. It also possesses a foot-like abductor muscle that allows the abalone to cling to rocks. It is this strong, low-fat muscle that we eat.

Roughly one hundred species of abalone exist worldwide. All edible, they live on rocks in deep waters, which means they are quite difficult to obtain.

Despite challenging harvesting conditions, the wild abalone population has been devastated worldwide. Thankfully, the news concerning farmed abalone is far more positive, with fifteen species now grown around the globe. China and Taiwan are by far the largest producers, generating over ninety percent of the world's aquaculture supply. As long as you avoid wild abalone, you can consume this mollusk with a clear conscience. Farmed abalone is considered by experts to be an eco-best seafood.

Farmed abalone ranges in size from two to four inches across. Wild averages about twelve inches across but its meat is much tougher than farmed. You will find fresh or frozen, canned, dried, or salted abalone at markets.

When I want live abalone, I first check to see if it's clinging to its tank. If not, I ask to touch the gastropod's foot muscle. It should flinch when I touch it. If it doesn't move or if my finger leaves a dent in its flesh, the abalone is dead.

Frozen abalone should be firm-fleshed and ivory in color. As is the case with other kinds of seafood, you don't want to see brown or discolored spots on it. Fresh or frozen, abalone should smell clean and sweet. Since it's highly perishable, store abalone on ice in your refrigerator and use it on the day of purchase.

Abalone takes less than two minutes to cook. Just fry or sauté it in hot oil for thirty to forty seconds per side. When the flesh seems tender in texture and appears white to creamy in color, it's done cooking.

Herbs such as basil, cilantro, dill, and mint enliven abalone's moist, sweet meat. Likewise, capers, coconut, cucumbers, ginger, lemon, oyster sauce, rice wine, sesame, soy sauce, tomatoes, and white wine enrich it.

PREPPING ABALONE FOR COOKING

You'll need to take the abalone out of its shell before you cook it. To do this, grab a flat, metal spatula and slide its blade between the meat and shell. **1)** Pry out the meat and place it on a cutting board. Cut off the dark organs and discard them.

Using a soft brush, **2)** scrub the abalone under running water. Return it to the cutting board and **3)** trim off the curled, hard edges, known as the skirt. Rinse it off again. When finished, you should have a clean, ivory-colored hunk of meat.

At this point you can **4)** slice the meat into steaks. If the meat seems too soft to handle, wrap it in plastic wrap and place it in the freezer until it firms up, about 30 minutes. Use a sharp chef's or filleting knife to cut your steaks somewhere between $^1/_2$ and $^3/_4$ inch thick.

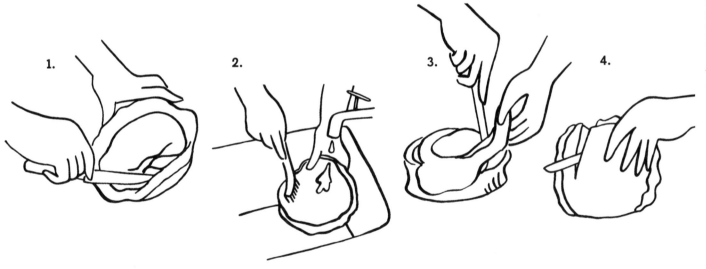

1.

2.

3.

4.

Pan-Seared Abalone

Pan-searing and sautéing are the customary techniques for cooking abalone. Here the sweet mollusk gets a kick from the addition of a few spices. This recipe can also be used with bluefish, carp, and tuna. If substituting those fish, adjust your cooking time accordingly.

SERVES 4

1/4 teaspoon chili powder

1/4 teaspoon sweet paprika

1/2 teaspoon garlic powder

1/3 cup unbleached all-purpose flour

2 tablespoons unsalted butter

1 pound abalone, cut into 4 steaks and tenderized (page 201)

Sea salt, to taste

Freshly ground black pepper, to taste

On a plate mix together the chili powder, paprika, garlic powder, and flour.

Heat the butter in a large nonstick frying pan over medium-high heat.

Season the abalone with salt and pepper. Dredge the steaks through the seasoned flour, coating completely. Place them in the pan and cook on one side until the abalone begins to turn creamy in color, 30 seconds to 1 minute. Turn over the steaks and cook on the other side for another 30 seconds to 1 minute or until tender. Remove and serve immediately.

Abalone in Mushroom-Oyster Sauce

Abalone is often sold in dried and canned form all over Asia and in the United States. If you cannot find canned abalone, you can substitute three (6.5-ounce) cans chopped clams. You'll find glass or cellophane noodles in Asian markets and in the Asian sections of some supermarkets.

SERVES 4

2 tablespoons olive oil

3 ounces shiitake mushrooms, stems discarded and caps sliced

3 ounces oyster mushrooms, sliced

$1^1/_2$ tablespoons oyster sauce

1 teaspoon soy sauce

1 teaspoon sesame oil

$^1/_2$ teaspoon fish sauce

1 (15-ounce) can abalone, drained and chopped

Sea salt, to taste

Freshly ground black pepper, to taste

7 ounces glass or cellophane noodles

Bring a small stockpot filled with salted water to a boil.

Heat the olive oil in a large, nonstick frying pan over medium heat. Add the mushrooms to the frying pan and sauté until softened, 3 to 4 minutes.

Whisk together $^1/_4$ cup of water with the oyster sauce, soy sauce, sesame oil, and fish sauce and pour into the frying pan. Increase the heat to high and cook, stirring occasionally, for 1 minute until blended and fragrant.

Season the chopped abalone with salt and pepper. Add the abalone to the frying pan and sauté for 1 minute until cooked through.

Add the glass noodles to the boiling water. Cook for 1 to 2 minutes or until done. Drain and evenly distribute the noodles onto four plates. Spoon equal amounts of abalone onto the noodles. Serve immediately.

 *Eel*

For years I remained a holdout on eel. Long, slender, slippery, and snake-like in its ability to slither across land in search of new waters, it seemed too creepy, too reptilian. Plus, the few times that I had eaten it, it had been unpleasantly mushy. But then I went to Spain, where this silver, freshwater fish has been considered a delicacy since Roman times. As a result, Spanish chefs and home cooks know how to handle eel. They keep it alive until just ready to cook, which avoids the mushiness that I had experienced. They stick to simple preparations—simmering it in olive oil with sliced garlic and chiles—allowing the firm, full-bodied, unique tasting meat to shine. Their skill in preparing eel changed my mind.

Although an eel can grow to ten feet in length, its average size is between two and five feet. Young eels, which are known as glass eels or elvers, are less than six inches in length and look a bit like cooked linguine. The smaller the eel, the more tender the meat. Raw eel meat is gray, and it lightens in color as it cooks.

Eel is sold whole and live or filleted and frozen. If you can, purchase it live, and have your fishmonger kill, skin, and cut it for you. This way you'll get the firmest, freshest meat possible. As it's quite perishable, you must use it within a day. If you buy frozen eel, keep it frozen until you're ready to cook it.

Eel's fatty meat is ideal for baking, braising, poaching, roasting, stewing, and hot-smoking. Its rich flavor is balanced out by such acidic foods as lemon, lime, soy sauce, tomatoes, and white wine. It also goes well with chiles, cilantro, garlic, black pepper, sage, sesame, shallots, and truffles.

Unfortunately, freshwater eel ranks as one of the environmentally worst fish available. The reasons are somewhat complicated. Eels spawn at sea, particularly in the Sargasso Sea, leaving their offspring to drift toward coastal waters. It takes the tiny elvers about one year to arrive in American waters. They may float along for up to three years before landing along the European coast.

In recent years the number of elvers arriving on either coastline has dropped sharply. Presumably this is due to climate change, which has caused their courses to shift and the young fish to be lost at sea. As a result, the number of baby eels available for stocking eel farms has also declined. Fewer elvers mean fewer eels. Additionally, American eels possess elevated levels of mercury and PCBs, only adding to the eels' status as an unsound seafood option.

Its one-of-kind flavor means the eel has no true substitutes. Enjoy it sparingly.

Matelote

This French fish stew gets its name from the French word matelot, which means "sailor." Ironically, it doesn't feature saltwater fish but instead such freshwater fish as eel or carp. In matelote you can successfully use another fish, such as carp or monkfish, in place of the eel.

SERVES 6

3 tablespoons extra-virgin olive oil

3 shallots, halved and sliced

4 garlic cloves, sliced

4 celery stalks, chopped

2 carrots, sliced

2¹/₂ cups dry red wine

2 sprigs fresh rosemary

2 sprigs fresh thyme

1 bay leaf

8 red peppercorns, crushed

13 yellow pearl onions

4 cups chicken or fish stock (see page 158 for steps on making fish stock)

2 pounds eel, skinned and cut into 2-inch chunks

1 scant teaspoon sea salt, plus more as needed

4 ounces white mushrooms, stems discarded and caps quartered

Freshly ground black pepper, as needed

Heat the olive oil in a medium stockpot over medium-high. Add the shallots, garlic, celery, and carrot. Cook until the garlic and shallots have softened, 2 to 3 minutes. Pour in the red wine and simmer for 5 minutes.

Bundle the rosemary, thyme, bay leaf, and peppercorns into a square of cheesecloth and tie the cloth together to make a *bouquet garni;* alternatively, you can put these ingredients in a spice ball. Add the spices, pearl onions, and stock to the pot and bring to a boil. Allow the ingredients to bubble away until aromatic, 5 minutes.

Add the eel and mushrooms and reduce the heat to medium. Simmer until the fish is tender and cooked through, 6 to 8 minutes.

Remove the herbs. Skim off any scum that has accumulated on top. Taste and adjust the seasonings as desired. Serve hot.

Roasted Eel with Ratatouille

Here, eel's sweet flavor is comple-
mented by the hearty stewed vegetable dish known
as Ratatouille (page 231). You can also make this
recipe with monkfish.

SERVES 4

1^1/$_2$ pounds eel, cut into 4-inch-long pieces
Sea salt, to taste
Freshly ground black pepper, to taste
^{1}/$_4$ cup olive oil
4 tablespoons unsalted butter
1 garlic clove, crushed
^{1}/$_2$ teaspoon kosher salt
^{1}/$_4$ teaspoon freshly ground white pepper
Ratatouille, for serving (page 231)

Preheat the oven to 450°F.

Season the eel with salt and black pepper.

Pour half of the olive oil into a large baking dish.
Place the seasoned eel in the dish and drizzle the
remaining olive oil over top.

Roast, turning over once halfway through the cooking time, until the eel is tender and cooked through,
15 to 20 minutes.

Put the butter, crushed garlic, kosher salt, and
white pepper in a small saucepan. Cook over medium
heat, swirling the pan periodically, until the butter
froths but hasn't yet begun to brown, 3 to 5 minutes.
Remove from the heat and discard the garlic.

Place equal amounts of ratatouille on four dinner
plates and lay the eel over top. Pour the seasoned butter over the eel and serve immediately.

Octopus

With its bulbous head and eight, sucker-lined tentacles, octopus is one of the most recognizable sea creatures known to man. It's also one of the most intelligent sea creatures, possessing the ability to open jars and cages, use tools, and mimic other aquatic life. Thanks to its diet of crustaceans and other mollusks, which leaves its flesh flavor-packed and a tad lobster-like, this bright, peculiar looking cephalopod has long been the darling of countless cuisines.

Octopus favors temperate and tropical waters, which has made it quite popular in Mediterranean, Portuguese, and Hawaiian cooking. Somewhat of a hermit, it lives on its own in these warm waters in rock crevices or houses that it creates from shells, stones, discarded tires, or pottery.

At markets octopi weigh around three pounds, with an extended tentacle length of between one to and two feet. In the wild they can grow to up to sixteen feet in length and weigh as much as thirty pounds.

An octopus's skin, body, tentacles, and black ink are edible. The beak, eyes, and organs should be removed and discarded before cooking. If you can, purchase an already cleaned octopus. If you must clean it yourself, see the steps on page 208 for instructions. Good fresh octopus will appear to glisten and look alive. The skin should not have any brown spots. It should likewise smell clean and not at all funky.

Before cooking, octopus must be poached to tenderize its rubbery flesh. Depending on its size, it should poach for thirty to sixty minutes in seasoned water; the larger the octopus, the longer it will need to poach. See Tenderizing Octopus, page 209, for further details.

After tenderizing the octopus, you can deep-fry, grill, sauté, or stew it. You can also use its black ink to enrich soups and pasta. If you aren't going to cook it immediately, leave the octopus in its poaching liquid and refrigerate it for up to two days.

Octopus's flavorful meat pairs with herbs such as bay leaves, dill, oregano, and thyme. It also accompanies such tart foods as capers, cured olives, lemon, pomegranate, red onion, vinegar, tomatoes, and white wine.

Fishery mismanagement has lead to overfishing, habitat destruction, and high bycatch, making octopus another seafood receiving the dreaded "eco-worst" rating. If you do purchase it, look for octopus from Spain. This country appears to have the most stable octopus population. You can substitute clams, squid, and monkfish in recipes calling for octopus.

CLEANING THE EIGHT-LEGGED WONDER

To clean an octopus; **1)** Start by laying it on your cutting board and slicing off the head right below the eyes; this will free the tentacles. Remove and set the tentacles aside.

Cut off and discard the eyes. Make a lengthwise slit in the head. Reach into this opening and pull out the organs. If you want to use the ink sac for flavoring, set it aside. Otherwise, discard everything but the head.

Octopus skin is edible, albeit a bit tough. If you want to peel off the skin, do so now. Just grab the skin with your fingers and peel. Either way, you should wash off the head and set it aside for later use.

Returning to the tentacles, **2)** press on the center where they meet and push up on the shell-like beak. You'll want to tear off or cut out this hard piece.

If you're working with a larger octopus, you'll also want to **3)** cut the tentacles into individual sections. Slice them apart and then move on to tenderizing and cooking the octopus.

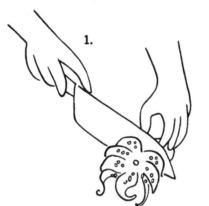
1.

2.

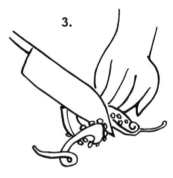
3.

Octopus, Crushed Tomatoes, and Kalamatas over Pappardelle

You can also serve the octopus with

Parmesan Polenta (page 237). Feel free to use squid or clams in place of octopus. If making this recipe with clams, pair them with pasta rather than polenta.

SERVES 4

2 pounds cleaned and tenderized Spanish octopus
Sea salt, to taste
Freshly ground black pepper, to taste
1 pound pappardelle pasta, for serving
2 tablespoons olive oil
2 (14.5-ounce) cans crushed tomatoes, drained
$1/2$ teaspoon crushed red pepper flakes
1 teaspoon capers, drained and rinsed

12 kalamata olives, pitted and halved

Using a sharp, chef's knife, cut the tentacles and head of the octopus into $1^{1}/_{2}$-inch pieces. Season with salt and pepper and set aside.

Bring a small stockpot filled with salted water to a boil. Cook the pasta according to the package's instructions.

As the pasta is cooking, heat the oil in a large frying pan over medium-high heat. Once the oil has begun to shimmer, add the octopus, tomatoes, red pepper flakes, capers, and olives. Cook for 5 minutes, stirring occasionally. Taste and adjust the seasonings before serving over the cooked and drained pappardelle.

TENDERIZING OCTOPUS

To tenderize your cleaned octopus, bring a stockpot filled with water to boil over high heat. Add 1 small quartered white onion, 1 large chopped celery stalk, 2 crushed garlic cloves, 1 sprig fresh rosemary, and 1 teaspoon coarse sea salt. Boil for 5 minutes. Add the octopus and reduce the heat to medium-low. Simmer uncovered for 30 to 60 minutes, or until the octopus feels tender when poked with a knife. Remove from the heat. Allow the octopus to cool in the stock for about 45 minutes.

If you aren't going to cook the octopus immediately, cover and refrigerate the cooled cephalopod. If you are using it right away, pat the cooled octopus dry with a clean cloth before cooking and then discard the poaching liquid.

Charred Octopus Salad

In this summery salad the smokiness of the charred octopus is balanced out by the sweetness of the tangerines and saltiness of the olives. You can substitute three clementines for the tangerines.

SERVES 6

2 pounds Spanish octopus, cleaned (page 208) and tenderized (page 209)

2 tablespoons olive oil

1/4 teaspoon crushed red pepper flakes

Sea salt, to taste

Freshly ground black pepper, to taste

2 tangerines, sectioned, seeds removed

1 small cucumber, chopped

1 small thinly sliced Vidalia or sweet onion

18 to 24 kalamata olives

4 1/2 firmly packed cups (about 4 ounces) arugula

1/4 cup aged balsamic vinegar

Preheat a grill on medium.

Place the octopus on a cutting board and slice the head and tentacles into 1 1/2-inch pieces. Toss the pieces together with the oil and crushed red pepper flakes; season with salt and pepper.

Toss together the tangerines, cucumber, onion, olives, and arugula. Set aside.

Lay a piece of foil on the grill and place the octopus on top of it.

Cover and grill the octopus until lightly crisped, 6 minutes. Turn the pieces over and cook for another 5 to 7 minutes, until the other side is crisp and browned. Remove from the grill.

Distribute the arugula salad evenly among 4 plates. Lay equal portions of octopus on the salads. Drizzle the balsamic vinegar over each salad before serving.

Squid

Some people claim that it looks like a cigar. Others liken it to a torpedo. I think it resembles the aliens Kang and Kodos from the animated series *The Simpsons*. No matter how you perceive this fleshy, ten-armed creature, you probably can envision what I'm talking about when I say, "squid."

Found in oceans around the globe, squid is known for its swimming prowess as well as its dark ink. It shoots this black ink at predators that come too close. In addition to being a defense mechanism for the squid, this salty fluid is also a coveted food flavoring.

A cephalopod from the mollusk family, squid varies in length from one inch to forty feet. What you'll find at markets usually falls between one and two feet long. The eco-friendly American longfin squid weighs up to five pounds. Keep in mind that the smaller the squid, the more delicate and mild it will be.

When buying squid, look for bright eyes and shiny purple to white skin. You don't want to see any browning; that's a sure sign that you should choose another squid. The flesh should smell clean and sweet.

You can purchase whole or frozen squid, squid rings, tubes, or steaks. To save yourself a little time and work, ask your fishmonger to clean whole squid for you. If you'd like to clean it yourself, see Cleaning Squid on page 212.

Whole, large squid is perfect for stuffing and baking. Rings and steaks respond well to braising, deep-frying, pan-frying, stir-frying, poaching, and sautéing.

Squid pops up in a wide range of cuisines. In Italian cooking it's breaded and fried. In Japan it's served in sushi. You'll also find it in Greek, Spanish, Chinese, and Korean recipes.

This mollusk's nutty flavor shines when paired with such tart foods as lemon, lime, tomatoes, vinegar, and white wine. It's also enhanced by chili powder, chorizo, cumin, garlic, ginger, lobster, paprika, rosemary, scallions, sesame, shallots, thyme, and zucchini.

Longfin squid from the U.S. is one of the environmentally friendliest seafood available. Low in contaminants, it reproduces quickly and has a healthy population. If you cannot track down longfin squid in your local market, you can substitute clams, sea scallops, or farmed North American shrimp in recipes.

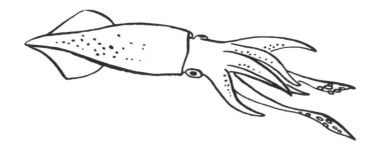

CLEANING SQUID

Before you start, bear in mind that squid will lose 25 percent of its weight during cleaning. If your recipe calls for 1 pound cleaned squid, purchase 1¼ pounds whole squid, to compensate for the weight loss.

The first step is to pull off the head. Grab the head at the point where it enters the body and pull, taking off the head and with it as much of the internal organs, including the ink sac, as you can. If you plan on using the ink for flavoring, set aside the sac for later use. Otherwise, discard it along with the other internal organs. Likewise, if the transparent body tube remains, yank this out and discard, too.

Using a knife, slice the body open lengthwise. If any viscera remain, cut or scrape this out. Rinse it off and move on to skinning.

To skin the squid's body, you simply grasp the skin and start peeling. Once it's peeled, rinse and pat it dry.

Next you'll separate the tentacles from the head. With the head facing you, place your knife right above the beak; this is the bulging spot directly over the eyes. Cut across, releasing the tentacles. Discard the head. Rinse and dry off the tentacles. With that you're ready to start cooking.

Salt 'n' Pink Pepper Squid

To boost the flavor of this simple but delicious dish, set out a small bowl of hot sauce for dipping.

SERVES 4

1¼ teaspoons coarse sea salt
1 tablespoon pink or red peppercorns
2 tablespoons olive oil
1 pound cleaned squid (facing page)
2 to 3 tablespoons sesame oil, for serving

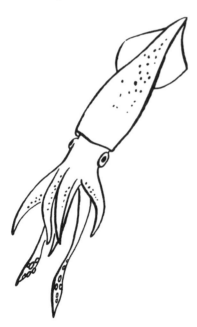

Using a mortar and pestle, crush the salt and peppercorns together so that you have a rough mixture of the two.

Heat the olive oil in a large frying pan over medium-high heat.

Using a knife, score one side of these sections in a crisscross pattern. Cut the squid into 4 equal, bite-sized sections; if you have small squid, just cut them in half. Season the squid on both sides with the salt and pepper mixture. Shake off any excess coating and place the squid in the pan.

Cook until the pieces start to curl up at the edges or bulge in the center, 1 to 2 minutes. Flip over and cook on the other side until it also curls, about 1 minute more. Remove and place the squid on a platter. Drizzle the sesame oil over the squid. Serve immediately.

Oh-So-Simple Calamari

For many, their first and possibly only taste of squid comes in the form of fried calamari. Served primarily as an appetizer, this preparation of battered and fried squid makes a frequent appearance on bar menus as well as in Italian, Mediterranean, and seafood restaurants.

The following recipe couldn't be much simpler. I've learned, though, that with calamari, the fewer the ingredients, the tastier the fried squid.

SERVES 2

Grapeseed oil, for frying
1 pound cleaned squid (page 212), cut into rings
$^3/_4$ cups plus 1 tablespoon unbleached all-purpose flour
1 teaspoon sea salt
1 teaspoon ground black pepper
Tomato sauce or aïoli for dipping

Heat 4 inches of oil in a large stockpot or deep fryer over medium-high heat. When the temperature reaches 350°F, you're ready to start cooking.

Using a clean towel, pat the squid rings dry so that they don't splatter when they hit the hot oil.

Place the flour, salt, and pepper in a bowl. Add the squid rings and toss to coat.

If you own a fryer basket, put the coated squid in it. Otherwise, gently lower the squid into the hot oil, using a slotted spoon. Allow the squid to fry for 2 to 3 minutes, until golden.

Using a slotted spoon or strainer, remove the fried calamari and place them on paper towels to dry. Serve hot with tomato sauce or aïoli for dipping.

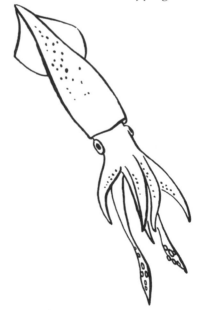

Stir-Fried Squid

I serve this stir-fry over steamed white rice. If using rice as your side, make it before stir-frying the squid. Otherwise, your stir-fry will grow cold as you wait for the rice to cook.

SERVES 4

1 pound precut squid rings, or cleaned squid (page 212), sliced into rings

2 tablespoons reduced-sodium soy sauce, plus more for dressing

2 tablespoons peanut oil

2 garlic cloves, sliced

1 small yellow onion, halved and sliced ½ inch thick

1 large zucchini, halved lengthwise and sliced

1 large red bell pepper, sliced ¼ inch thick

¼ teaspoon crushed red pepper flakes

Sea salt, to taste

Freshly ground black pepper, to taste

Place the squid rings and soy sauce in a bowl and toss to coat.

Heat the peanut oil in a wok or large frying pan over high heat. Add the garlic, onion, zucchini, and bell pepper. Reduce the heat to medium-high and cook, stirring frequently, until the vegetables are softened and slightly translucent, 3 to 4 minutes.

Draining off and reserving the soy sauce, add the squid rings and the crushed red pepper flakes. Cook the squid, stirring often, until it turns opaque and becomes tender, 1 to 2 minutes.

Add the reserved soy sauce and simmer for 1 minute. Taste and add salt, pepper and more soy sauce if needed. Serve immediately.

Sweet and Savory Stuffed Squid

Born from a Saturday spent in the
kitchen with my friends Vince Smith and Sharon
Burke, Sweet and Savory Stuffed Squid is a delightful
dish that defies the old adage, "Too many cooks spoil
the broth." Serve this squid alongside pasta or Parmesan Polenta (page 237).

SERVES 4

1 teaspoon dried thyme

2 tablespoons (about $^1/_2$ stalk) minced celery

$^1/_4$ cup dried currants

$^1/_4$ cup roughly chopped walnuts

$^1/_2$ cup plain white breadcrumbs

$^1/_4$ to $^2/_3$ cup vegetable or fish stock, warmed

2 tablespoons olive oil

2 garlic cloves, crushed

4 (8-inch-long) squid tubes

1 teaspoon sea salt, divided, plus more
   for seasoning

Freshly ground black pepper, to taste

1 (28-ounce) can crushed tomatoes (2 cups)

2 tablespoons minced fresh basil

$^1/_4$ cup dry rosé wine

In a small bowl toss together the thyme, $^1/_2$ teaspoon of the salt, celery, currants, walnuts, and bread-crumbs. Add $^1/_4$ cup of the vegetable or fish stock to the stuffing and stir until softened. If the stuffing still seems dry, gradually add more stock. The stuff-ing should be moist but not soggy.

Heat the oil and crushed garlic in a large sauté or frying pan over medium heat, swirling the garlic around once or twice so that all of the oil gets fla-vored, 1 to 2 minutes. Remove the garlic and set aside.

As the oil is heating, season the squid with the remaining salt and pepper. Fill each body with 2 to 3 tablespoons of stuffing, making sure to evenly dis-tribute. Thread each opening closed with a toothpick.

Once the oil has started to shimmer, lay the stuffed squid in the pan. Cook until a light crust forms, 2 minutes, and then turn over and cook on the other side for another 2 minutes. Remove from the pan and cover.

Return the garlic to the pan and add the tomatoes, basil, $^1/_2$ teaspoon of the salt, and wine. Cook over medium heat until the sauce has cooked down by a third, 3 to 4 minutes. Put the squid back in the pan and warm for 1 minute. Serve hot.

Whelk

Until recently, my only experiences with the spiral-shelled sea snails known as whelk involved seeing their shells displayed as decorative tchotchkes in seaside homes, inns, and restaurants. If I had ever lived by the ocean, it no doubt would have a richer history for me. This large, flavorful gastropod has been feeding coastal communities since the Stone Age.

Like abalone, the edible part of whelk is its foot-like muscle. Its chewy meat is juicy, a smidge salty, and a tad sweet. It reminds me a bit of the quahog clam and works well in any soups and chowders that feature that bivalve.

Although whelk is available worldwide, you'll have to frequent a well-stocked Asian, Italian, or seafood shop to buy it. With the introduction of U.S. whelk fisheries and an increasing culinary interest in the sea snails, though, this scarcity should soon change.

Whelks are generally sold precooked and shelled. Sometimes they're taken a step further and canned or jarred in spiced vinegar. On a rare occasion, you may come across fresh or frozen whelks.

If you buy whole whelks in their shells, you must scrub them under running water until clean. Place them in a pot of cold water and bring it to a boil. Simmer the whelks for ten minutes and then scoop them out with a slotted spoon. Lay them on a mound of clean towels and, using a paring knife, pick out the meat and cut out the hard circlet that covers the whelk's mouth. Once this is accomplished, you're ready to dig in.

In addition to boiling and serving whelks with a sprinkle of salt and ground white pepper, you can bake, pan- or deep-fry, sauté, or steam them. Their sweet, chewy meat partners deliciously with bacon, celery, green peppers, onion, potato, scallion, shallot, sweet onion, and tomato. They also perk up with chiles, cilantro, fennel, garlic, lime, parsley, white pepper, thyme, and malt, red wine, and cider vinegar.

At present there are no eco-recommendations for whelk.

GETTING TO KNOW THE WHELK FAMILY

More than fifteen hundred species exist in the Buccinum, or whelk, family, with members scattered around the world in tropical to frigid ocean waters. Although differing in habitats, they all possess whorled, top-shaped shells that, depending upon the species, can grow to over a foot in height. They love to eat mollusks, particularly live mussels, but will also consume carrion if necessary.

Although a multitude of varieties exist, Americans typically encounter two or three types of whelks:

Channeled: Possessing deep grooves or channels in its shell, the channeled whelk is one of two species popular in American markets. Growing to almost eight inches in length, this species is bigger and more elongated than its Europe relation, the common whelk.

Common: The favorite species of Europeans, common whelk has a wavy, coiled, ivory-colored shell and ranges between four to six inches long.

Knobbed: As its name indicates, the knobbed whelk has pointed projections near the top of its shell; it uses these knobs to crack open the shells of prey. A large creature, its shell can measure up to a foot in height.

Tangy Whelk Salad

If you can track down fresh, whole whelks, use them in this salad. Keep in mind that you'll need to clean, boil, and slice them before adding them. Otherwise, precooked, canned whelks are perfectly acceptable.

SERVES 4

1 small red onion, halved and thinly sliced

1 small cucumber, diced

2 garlic cloves, thinly sliced

1 small serrano chile, seeded and diced

3 tablespoons chopped fresh cilantro

$1/2$ cup red wine vinegar

2 tablespoons extra-virgin olive oil

$1/2$ teaspoon kosher salt

Freshly ground black pepper, to taste

1 pound whelks, cleaned, boiled (page 217), and sliced $1/2$-inch thick

In a medium bowl, mix together the onion, cucumber, garlic, chile, cilantro, vinegar, oil, salt, and pepper. Add the whelks and stir to combine. Cover the bowl with plastic wrap and refrigerate for 1 hour so that the flavors meld together.

Before serving, taste and add more salt and pepper if needed. Spoon the salad into small bowls and serve chilled.

Whelk Crêpes

To make the thinnest, most authentic crêpes possible, I use a well-oiled, ten-inch, cast-iron crêpe pan. You could also make these in a nonstick crêpe pan or a low-sided, ten-inch frying pan.

If you can't find whelks, substitute canned clams.

SERVES 6

1 cup unbleached all-purpose flour, sifted

2 teaspoons kosher salt, divided

$^1/_4$ teaspoon freshly ground black pepper

1 tablespoon minced fresh parsley or $1^1/_2$ teaspoons dried parsley

2 large eggs, at room temperature

$1^1/_2$ cups skim milk, at room temperature

2 tablespoons unsalted butter, melted and cooled to room temperature

2 tablespoons olive oil

1 small shallot, minced

$^1/_2$ teaspoon dried thyme

8 ounces whelks, cleaned, boiled (page 217), and minced

$^1/_2$ teaspoon freshly ground white pepper

Unsalted butter, for greasing the pan

2 large ripe tomatoes, chopped

$1^1/_2$ firmly packed cups (about $1^1/_2$ ounces) mixed greens

2 to 4 tablespoons red wine vinegar, for dressing the crêpes

In a medium bowl, whisk together the flour, 1 teaspoon salt, black pepper, and parsley.

In a separate bowl, whisk together the eggs, milk, and melted butter.

Add the liquids to the flour mixture and whisk the ingredients together until most of the lumps have been removed. Refrigerate the batter for 1 hour.

Heat the olive oil in a medium sauté or frying pan over medium-high heat. Add the shallot and thyme and sauté until the shallot starts to soften and becomes slightly golden in color, 2 to 3 minutes. Add the whelk, white pepper, and the remaining teaspoon of salt and sauté until golden, about 8 to 10 minutes. Remove the pan from the heat and cover.

Remove the batter from the refrigerator. If there are any lumps in it, strain them out.

Heat a 10-inch crêpe pan or low-sided frying pan over medium-high heat and then add a dab of butter. Coat the entire surface of the pan with the butter.

Holding the pan off the heat, pour 2 to 3 tablespoons of batter onto the pan. Swirl the batter so that the entire surface is evenly coated.

Return the pan to the heat and cook until the bottom of the crêpe is light brown and the top has set, 2 to 3 minutes. Using either a spatula or your fingers, flip the crêpe over and allow the other side to cook for 1 minute.

Place the crêpe on a plate and spoon 2 to 3 tablespoons of the whelk mixture in the center. Add a handful of chopped tomatoes, mixed greens, and a splash of red wine vinegar. Fold the crêpe in half, then into a triangle. Cover to keep warm.

Repeat with the remaining batter and serve immediately.

Farfalle with Whelk Sauce

A favorite of mine since early child-hood, jaunty, ruffled farfalle adds a touch of whimsy to this savory dish. You can also use canned clams in place of the whelk to dress up your bow tie–shaped pasta.

SERVES 4

1 pound farfalle pasta

$1/2$ cup olive oil

3 garlic cloves, thinly sliced

2 teaspoons crushed red pepper flakes

8 ounces whelks, cleaned, boiled (page 217), and coarsely chopped

$1/3$ cup dry white wine

$1/2$ teaspoon sea salt

$1/4$ teaspoon freshly ground black pepper

$1/4$ cup chopped fresh flat-leaf parsley

$1/4$ cup grated Pecorino Romano cheese

Bring a medium stockpot filled with salted water to a boil. Cook the pasta according to the package's instructions. Drain, reserving $1/2$ cup of the cooking water.

Heat the olive oil in a large frying pan over medium heat. Add the garlic and red pepper flakes and cook until the garlic begins to brown, 2 to 3 minutes.

Add the whelk, wine, salt, and pepper. Simmer until the whelk softens, 10 to 12 minutes. Taste and adjust the seasonings.

Add the pasta and half of the reserved water to the frying pan. Toss to coat, adding more water as needed to achieve a sauce-like consistency. Add the parsley and cheese. Toss until well combined and serve hot.

Chapter

9

Seafood Sides

Seafood avoiders often confess to me their various reasons for keeping fish out of their kitchens. Not only are they unsure how to prepare it, but they also struggle over what foods go with fish and shellfish, beyond, that is, green salads, baked potatoes, or thick slices of bread. Luckily, I can think of dozens of dishes that partner well with seafood.

The following pages contain a few of my favorite seafood-friendly sides. In all of them versatility is key. Many also go nicely with meat and poultry.

In each recipe I indicate which seafood works with the side dish, and in many cases I point out particular recipes that make good matches. By offering this information, I aim to take the guesswork out of side and entrée pairings.

Mango-Tomato Salsa

Ridiculously simple and quick, this refreshing salsa is a great as a side dish for a variety of seafood. This includes such crustaceans as crayfish, lobster, and shrimp. You can also use this salsa as a dressing, spreading it across the top of grilled mahi mahi, salmon, swordfish, or tuna. It makes a tasty accompaniment to Open-Faced Lobster-Avocado Rolls (page 56), Blackened Shad (page 85), Spicy Citrus Cobia (page 96), or Saffron and Cinnamon-Scented Monkfish Kebabs (page 138).

SERVES 4

2 ripe tomatoes, diced
1 large, ripe mango, peeled and diced
3 scallions, whites and 1 inch of greens diced
Juice of $\frac{1}{2}$ lime

In a small bowl toss together the tomatoes, mango, scallions, and lime juice. Cover and refrigerate for at least 30 minutes or until ready to use.

Tomato-Onion-Cucumber Salad

Inspired by the rejuvenating salads of the Mediterranean, Tomato-Onion-Cucumber Salad is a longstanding favorite in my household. It's so tasty that you may want to skip the fish and just eat this easy dish on its own. Serve it alongside swordfish or any other oily, meaty fish. It has a strong affinity for such recipes as Blackened Shad (page 85) and Turkish Bluefish Grill (page 88).

SERVES 4 TO 6

4 large tomatoes, seeded and cut into chunks
1 small red onion, quartered and thinly sliced
2 large scallions, whites only, chopped
1 garlic clove, minced
2 cucumbers, peeled, seeded, quartered, and sliced
Handful of fresh mint, chopped
Handful of fresh, flat-leaf parsley, chopped
$\frac{1}{4}$ cup extra-virgin olive oil
3 tablespoons red wine vinegar
$\frac{1}{2}$ teaspoon sea salt
$\frac{1}{4}$ teaspoon freshly ground black pepper

In a large bowl, toss together the tomatoes, onion, scallions, garlic, cucumbers, mint, and parsley. Whisk together the olive oil, vinegar, salt, and pepper. Pour the dressing over the salad and toss to coat. Refrigerate for 30 minutes. Serve chilled.

Moroccan Carrots

Preserved lemons play an especially prominent role in Moroccan cuisine. You'll see them in everything from meaty tagines to vegetable dishes. If you cannot find preserved lemons online or at gourmet shops, you can always make your own. See Lemon Preservation (page 226) for details.

If you can't find golden raisins, you can replace them with regular raisins. Just reduce the amount by 1 tablespoon.

Sweetly spicy Moroccan Carrots are spectacular with Saffron and Cinnamon-Scented Monkfish Kebabs (page 138), Chermoula-Coated Striped Sea Bass (page 143), and Sea Bass Satay (page 172). The combined crunch of the carrots and slight chewiness of the raisins provide a pleasant contrast to these tender-fleshed fish.

SERVES 6

$1^{1}/_{2}$ tablespoons honey

1 teaspoon ground cinnamon

$^{1}/_{4}$ teaspoon ground allspice

$^{1}/_{4}$ teaspoon ground cumin

3 tablespoons olive oil

10 medium carrots, peeled and cut into $^{3}/_{4}$-inch-long and $^{1}/_{4}$-inch-wide matchsticks

$^{1}/_{3}$ cup golden raisins

3 tablespoons pine nuts, toasted

$^{1}/_{2}$ preserved lemon rind and flesh rinsed and diced

In a small bowl, whisk together the honey, cinnamon, allspice, cumin, and olive oil.

In a medium bowl, toss together the carrots, raisins, and pine nuts.

Pour the dressing over the carrot mixture and toss again. Cover and refrigerate until chilled, 45 minutes or overnight if making a day ahead.

Once the carrots have chilled, add the preserved lemons and toss to combine. Serve cold or at room temperature.

Lemony Fennel

The tart freshness of Lemony Fennel makes it a good match for such oily, strongly flavored fish as sardines, shad, mackerel, bluefish, sablefish, swordfish, and salmon. Couple this side with Herb-Stuffed Sardines (page 82), Turkish Bluefish Grill (page 88), or Spicy Citrus Cobia (page 96).

SERVES 4

2 fennel bulbs
1 can (about 10 to 12) artichoke hearts, rinsed, drained, and quartered
1 large, ripe tomato, seeded and diced
2 garlic cloves, minced
1/2 cup roughly chopped flat-leaf parsley
Freshly squeezed juice of 1 lemon
1/4 preserved lemon (page 226), peel and flesh diced
1/4 cup extra-virgin olive oil
1/2 teaspoon kosher salt
1/2 teaspoon freshly ground black pepper

Remove any remaining stalks from the fennel bulbs. Wash the bulbs and then cut them into quarters and discard the cores. Thinly slice the quarters and place them in a large salad bowl.

Add the artichoke hearts, diced tomato, garlic, and parsley to the bowl and toss to combine.

In a small bowl, whisk together the lemon juice, preserved lemon, oil, salt, and pepper.

Pour the dressing over the salad and toss to combine. Cover and refrigerate for 30 minutes to allow the flavors to meld. Serve chilled or at room temperature.

LEMON PRESERVATION

Preserving lemons couldn't be simpler. Just add salt to lemons and—*Voila!*—you have preserved lemons. Okay, so it's a tad more complicated than that. To make preserved lemons, you will need four unwaxed, preferably organic lemons, $1/3$ cup coarse sea salt, a sterilized canning jar with a lid, and an optional $1/4$ cup of freshly squeezed lemon juice.

Soak the lemons overnight in a tub of lukewarm water, then drain them and pat them dry. Use a sharp knife to cut the fruit into four equal sections from their tops to $1/2$ inch from their bottoms, making sure not to completely cut the sections apart. Sprinkle a little salt on the pulp and then close up the lemons.

Spread a $1/2$-inch layer of salt on the bottom of the canning jar. Drop a lemon into the jar, add more salt, and then add another lemon. Repeat the process, pressing down on each lemon so that others can be packed into the jar. When finished, you should have an ample amount of juice, along with lemons and salt, in the jar. If the lemons look a bit dry, add the optional juice, leaving a little room at the top.

Seal and store the lemons for one month, periodically shaking the jar to distribute the salt and juice. Before using, rinse off the lemons.

Sweet Peas

Inspired by the flavors of Greece, these sweet yet salty peas form a wonderful partnership with meaty fish such as sablefish, salmon, and tuna, and with milder fish such as cod, halibut, and trout. I serve these alongside Olive Oil-Poached Sable (page 105), Seven Spice Salmon (page 110), Beer Battered Cod (page 154), or Pollock Fingers (page 165).

SERVES 4

2^1/$_2$ cups fresh or frozen green peas

2 tablespoons unsalted butter, at room temperature

1 teaspoon sugar

^{3}/$_4$ teaspoon sea salt

^{1}/$_4$ teaspoon freshly ground black pepper

2 teaspoons minced fresh mint

Fill a large saucepan with water and bring to a boil. Add the peas and cook until just tender, about 5 minutes.

In a small bowl, mash together the butter, sugar, salt, pepper, and mint.

Drain the peas and return them to the hot saucepan. Add the flavored butter and toss to combine. Serve immediately.

Warm Summer Corn Salad

Light yet flavorful, this salad of corn and red peppers goes with most fish and remarkably well with shellfish such as crab and lobster. I often pair this salad with Crab Cakelets (page 44), Grilled Lobster with Lime-Herb Butter (page 55), Breadcrumb-Crusted Croaker (page 127), and Lime-Marinated Swordfish Kebabs (page 114).

SERVES 6

2 tablespoons salted butter
1 large garlic clove, grated
4 cups fresh or frozen corn kernels
1 large red bell pepper, chopped
1 1/2 teaspoons minced fresh basil
Sea salt (optional)
Freshly ground black pepper (optional)

Heat the butter in a medium sauté pan over medium-high heat. Add the garlic and sauté until softened but not browned, 2 minutes.

Add the corn and bell pepper, toss to combine, and cook for another 5 minutes. Add the basil and stir to combine. Taste and add salt and pepper if desired. Serve immediately.

Haricot Verts

As I kid, I referred to haricot verts as "French string beans." Essentially, that's what they are. Simmered in chicken or vegetable stock, these slender, green legumes make a lovely addition to any meal featuring flavorful, mild, delicate fish. I offer these beans alongside Sautéed Char with Mushrooms (page 123), Braised Halibut with Shallot-Herb Butter (page 131), Paprika Orange Roughy (page 162), or Pecan-Crusted Trout (page 198).

SERVES 6

2 tablespoons unsalted butter
1 small shallot, minced
2 pounds fresh French green beans, stems removed
2 cups chicken stock, plus more as needed
Sea salt, to taste
Freshly ground white pepper, to taste

Melt the butter in a medium sauté pan over medium heat.

Add the shallot and cook until it is softened but not browned, 3 to 4 minutes.

Add the beans and the chicken stock. Add more stock if 2 cups is not enough to partially cover the beans.

Turn the heat up to medium-high and bring the stock to a low boil. Reduce the heat to medium and allow the beans to simmer until tender, about 5 minutes.

Season to taste with salt and pepper. Serve immediately.

Chilled Red Lentils

These hearty lentils could be a meal on their own. When served as a side, they pair with firm, white fish as well as oilier, meaty dishes such as Simple Shad (page 84), Baked Bluefish (page 89), and Lime-Marinated Swordfish Kebabs (page 114). If you can't track down red lentils, brown lentils are a good replacement.

SERVES 4

³/₄ cup red lentils, sorted and rinsed

1¹/₂ tablespoons sherry vinegar

1 teaspoon Dijon mustard

¹/₂ teaspoon sea salt

¹/₂ teaspoon ground cumin

¹/₄ cup olive oil

1 large shallot, minced

1 large red bell pepper, diced

1 medium cucumber, seeded and diced

1 large carrot, peeled and diced

1 ounce crumbled feta cheese (optional)

Bring 4 cups of salted water to a boil. Add the lentils and cook, uncovered, until tender, about 20 minutes.

As the lentils are cooking, whisk together the vinegar, mustard, salt, cumin, olive oil, and shallot.

Drain the lentils, place them in a medium bowl, and allow them to cool for 30 minutes.

Once the lentils are no longer steaming-hot, add the dressing, bell pepper, cucumber, and carrot and toss to combine. Taste and adjust the seasonings.

Refrigerate for at least 1 hour to allow the flavors to meld. If including the feta cheese, stir it in just before serving. Serve chilled.

Ratatouille

This aromatic, vegetable-based, Provençal classic goes with a host of seafood. It can pep up milder fish such as grouper and tilapia and temper such bold fish as monkfish, swordfish, mahi mahi, and eel. It is quite nice with Breadcrumb-Crusted Croaker (page 127), Pecan-Crusted Trout (page 198), and Roasted Eel (page 206).

Ratatouille can be served hot, cold, or at room temperature. In a larger serving, it makes for a filling vegetarian entrée.

SERVES 8

2 pounds eggplant, peeled and cut into 1-inch cubes

1 teaspoon sea salt, plus more for seasoning

1/4 cup extra-virgin olive oil, divided

3 pounds zucchini, quartered and sliced

1 small yellow squash, quartered and sliced

2 large red bell peppers, cut into 1-inch squares

4 garlic cloves, sliced

1 large yellow onion, chopped

1 (14.5-ounce can) diced tomatoes, drained

1 1/2 tablespoons dried oregano

1 1/2 tablespoons dried thyme

1 teaspoon dried basil

1 teaspoon freshly ground black pepper

Place the chopped eggplant in a strainer or colander, sprinkle with 1 teaspoon of salt, and toss to coat. Leave the eggplant to drain for 20 minutes.

Heat 2 tablespoons of the oil in a medium stockpot or Dutch oven over medium heat. Pat the eggplant dry and add it and the zucchini and yellow squash to the pot. Sauté for 6 to 8 minutes or until the eggplant and squash have become golden in color. Add the remaining olive oil, bell pepper, garlic, and onion and sauté for 5 minutes. Add the tomatoes, oregano, thyme, basil, and black pepper and stir to combine.

Reduce the heat to low and allow the ingredients to simmer until the vegetables have softened and the flavors have melded together. Depending on how soft you like your vegetables, this could be anywhere from 10 to 30 minutes.

Taste and adjust the seasonings. Serve the ratatouille warm or at room temperature.

Wild Rice-Mushroom Pilaf

Earthy and filling, wild rice-mush- room pilaf is a scrumptious side for mild, delicate fish such as cod, haddock, halibut, and trout, as well as for bold, firm fish such as mahi mahi, monkfish, and salmon. I frequently partner this pilaf with Cedar Planked Char (page 124) or Braised Halibut with Shallot-Herb Butter (page 131).

SERVES 6

3 cups chicken stock

2 cups wild rice

6 tablespoons unsalted butter, plus more as needed

2 leeks, finely chopped

2 garlic cloves, minced

12 ounces cremini mushrooms, stems discarded and caps diced

2 tablespoons dried parsley

2 teaspoons dried thyme

Freshly ground black pepper, to taste

$1/2$ cup slivered almonds, toasted and roughly chopped

In a medium saucepan bring the chicken stock and rice to a boil. Reduce the heat to medium-low, cover the pan, and simmer until all the liquid has been absorbed, 45 to 55 minutes. The rice will still be slightly firm. If the stock has evaporated before the rice has finished cooking, add up to $1/4$ cup stock or water as needed.

Preheat the oven to 350°F. Grease a large baking dish with butter.

Melt the 6 tablespoons of butter in a medium sauté or frying pan over medium heat. Add the leeks, garlic, and mushrooms and sauté until lightly browned, 5 to 8 minutes.

Add the parsley, thyme, black pepper, almonds, and cooked rice and stir until well combined. Spoon the mixture into the buttered baking dish. Cover the dish with foil and bake for 30 to 40 minutes, until the rice is evenly heated. Serve warm.

Golden Brown Cauliflower

This robust dish boosts the flavors of subtler fish such as trout, sole, and barramundi but also holds its own with stronger fish such as carp and salmon. I serve Golden Brown Cauliflower with Czech Christmas Carp (page 91), Picholine-Caper Sole (page 189), and Pearl Onion, Orange, and Thyme–Stuffed Striped Bass (page 146).

SERVES 4

3 pounds cauliflower, cut into 1-inch-wide florets
2 tablespoons olive oil
1 teaspoon sea salt
$1/2$ teaspoon freshly ground black pepper
$1/4$ teaspoon ground nutmeg
Good-quality aged balsamic vinegar (optional)

Preheat the oven to 450°F.

In a large bowl, toss together the cauliflower, olive oil, salt, pepper, and nutmeg.

Spread the cauliflower evenly over a large baking sheet. Roast for 25 to 35 minutes, turning the florets periodically, until they become soft and golden brown. Serve with an optional drizzle of aged balsamic vinegar.

Parsnip Chips

This version of the sweet root veg-etable pairs beautifully with such mild, white-fleshed fish as cod, orange roughy, and pollock. I often eat Parsnip Chips with Beer-Battered Cod (page 154) or Pollock Fingers (page 165).

SERVES 4

2 pounds parsnips, peeled and sliced
 into $1/4$-inch-thick rounds

3 tablespoons olive oil

1 teaspoon sea salt

$1/2$ teaspoon freshly ground white pepper

$1/2$ teaspoon garlic powder

Preheat the oven to 375°F.

In a large bowl toss together the parsnips, oil, salt, pepper, and garlic powder. Spread the parsnips evenly over a large baking sheet.

Roast the parsnips for 40 to 45 minutes, flipping them once or twice, until they are crispy and browned. Serve hot.

Roasted Chestnut-Garlic Brussels Sprouts

The complex texture and nutty taste of these Brussels sprouts balances out the delicateness of such fish as barramundi, flounder, halibut, sole, and trout. These sprouts also make great partners for Czech Christmas Carp (page 91) and Pecan-Crusted Trout (page 198).

SERVES 6

2 pounds fresh or frozen Brussels sprouts, halved from top to bottom

$1/2$ cup steamed chestnuts, roughly chopped

2 garlic cloves, minced

2 tablespoons olive oil

$1/2$ teaspoon sea salt

$1/4$ teaspoon freshly ground black pepper

Preheat the oven to 425°F.

Place the Brussels sprouts, chestnuts, garlic, oil, salt, and pepper in a large baking dish and toss together.

Spread the sprouts and chestnuts in a single layer on a baking sheet and bake for 25 minutes, or until tender. Serve immediately.

SELECTING SPROUTS

Prized for their sweet nuttiness and petite form, Brussels sprouts are most tender and flavorful at 1 to $1/2$ inches in diameter. When shopping for fresh Brussels sprouts, look for small, firm, bright green heads and compact leaves. Avoid large, soft, or yellow ones, as they tend to be old and bitter. If you happen upon sprouts that are still attached to their stalk, opt for the smallest stalk; these will contain the youngest and best tasting sprouts.

Unwashed, individual sprouts will keep in a plastic bag in the refrigerator crisper for up to three days.

Crispy Rosemary Potatoes

One of my all-time favorite sides, these potatoes are a pleasure not only at dinner with Paprika Orange Roughy (page 162) or Pearl Onion, Orange, and Thyme–Stuffed Striped Bass (page 146) but also at breakfast with a Sable and Goat Cheese Omelet (page 103).

SERVES 6

2¹/₂ pounds russet potatoes, peeled, quartered, and cut into ¹/₂-inch-thick slices

¹/₃ cup plus 1 tablespoon olive oil

1 garlic clove, minced

1¹/₂ tablespoons minced fresh rosemary

Sea salt, to taste

Freshly ground black pepper, to taste

Bring a medium stockpot of salted water to a boil. Add the potatoes and boil for 4 to 6 minutes, or until they are slightly tender. Drain the potatoes and set aside.

Heat the olive oil in a large frying or sauté pan over medium-high heat.

Add the potatoes and cook for 15 minutes, tossing periodically, until browned.

Add the garlic, rosemary, salt, and pepper, stir to combine, and cook for 5 minutes, or until the potatoes appear crispy. Taste and adjust the seasonings if necessary. Serve immediately.

Parmesan Polenta

On nights when you're rushing to prepare dinner, you could substitute the cornmeal in this recipe with instant polenta and follow the cooking instructions on the package. The resulting dish won't possess the richness of slow-cooked polenta, but it will save time. If you opt for instant, use it with such full-flavored fish as mahi mahi, salmon, and shad, and recipes such as Spice-Peppercorn Shrimp (page 62), Pan-Seared Scallops with Sherry Vinegar Reduction (page 39), Seven Spice Salmon (page 110), or Fish Plaki (page 187). The boldness of these foods compensates for instant polenta's relative blandness.

In general, you can serve slow-cooked Parmesan Polenta with any seafood.

SERVES 4

2 cups chicken stock
1 cup coarse yellow cornmeal
2 tablespoons salted butter
$^2/_3$ cup grated Parmesan cheese
$^1/_4$ tablespoon freshly ground black pepper

Place the chicken stock and 2 cups of water in a large saucepan and bring the liquids to a boil over medium-high heat. Slowly pour in the cornmeal, stirring constantly with a wooden spoon as you add it. Reduce the heat to low and continue stirring until the polenta is extremely thick and the spoon can support itself in the pan, about 30 minutes.

Add the butter, cheese, and black pepper to the polenta, stirring until well combined. Transfer the finished polenta to individual plates or a warmed serving bowl and serve immediately.

SEAFOOD'S LONGTIME COMPANION

A staple of Northern Italian cuisine, modern polenta dates back to the mid seventeenth century. It was during this time that the Venetians introduced American corn to the region. Prior to the 1600s a form of polenta was made using chestnut flour or barley.

Cooked in an unlined, copper kettle, this combination of ground corn and water was vigorously stirred until a thick mush formed. To test for doneness, the cook would insert his wooden spoon in the center of the mixture. A standing, unmoving spoon meant the polenta was done.

Once finished, the polenta was either served immediately in its porridge-like state or spooned out of the pot, spread out on a flat surface to cool and solidify, and then cut into squares. The pieces would then be grilled or fried and paired with seafood, vegetables, or a sauce.

Garlic Mashed Potatoes

Based on a recipe in Julia Child's *Mastering the Art of French Cooking, Volume 1*, these mashed potatoes go well with a myriad of seafood recipes. Try them with Seven Spice Salmon (page 110), Steamed Ginger-Sesame Snapper (page 141), and Picholine-Caper Sole (page 189). Similar to Parmesan Polenta (page 237) and Crispy Rosemary Potatoes (page 236), this dish complements truly any fish.

SERVES 6

4 tablespoons unsalted butter, plus more as needed
25 garlic cloves, peeled
2 tablespoons unbleached all-purpose flour, sifted
1 cup skim milk, boiled
2½ pounds russet potatoes, peeled and quartered
¼ cup skim milk, warmed
1 teaspoon sea salt

Place the butter and garlic in a small sauté pan. Cover and cook on medium-low for about 20 minutes, stirring occasionally, until the garlic is tender but not browned.

Reduce the heat to low and slowly add the flour, stirring until blended and frothy. Remove the pan from the heat and whisk in the boiled milk. Pour this mixture into a blender or food processor and purée.

Return the garlic purée to the pan and simmer over medium-low heat for another 2 minutes before removing from the heat. Dot the top with chunks of butter to stop a skin from forming.

Boil the potatoes in a large pot of salted water until tender, 10 to 12 minutes. Drain the potatoes and either mash them by hand or push them through a potato ricer. Do not pulse the potatoes in a food processor; this will make them pasty and unappealing.

Once the potatoes have been mashed, beat in the warmed milk, followed by the garlic purée. Taste and add up to 1 teaspoon salt. Serve immediately.

Eco-Rating Chart

FISH	ECO RATING
ABALONE	Eco-best (farm-raised)
ANCHOVY	Eco-best
BARRAMUNDI	Eco-best
BLUEFISH	Eco-okay (U.S. wild)
BUTTERFISH	No eco-rating at present
CARP	No eco-ratings at present
CATFISH	Eco-best (U.S.)
CHAR	Eco-best
CLAMS	Eco-best (farm-raised, soft-shell)
COBIA	Eco-best (U.S.)
COD	Eco-best (AK); Eco-okay (Pacific)
CRAB	Eco-best (Dungeness, stone)
CRAYFISH	Eco-best (U.S.)
CROAKER	Eco-okay
EEL	Eco-worst
FLOUNDER	Eco-okay (Pacific)
GROUPER	Eco-okay (U.S. Gulf of Mexico)
HALIBUT	Eco-best (Pacific)
HADDOCK	Eco-best (U.S.)
HERRING	Eco-okay
LOBSTER	Eco-okay
MACKEREL	Eco-best (King, Spanish, Atlantic from Canada)
MAHI MAHI	Eco-best (U.S. pole-caught)
MONKFISH	No eco-rating at present
MUSSELS	Eco-best

FISH	ECO RATING
OCEAN PERCH	Eco-okay (Pacific line-caught)
OCTOPUS	Eco-worst
ORANGE ROUGHY	Eco-worst
OYSTERS	Eco-best (farm-raised); Eco-okay (wild)
POLLOCK	Eco-best (Norway); Eco-okay (U.S.)
PORGY	Eco-okay (U.S.)
SABLEFISH	Eco-best
SALMON	Eco-okay (Pacific NW)
SARDINES	Eco-best
SCALLOPS	Eco-best (farm-raised bay); Eco-okay (sea from Canada and U.S.)
SEA BASS	Eco-okay (line-caught)
SHAD	No eco-rating at present
SHRIMP	Eco-okay (U.S. farm-raised, wild)
SNAPPER	Eco-okay
SOLE	Eco-okay (Pacific wild)
SQUID	Eco-best (U.S. longfin)
STRIPED BASS	Eco-best (U.S. farm-raised)
SWORDFISH	Eco-okay (U.S., Canada)
TUNA	Eco-best (albacore); Eco-okay (pole-caught bonito and skipjack)
TURBOT	No eco-rating at present
TILAPIA	Eco-best (U.S.)
TROUT	Eco-best (U.S. farm-raised rainbow)
WHELK	No eco-rating at present

Bibliography

BOOKS

Allen, Darina. *Forgotten Skills of Cooking.* London: Kyle Books, 2009.

Bittman, Mark. *Fish.* New York: Wiley Publishing, Inc., 1994

Child, Julia. *Mastering the Art of French Cooking, Vol. 1.* New York: Alfred Knopf, 2002.

The Culinary Institute of America. *The Professional Chef 7th Edition.* New York: John Wiley and Sons, Inc., 2002.

Davidson, Alan. *Mediterranean Seafood.* Berkley: Ten Speed Press, 2002.

Davidson, Alan. *The Oxford Companion to Food.* Oxford: Oxford University Press, 2006.

Fabricant, Florence (ed). *The New York Times Seafood Cookbook.* New York: St. Martin's Press, 2003.

Fearnley-Whittingstall, Hugh and Fisher, Nick. *The River Cottage Fish Book.* London: Bloomsbury, 2007.

Folse, John D. *The Encyclopedia of Cajun and Creole Cuisine.* Gonzales, LA: Chef John Folse and Company Publishing, 2006.

Garmey, Jane. *Great British Cooking.* New York: William Morrow, 1992.

Green, Aliza. *Field Guide to Seafood.* Philadelphia: Quirk Books, 2007.

Green, Aliza. *Field Guide to Herbs and Spices.* Philadelphia: Quirk Books, 2006.

Grigson, Jane. *Jane Grigson's Fish Book.* London: Penguin Books, 1993.

Herbst, Sharon Tyler and Herbst, Ron. *The New Food Lover's Companion.* Hauppauge, NY: Barron's Educational Series, Inc., 2007.

Hutton, Wendy. *Authentic Recipes from Malaysia.* Singapore: Periplus, 2005.

Iyer, Raghavan. *660 Curries.* New York: Workman, 2008.

Kenney, Matthew. *Matthew Kenney's Mediterranean Cooking.* San Francisco: Chronicle Books, 1997.

Lilja, Agneta and Tidholm, Po. *Celebrating the Swedish Way.* Stockholm: The Swedish Institute, 2004.

Long, Sorey and Linden, Kanika. *Authentic Cambodian Recipes.* London: Marshall Cavendish Cuisine, 2010.

Mariani, John F. *The Encyclopedia of American Food and Drink.* New York: Lebhar-Friedman Books, 1999.

McGee, Harold. *On Food and Cooking.* New York: Scribner, 2004.

Nilsen, Angela (ed.). *Good Food Magazine 101 Mediterranean Dishes.* London: BBC Books, 2008.

Ojakangas, Beatrice. *Scandinavian Feasts.* Minneapolis: University of Minnesota Press, 1992.

Page, Karen and Dornenburg, Andrew. *The Flavor Bible*. New York: Little, Brown and Company, 2008.

Raichlen, Steven. *Planet Barbecue!* New York: Workman Publishing, 2010.

Rombauer, Irma S., Rombauer Becker, Marion and Becker, Ethan. *The All New Joy of Cooking*. New York: Scribner, 1997.

Stein, Rick. *Rick Stein's Complete Seafood*. Berkley: Ten Speed Press, 2004.

Whiteman, Kate. *The World Encyclopedia of Fish and Shellfish*. London: Hermes House, 2010.

Wolfert, Paula. *Couscous and Other Good Food from Morocco*. New York: Quill, 2001.

Woodward, Sarah. *Tastes of North Africa*. London: Kyle Cathie Limited, 1998.

WEB RESOURCES

Gulf of Maine Research Institute. www.gmri.org

Environmental Defense Fund. www.edf.org

Monterey Bay Aquarium: Seafood Watch. www.montereybayaquarium.org/cr/seafoodwatch.aspx

Index

A

abalone, 200–203
    Abalone in Mushroom-Oyster Sauce, 203
    about, 199, 200
    eco-rating, 200
    Pan-Seared Abalone, 202
    prepping, 201
albacore tuna, 116. *see also* tuna
anchovy, 65–70
    about, 64, 65
    Caesar Salad, 66
    Cannellini-Anchovy-Tomato Pita, 68
    cleaning, 66
    eco-rating, 65
    Fettucine with Anchovy Sauce, 69
    Jansson's Temptation, 70
    Marinated Anchovies, 67
Atlantic salmon, 107. *see also* salmon

B

bamboo steamers, 16
banana leaf baskets, 145
barramundi, 177–180
    about, 176, 177
    Banana Leaf Barramundi, 178
    Barramundi Pilaf, 180
    eco-rating, 177
    Miso-Glazed Barramundi, 179
bay scallops. *see also* scallops
bay scallops, 36
bivalves, 19
black cod. *see* sablefish
black sea bass. *see* sea bass
bluefin tuna, 116. *see also* tuna

bluefish, 87–89
    about, 86, 87
    Baked Bluefish, 89, 230
    eco-rating, 87
    Pan-Seared Bluefish, 202
    smoking, 102
    Turkish Bluefish Grill, 88, 223, 225
boning knives, 15
bonito, 116. *see also* tuna
branzino, 170
brown trout, 195. *see also* trout
Brussels sprouts
    Roasted Chestnut-Garlic Brussels Sprouts, 91, 198, 235
    selecting, 235
butterfish, 71–73
    about, 64, 71
    Grilled Cambodian Butterfish, 73
    Sautéed Butterfish, 72

C

carp, 90–93
    about, 86, 90
    Asian-Style Carp, 93
    Czech Christmas Carp, 91, 233, 235
    Czech Republic Carp Festival, 92
    eco-rating, 90
    Matelote, 205
    Pan-Seared Carp, 202
    smoking, 102
carrots
    Moroccan Carrots, 138, 143, 224
catfish, 148–151
    about, 147, 148
    Catfish Curry, 150
    Catfish Gratin, 159

Catfish Puff Pie, 151
    Catfish Tacos, 113
    Chunky Catfish Stew, 149
    Creamy Pasta with Catfish and Peas, 182
    eco-rating, 148
    Indian Spiced Catfish, 163
    Paprika Catfish, 162
cauliflower
    Golden Brown Cauliflower, 91, 146, 189, 233
char, 122–124
    about, 121, 122
    Cedar Planked Char, 124, 232
    eco-rating, 122
    Sautéed Char with Mushrooms, 123, 229
chef's knives, 11, 15
chermoula, 143, 153
cherrystone clams, 20. *see also* clams
Chilean sea bass, 170
Chinook salmon. *see also* salmon
chinook salmon, 107
chum salmon, 107. *see also* salmon
clam knives, 16
clams, 20–24
    about, 19, 20
    Clam Crêpes, 220
    Clam Fritters with Spicy Rémoulade, 21–22
    cleaning, 22
    Grilled Clams with Lemon-Basil Butter, 24
    Littleneck Linguine with Brown Butter, 23
    shucking, 22
cleaning
    anchovy, 66
    clams, 22
    crab, 42
    fish, 11–12
    mussels, 26
    octopus, 208
    oysters, 33
    squid, 212
cobia, 94–96
    about, 94
    eco-rating, 94

    Malaysian Fish Soup, 95
    Spicy Citrus Cobia, 96, 223, 225
cod, 152–154
    about, 147, 152
    Beer-Battered Cod, 154, 227, 234
    Cod Tacos, 113
    eco-rating, 152
    Fish Plaki, 187
    Indian Spiced Cod, 163
    Paprika Cod, 162
    Tagine of Cod, 153
coho salmon, 107. *see also* salmon
cooking equipment, 15–16
corn
    Warm Summer Corn Salad, 44, 114, 127, 228
crab, 41–45
    about, 40, 41–42
    cleaning, 42
    Crab Cakelets, 44, 228
    Dungeness Crab Salad, 43
    eating, 42
    eco-rating, 41, 42
    Spicy Crab Stew, 45
crayfish
    about, 40, 46–47
    Crayfish and Mushroom Risotto, 50
    Crayfish Étouffée, 48
    eco-rating, 46
    Louisiana Crayfish Boil, 49
    Swedish Crayfish Boil, 47
croaker, 125–129
    about, 121, 126
    Barbecued Croaker Salad, 128–129
    Breadcrumb-Crusted Croaker, 127, 228, 231
    eco-rating, 126
crustaceans, 40

E

eco-ratings chart, 239

eel, 204–206
    about, 199, 204
    eco-rating, 204
    Matelote, 205
    Roasted Eel with Ratatouille, 206, 231

F

fennel
    Lemony Fennel, 82, 88, 225
fillet knives, 16
fish
    cleaning, 11–12
    cutting fillets, 14–15
    cutting steaks, 13–14
    descaling, 12
    fish stock, 158
    indirect grilling, 125
    skin, 13
    smoking, 102
flounder, 181–183
    about, 176, 181
    Creamy Pasta with Flounder and Peas, 182
    eco-rating, 181
    Flounder Braciole, 183
frying pans, 15

G

gloves, cut-resistant, 16
grilling planks, 16
grouper, 155–157
    about, 147, 155
    Caribbean Stir-Fry, 157
    eco-rating, 155
    Souper Grouper, 156

H

haddock, 184–187
    about, 176, 184
    eco-rating, 184
    Fish Plaki, 187, 237
    Haddock Couscous, 186
    Haddock Pilaf, 180
    Smoked Haddock Frittata, 185
halibut, 130–132
    about, 121, 130
    Braised Halibut with Shallot-Herb Butter, 131, 229, 232
    eco-rating, 130
    Halibut Cassoulet, 132
    Mediterranean Halibut Packets, 194
hard-shell clams, 20. *see also* clams
haricot verts, 123, 131, 162, 198, 229
herring, 74–78
    about, 64, 74–75
    deboning, 75
    Pickled Beet and Herring Salad, 76
    Scottish Fried Herring, 77
    Smoked Herring Tea Sandwiches, 78

K

king salmon, 107. *see also* salmon
knives, 11, 15–16, 17
kroeung, 145

L

lemon preservation, 224, 226
littleneck clams, 20, 23. *see also* clams
lobster, 51–57
    about, 40, 51–52
    Boiled Lobster, 51
    eco-rating, 52
    Grilled Lobster with Lime-Herb Butter, 55, 228
    Lobster-Corn Chowder, 54
    Lobster Roll, 57

Open-Faced Lobster-Avocado Roll, 56, 223
preparing live, 53
removing meat from, 52

m

mackerel, 97–100
about, 86, 97
eco-rating, 97
Lime-Marinated Mackerel Kebabs, 114
Mackerel Escabèche, 98
Smoked Mackerel Jackets, 99
Zesty Lime Mackerel, 100
mahi mahi, 133–135
about, 121, 133
eco-rating, 133
Indian Spiced Mahi Mahi, 163
Jamaican Jerk Mahi Mahi, 134
Mahi Mahi Gratin, 159
Tropical Mahi Mahi, 135
monkfish, 136–138
about, 121, 136
Bouillabaisse, 137–138
eco-rating, 136
Matelote, 205
Saffron and Cinnamon-Scented
    Monkfish Kebabs, 138, 223, 224
mushrooms
Wild Rice-Mushroom Pilaf, 131, 232
mussels, 25–29
about, 19, 25–26
Belgian Steamed Mussels, 27
Broiled Stuffed Mussels, 29
cleaning, 26
eco-rating, 26
Mussels Provençal, 28

O

ocean perch, 158–160
about, 147, 158

eco-rating, 158
Ocean Perch Gratin, 159
Red, White, and Green Perch, 160
octopus, 207–210
about, 199, 207
Charred Octopus Salad, 210
cleaning, 208
eco-rating, 207
Octopus, Crushed Tomatoes, and Kalamatas
    over Pappardelle, 209
tenderizing, 209
omega-3 fatty acids, 7
orange roughy, 161–163
about, 147, 161
eco-rating, 161
Indian Spiced Orange Roughy, 163
Paprika Orange Roughy, 162, 229, 236
oyster knives, 16
oysters, 30–35
about, 19, 30–31
Angels on Horseback, 33
cleaning, 33
eco-rating, 30
on the half shell, 32
Oyster Po' Boys, 34
Oyster Shooters, 32
Oysters Rockefeller, 35
shucking, 31

p

paring knives, 15
Parsnip Chips, 154, 165, 234
peas
Sweet Peas, 123, 154, 165, 227
pilaf
Barramundi Pilaf, 180
Wild Rice-Mushroom Pilaf, 131, 232
pink salmon, 107. *see also* salmon
pliers and tweezers, 16
po' boy sandwich, 34, 35

polenta
  Parmesan Polenta, 39, 100, 131, 160, 166, 189, 209, 216, 237
pollock, 164–166
  about, 147, 164
  eco-rating, 164
  Hazelnut Pesto Pollock, 166
  Pollock Fingers, 165, 227, 234
porgy, 167–169
  about, 147, 167
  eco-rating, 167
  Garlic Porgy, 169
  Porgy Pie, 168
potatoes
  Crispy Rosemary Potatoes, 89, 146, 162, 236
  Garlic Mashed Potatoes, 89, 160, 165, 238

Q

quahog clams, 20. *see also* clams

R

rainbow trout, 195. *see also* trout
Ratatouille, 127, 198, 206, 231
razor clams, 20. *see also* clams
red salmon, 107. *see also* salmon
rémoulade, 21
Rémoulade, Clam Fritters with Spicy, 21–22
rice
  Barramundi Pilaf, 180
  Wild Rice-Mushroom Pilaf, 131, 232
rock bass. *see* sea bass

S

sablefish, 101–105
  about, 86, 101
  eco-rating, 101
  Olive Oil-Poached Sablefish, 105, 227

  Pan-Seared Sablefish with Soy-Sesame Glaze, 104
  Sable and Goat Cheese Omelet, 103, 236
  Smoked Sablefish Frittata, 185
  smoking, 102
salads
  Caesar Salad, 66
  Tomato-Onion-Cucumber Salad, 85, 88, 114, 166, 223
  Warm Summer Corn Salad, 44, 114, 127, 228
salmon, 106–111
  about, 86, 106–107
  eco-rating, 106, 107
  Great Gravlax, 108
  Salmon, Spinach, and Watercress Salad, 196
  Salmon Gratin, 159
  Salmon Patties with Dijon-Caper Mayo, 193
  Salmon Pilaf, 180
  Sesame-Crusted Salmon with Sweet Tamarind Sauce, 111
  Seven Spice Salmon, 110, 227, 237, 238
  Smoked Salmon-Avocado-Tomato Tartare, 109
  Smoked Salmon Frittata, 185
  smoking, 102
  types, 106, 107
salmon trout, 196. *see also* trout
salsa
  Mango-Tomato Salsa, 56, 85, 138, 223
sardines, 79–82
  about, 64, 79–80
  eco-rating, 79
  Herb-Stuffed Sardines, 82, 225
  Onion-Sardine Pissaladiè, 81
  Sardine Spread, 80
sauté pans, 16
scallops, 36–39
  about, 19, 36
  eco-rating, 36
  Pan-Seared Scallops with Sherry Vinegar Reduction, 39, 237
  Scallop and Mushroom Pie, 38
  Vietnamese Scallop Boat Salad, 37
scrod, 153
scup. *see* porgy

sea bass, 170–172
    about, 147, 170
    eco-rating, 170
    Sea Bass Ceviche, 171
    Sea Bass Satay, 172, 224
sea bream. *see* porgy
sea scallops, 36. *see also* scallops
sea trout, 196. *see also* trout
seafood
    cleaning fish, 11–12
    ease of preparation, 8
    eco-ratings, 10–11
    health benefits, 7
    ingredients, 18
    selecting, 9–10
    sellers of, 9–10
    sustainability, 7, 8, 10–11
seafood crackers, 16
sergeant fish. *see* cobia
shad, 83–85
    about, 64, 83
    Blackened Shad, 85, 223
    eco-rating, 83
    Sautéed Shad Roe, 84
    Simple Shad, 84, 230
shrimp, 58–63
    about, 40, 58–59
    deveining, 59
    eco-rating, 58
    Sautéed Ginger-Scallion Shrimp, 60
    Shrimp Cocktail, 60
    Shrimp Paella, 63
    Sizzling Garlic Shrimp, 61
    Spice-Peppercorn Shrimp, 62, 237
side dishes, 222–238
    Chilled Red Lentils, 114, 230
    Crispy Rosemary Potatoes, 89, 146, 162, 236
    Garlic Mashed Potatoes, 89, 160, 165, 238
    Golden Brown Cauliflower, 91, 146, 189, 233
    Haricot Verts, 123, 131, 162, 198, 229
    Lemony Fennel, 82, 88, 225
    Mango-Tomato Salsa, 56, 85, 138, 223
    Moroccan Carrots, 138, 143, 224
    Parmesan Polenta, 39, 100, 131, 160, 166, 189, 209, 216, 237
    Parsnip Chips, 154, 165, 234
    Ratatouille, 127, 198, 206, 231
    Roasted Chestnut-Garlic Brussels Sprouts, 91, 198, 235
    Sweet Peas, 123, 154, 165, 227
    Tomato-Onion-Cucumber Salad, 85, 88, 114, 166, 223
    Warm Summer Corn Salad, 44, 114, 127, 228
    Wild Rice-Mushroom Pilaf, 131, 232
silver salmon, 107. *see also* salmon
skillets, 15
skipjack, 116. *see also* tuna
snapper, 139–141
    about, 121, 139
    eco-rating, 139
    Salt Baked Snapper, 140
    Steamed Ginger-Sesame Snapper, 141, 238
sockeye salmon, 107. *see also* salmon
soft-shell clams, 20. *see also* clams
sole, 188–190
    about, 176, 188
    Creamy Pasta with Sole and Peas, 182
    eco-rating, 188
    Parmesan-Coated Sole, 190
    Picholine-Caper Sole, 189, 233, 238
spatulas, 15
squid, 211–216
    about, 199, 211
    cleaning, 212
    eco-rating, 211
    Oh So Simple Calamari, 214
    Salt 'n' Pink Pepper Squid, 213
    Stir-Fried Squid, 215
    Sweet amd Savory Stuffed Squid, 216
steamers, 20. *see also* clams
steelhead trout, 196. *see also* trout
stockpots, 15
striped bass, 142–146
    about, 121, 142
    Angkor-Style Striped Bass, 144–145
    Chermoula-Coated Striped Bass, 143, 224

striped bass continued
    eco-rating, 142
    Pearl Onion, Orange, and Thyme-Stuffed Striped Bass,
        146, 233, 236
swordfish, 112–114
    about, 86, 112
    eco-rating, 112
    Lime-Marinated Swordfish Kebabs, 114, 228, 230
    smoking, 102
    Swordfish Tacos, 113

T

thermometers, deep-fry, 16
tilapia, 191–194
    about, 176, 191
    eco-rating, 191
    Mediterranean Tilapia Packets, 194
    Paprika Tilapia, 162
    Tilapia Patties with Dijon-Caper Mayo, 193
    Tilapia Tacos, 113
    Warm Potato and Tilapia Salad, 192
trout, 195–198
    about, 176, 195
    eco-rating, 195–196
    Pecan-Crusted Trout, 198, 229, 231, 235
    Smoke Trout-Topped Potato Pancakes, 197
    Smoked Trout Frittata, 185
    Trout, Spinach, and Watercress Salad, 196
    Trout Pilaf, 180
    types, 195–196
    Warm Potato and Trout Salad, 192
tuna, 115–120
    about, 86, 115
    Chilled Tuna and White Beans, 117
    Dive Bar Tuna Delight, 120
    eco-rating, 116
    Lime-Marinated Tuna Kebabs, 114
    Pan-Seared Tuna, 202
    Supper Club Tuna Salad, 118–119
    Tuna, Spinach, and Watercress Salad, 196
    Tuna Tacos, 113

    types, 116
    Warm Potato and Tuna Salad, 192
turbot, 173–175
    about, 147, 173
    eco-rating, 173
    Seasonal Simmered Turbot, 174
    Tarragon Turbot, 175

W

whelk, 217–221
    about, 199, 217–218
    Farfalle with Whelk Sauce, 221
    Tangy Whelk Salad, 219
    Whelk Crêpes, 220–221

Y

yellowfin tuna, 116. *see also* tuna